DOS for Non-Nerds

Michael Groh
Bill Camarda

New Riders Publishing, Carmel, Indiana

To Pam, Sarah and James:

"All my dreams would still be dreams, if there hadn't been you."

DOS for Non-Nerds

By Michael Groh

Published by
New Riders Publishing
11711 N. College Ave., Suite 140
Carmel, IN 46032 USA

Printed in the United States of America 1 2 3 4 5 6 7 8 9 0

Library of Congress Cataloging-in-Publication Data

```
Groh, Michael, 1951-
  DOS for non-nerds/Michael Groh.
        p.     cm.
  Includes index.
  ISBN 1-56205-151-2 : $18.95
  1. Operating systems (Computers) 2. MS-DOS (Computer file) 3. PC-DOS
  (Computer file) I. Title.
  QA76.76.063G763       1993
  005.4'469—dc20                                        93-14718
        CIP
```

Publisher
David P. Ewing

Associate Publisher
Tim Huddleston

Acquisitions Editor
John Pont

Managing Editor
Cheri Robinson

Product Directors
B. Rustin Gesner
Tim Huddleston

Production Editor
Nancy E. Sixsmith

Editors
Patrice Hartmann
Peter Kuhns
Lisa Wagner
Steve Weiss

Technical Editor
Lee Lackey

Editorial Secretary
Karen Opal

Book Design and Production
Amy Peppler-Adams
Katy Bodenmiller
Jodie Cantwell
Christine Cook
Dennis Clay Hager
Tim Montgomery
Roger S. Morgan
Juli Pavey
Angela M. Pozdol
Michelle M. Self
Dennis Sheehan
Gregory Albert Simsic
Sue VandeWalle
Alyssa A. Yesh

Proofreaders
Diana Bigham
Julie Brown
Mitzi Gianakos
Howard Jones
John Kane
Sean Medlock
Linda Quigley
Angie Trzepacz
Suzanne Tully

Indexed by
John Sleeva

About the Authors

Michael ("Anything for a Buck") Groh is a recovering nerd who works for New Riders Publishing as a book development specialist and product director. He's produced lots and lots of books in the past year or so that have helped unravel the mysteries of DOS and Windows for zillions of befuddled PC users. In the past, Mike has held such diverse nerdy jobs as selling car parts in a BMW shop, performing CBCs and WBC diffs as a Medical Technologist (ASCP), writing computer programs, and selling expert systems that weren't expert at anything. During his internment as a student at the University of Iowa, Mike slept through most of a Master's program in Clinical Chemistry (they gave him a diploma anyway). After moving to Boston he spent his weekends remodeling his Brookline condo and earning an MBA at Northeastern University.

Now rumored to be living in Indiananoplace, Mike has settled down, got married to Pam, and is the proud daddy of James Michael Groh and is stepdaddy of Sarah Allison Wood. He spends his scant spare time programming Otis, the Ultimate Stock and Mutual Fund Forecasting Machine, and washes the dishes *most* of the time

Bill Camarda specializes in writing about computer and telecommunications topics for large corporate clients. Formerly an editor at *Family Computing Magazine,* he is the author of *Bringing the Computer Home.*

About the Artists

Talmage "Tal" Burdine won an Academy Award for his work in "Star Wars." (Yeah, right.) Actually, he attended Herron School of Art in Indiana-polis, and has worked as a freelance illustrator for many years. Mr. Burdine lives in Indianapolis with his wife and child, and says that he works cheap.

Chris Rozzi earned his BFA in Fine Arts at Wabash College, and continued to study illustration at the Herron School of Art. Currently, he is an associate exhibit artist at the Children's Museum in Indianapolis, and is also a freelance illustrator.

Terry Hall designed the crossword puzzles for this series. He is the owner of Media Productions in Wheaton, Illinois, and has been a professional puzzle designer for several years. Hall uses computers in most of his design work, and has published several complete books of crossword puzzles, word searches, and other puzzles, including *Tyndale Crossword Puzzles, Volumes I* and *II* (Tyndale House Publishers, Inc).

Acknowledgments

Thanks to all those who pitched in and helped with getting this book done:

Dave Ewing for pushing this book project through and giving me the chance to see if I could write a whole book myself. Now I are a author. Dave: Can I have at least three weeks to write the next book?

Tim Huddleston for his nagging to get things done, bucking up when things fell down, and really good suggestions of less nerdy ways to say things (socks and underwear, indeed!)

Cheri Robinson and Rob Tidrow for their moral and practical support on this and the other projects I've been involved with.

Nancy Sixsmith, Lisa D. Wagner, Patrice Hartmann, Peter Kuhns, and Steve Weiss for making sure I conjugated my verbs, checking that I split infinitives where they needed to be split, and that I didn't dangle my participles most of the time.

Rusty Gestner ("AutoCAD god"), Kevin Coleman ("Bicycle Freak"), Brad Koch ("Marketing Geek Who Never Forgets Anything") for their last minute tech review and development passes. I still think magical magnetic goobers says it better than magnetic domains.

Bill Camarda for being such a nice guy and helping at the last possible minute. You're a darn good writer, Bill.

Lee Lackey, Supernerd Himself But A Really Funny Guy (SHBARFG), for making sure I didn't lie too often (or at least, not when it mattered).

Shelly Womack, Andy Thomas and the other Microsoft Wizards for their continued support of New Riders book projects.

Bill Gates, King of Nerds, for dropping out of Harvard and getting a job that is now helping me make a living. Thanks, Bill. Please don't ever trade your glasses for contacts or get your hair styled.

Trademark Acknowledgments

Warning and Disclaimer

Contents at a Glance

Contents

INSTRUCTION MANUAL
READ ME FIRST

Introduction

Since the early 1980s, the personal computer (PC) has touched the lives of many millions of people. Well, some have been touched; others may feel like they've been hit by a truck. About 100,000,000 PCs have been sold in the last 10 or 15 years. Whatever the number, it sure is big. And every year more millions of people join the ranks of the confused and unhappy users of these infernal machines. And it looks like you're one of them.

In some ways, it's a shame that the IBM-compatible PC has outsold the Macintosh by more than 10-to-1. A long time ago (and before anyone could stop them), IBM settled on Microsoft's disk operating system (DOS) as the standard *operating system* for its PCs. Many people think that IBM's selection of DOS was unfortunate—especially people who are using it for the first time (and definitely anyone who's ever used a Macintosh—people in this second group are sometimes called "Mac bigots.") For these computer users, DOS is ugly and hostile.

True enough, DOS does seem pretty unattractive and unfriendly, especially when you compare it to the friendly "graphical" interface of the Macintosh. Mac users work with their computers by looking at little pictures on the screen and using a cute little rolling soap bar (called a *mouse*) to tell the computer what to do.

If you've never really used a computer, some people would make you believe that it really is hard. These people, however, are known as "computer nerds," and they generally don't have anything better to do than play with a computer. Not only do most of these people not have real lives, they also are lying to you.

Sure, if you want to use a computer, you have to learn a few things. But you don't have to become a "computer nerd" yourself. The hardest part is memorizing a few silly sounding words (nerds call them *commands*), which you must type into the keyboard.

And with DOS, silly communication is a two-way street. Your computer won't blow up if you make a mistake, but DOS probably will show you some dorky message, which sounds vague but in reality is quite meaningless. Imagine seeing this on your screen:

```
Bad command or file name
```

Computer nerds love this kind of stuff. You'll probably still hate these messages (I know I do) when you finish this book, but at least you'll know what they mean.

The good news is that, in all honesty, DOS just ain't that hard. Trust me. There are billions and billions of people (okay, perhaps a few dozen) who aren't nearly as smart as you, but who have learned enough DOS to use a computer like real pros. If some Bozo wearing a pocket protector can figure out a computer, you can too. And that's what this book is about.

The Facts of DOS Life

If you hate the idea of dealing with a computer, you're in good company. But a PC can be a good thing to have, if you've got the right attitude about it. Here are some basic true-life facts of computing you should think about:

Computers should be fun. Zillions of kids own Nintendo and Sega games and Game Boys. Each of these games have a true computer buried somewhere inside. You can bet that your computer is a lot more powerful than these toys. Most of the same games available for these devices can be bought for your PC.

Think of it this way: if a kid can have a great time with nothing more than a glorified calculator, why shouldn't your computer be as much fun for you? If you want proof (or just want to enjoy using a computer for a change), just buy or borrow a computer game, get someone to help you install it on your machine and have some fun with it.

Computers should make your life easier. This is the bottom line. In just a few tedious hours, you can make your computer do things that would otherwise take many, many tedious hours. Really!

Computers are used every day. Yes indeed, you are already an experienced computer user. Have you ever used a microwave oven? Or an automated teller machine? Does your car have fuel injection, ABS brakes, or is it equipped with air bags? If the answer to any of these questions is "yes," then you have already used computers. And if you made popcorn, got some cash, or survived a car crash, you used that computer like a pro!

Why This Book Was Written

DOS is about the best thing that ever happened to computer book writers. In fact, before DOS there wasn't any such thing as a "computer book writer." After DOS was created by the wizards (some say demons) at Microsoft, an enormous market was built around supplying "how-to" books to millions of confused and unhappy DOS users.

Solving the "Mystery" of Your Computer

Your computer is somewhat less complicated than the average microwave oven or CD player. You don't need to know what goes on inside of a microwave in order to defrost a frozen bagel, do you? Well, you don't need to know what goes on inside your computer before you can use it to do useful work for you.

There's no mystery about personal computers. Just as you slip a CD into the CD player and push a few buttons to hear music, all you do on a computer is slip a disk into the box and push a few buttons on the keyboard to get your work done.

This book will help you learn exactly *what* buttons to push and *when* to push them. Oh yes, and it will help you know what to do when something doesn't happen the way it's supposed to.

Making Your Computer More Productive

Remember that your computer is only what you make of it. If you don't take advantage of its power, your computer may end up as nothing more than an expensive (and very large) paperweight. If you want to use your computer as a glorified typewriter, and do nothing else but write letters on it, that's your business. But that's like buying a Cadillac when a bicycle will do. Hey, you spent all that dough on that high-tech contraption (well, somebody did), so put it to use!

Your PC can do a lot of things. In fact, your PC is actually a lot more powerful than the computers that were used in the Apollo spacecraft! Just think: all that power, and you don't even need to go to the moon. Depending on which programs you use, you can use your PC to write letters, draw pictures, balance your checkbook, play a really cool game, or teach yourself to fly an airplane. Or maybe even a space ship.

This book will help you feel comfortable exploring your machine's capabilities. You won't break it (the computer, not the book), and, with few exceptions, there's really not much you can do to harm your system or its programs.

Being an Independent Computer User

Like Ann Landers, many other beginning computer books will tell you over and over again that you should go get help from an expert. That's a copout and a waste of your money. This book will never do that. Instead, this book will show you how to take control of DOS and your PC. Nothing is as degrading as having to suck up to some pimply-faced, 19-year-old nerd down the hall when you need help with your machine.

Having spent some time as a 19-year-old, pimply-faced computer nerd, I can tell you from personal experience that the geek really gets a kick out of knowing that you need his (or her) help. It's time to declare your independence from the nerds of the world!

You're the Boss—Not the Stupid Computer!

Finally, remember that the computer is the servant, and you're the boss. Not the other way around. There are ways to tame that beast, and you've already taken the first step by seeking help from this book. You won't need help reading this book and completing the exercises in it. Each time you complete a task at the keyboard, you prove that you really are smarter than that expensive paperweight on your desk.

Remember the basic relationship between you and your computer: *you* give the computer the commands (by typing them at the keyboard), and the *computer* obeys them. Not the other way around. The only time the computer doesn't obey is when it doesn't understand what you are trying to tell it, which usually comes from a typo.

NERDY DETAILS

I'll let you in on a well-kept secret: the whole big deal about using a PC is to know *what* commands to use and *when* to use them. The truly nerdy person will tell you that there's something special about being nerdy enough to understand something as "complicated" as a computer. This is a totally ridiculous idea!

As you read this book, I'm sure you'll come to the realization that your PC is no more complicated or difficult to understand than many things you already know. (Can you cook? Play a musical instrument? Fix cars?) This book takes you from the simplest PC concepts on through some pretty advanced commands, but we'll make the journey with small steps. Progress at your own rate, and I'm sure the confidence in growing "computerese" will reward you many times over for the effort to get through this book.

Chapter 0 of this book spells out the basic concepts and rules every computer user should understand. Please take a moment and read this very important material.

How This Book Is Different

First and foremost, *you're no dummy!* There are very few places in this book where you are told you shouldn't care about a topic, or not to bother with some detail. If something is truly unimportant to you, then it's not in this book.

This book respects you as an intelligent person who is trying to get a job done. That job might be part of your regular work week, or it could be preparing the newsletter for your kid's Brownie or Boy Scout troop. It makes no difference; the important thing is that your time is valuable and you don't want to waste any of it trying to learn how to use your computer.

This book also contains fewer pages than many computer books in the store. It contains more pages than some other books. In fact, *this book has exactly the right number of pages for the material in it.* What this means is that you aren't getting stuff you don't want or need, and you are not missing things that could be important to you.

Whenever they make sense, this book compares the computer to everyday things to help you learn more easily. For instance:

Driving a Car

You don't have to know how a car's engine works before you can drive. Yet, you do have to know how to put a car in gear, and how to use the gas pedal, steering wheel, and brakes to get where you're going. There are also certain rules of the road, such as staying on the right side of the road (at least, here in the U.S.), stopping when the light is red, and not driving too fast (or you'll get a ticket).

Computers are like driving. Always press the Enter (or Return) key after you've typed in a command, stop and read the message when DOS doesn't like something you've done, and don't turn off the computer while a program is running.

Cooking

You have to learn a few basics before you can whip up a complete Thanksgiving dinner. There are also certain rules: plan a meal before you start, don't get egg shells in the batter, and clean up after you're done.

Computers are like cooking. Think about what you're doing before you start, don't use *pirated* (stolen) software, and keep your hard disk organized.

Going to the Amusement Park

Amusement parks are interesting. They can be fun or terrifying. People pay good money to be whirled around until they get sick. Then they spend more money on corn dogs, cotton candy, and other junk food, just to make sure that when they do get sick, they get *good* and sick.

Computers are like amusement parks. People pay lots of money to buy a computer that just upsets and frustrates them, then spend good money on more upsetting and frustrating software and computer toys, such as printers and modems.

Who Should Read This Book?

So let's be honest and answer the following questions:

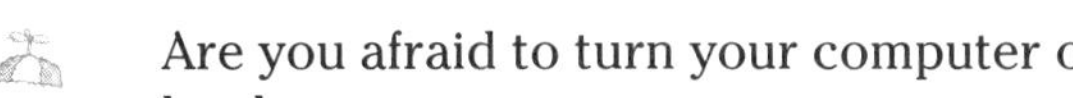

- Are you afraid to turn your computer on? If so, you need to read this book.
- Can you identify this thing? Does it look "friendly" to you? If not, you need to read this book.

  ```
  C:\>
  ```

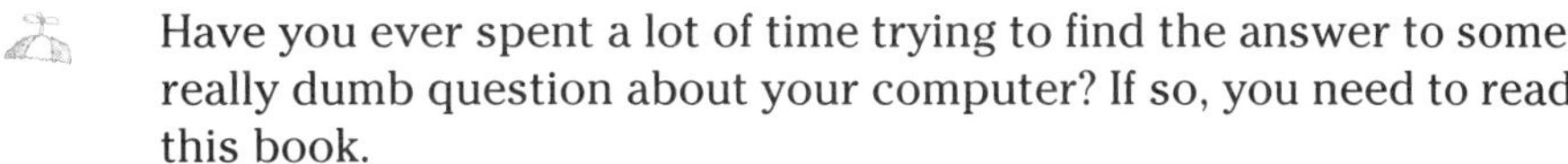

- Have you ever spent a lot of time trying to find the answer to some really dumb question about your computer? If so, you need to read this book.
- Are you tired of going to the local nerd (who might be a friend or neighbor, an office partner, or the new kid down the hall) to get help with things that you just *know* aren't hard to do (if only you knew how)? If you've had to make a humbling visit to your local nerd, you need to read this book.
- If you've ever been stuck on some darn DOS thing that kept you from getting your work done, you need to read this book.
- If you've ever had trouble getting help with your computer when you needed it, you need to read this book.

A beginning computer user who doesn't know what to do at the dreaded `C:\>` prompt should read this book. In fact, just about everybody (you, your mom, your boss) should read this book!

You may not even be a beginner. I've been using DOS a long time, and sometimes I feel that I need help with it. I usually turn to a book for help rather than go to some nerd who *might* know more about my problem than I do. You, too, may be an experienced computer user who knows very little or nothing at all about the computer. You may think that your machine can do only one thing, and wonder what *else* you could make it do if you only knew how. If so, this book can help you, too.

This book is also for the people who are sick of turning to the office nerd for help. This book is about *empowerment*, the ability to do things on your own. It's time to take charge of your work and your time, and to finally learn just how easy it is to conquer DOS. Books are the ideal way to learn a new subject like DOS. You can pick the book up when you need something, put it down when you're through, and you don't owe it any favors when it helps you with something.

How To Read This Book

You don't have to read *DOS for Non-Nerds* from cover to cover. If you do, you'll probably get really bored before you're through. Frankly, you've got better things to do than memorize a bunch of DOS commands. When you need some DOS things, just look them up. With only one exception, you can jump around and read only those parts that you need to.

Here's the exception: please, please, PLEASE read Chapter 0 first. It contains the very basic material you have to know and understand to get value from the rest of the book. Even if you don't read anything else in the whole book, Chapter 0 contains material that is essential for understanding DOS and your computer.

Chapter 0 contains "feel-good" stuff you won't read anywhere else. While researching this book, I consulted lots of other DOS books to see how the authors of those books approached and described different topics. None of these books take the time to tell you that you're smarter than the best and biggest computer ever built. No other book I've looked at describes the magic of personal computers, or explains why you, the user, can always wield ultimate control over the machine. Read Chapter 0, please!

What About You?

So what makes you tick? You are probably a professional, personal, or hobbyist computer user who is motivated to learn something about DOS.

 A *professional* user, of course, is someone who uses a PC in his or her daily work.

 By *personal* user, I mean someone who uses a computer for something of a personal nature (such as managing your homeowner's association meeting schedule).

- The *hobbyist* is a user whose hobby is using the computer, whether it be for playing games, communicating with other people via a modem, or just reading about computers in books and magazines.
- You are also someone who doesn't want to have to read 800 pages of highly technical discussions to learn the essentials of using your computer.
- You have no need for in-depth discussions of "just what, exactly, happens when I press the Return key."
- Also, you're not really concerned about specific details of different software packages, particularly if you don't own or use those packages. You just want the facts, and you want 'em fast.

You and Your Computer

I've assumed the following things about you and your computer:

- Your computer is usually referred to as *IBM-compatible* or as an *IBM-PC clone*. This doesn't mean it has to look like a genuine IBM-PC or PS/2 (if you've seen one). It just means that your PC can run software (computer programs) written for the original "personal computer" developed by IBM about a million years ago.
- Your PC is equipped with a hard disk. (If you don't know what a hard disk is, it's a thing inside your computer that stores your programs and data while the power is off.) Without a hard disk, you have to put a floppy disk into the floppy drive every time you use the machine. (You know what a floppy disk is, right? If not, go ahead and read Chapter 0 right now!)
- Finally, your computer is equipped with a color monitor (the TV-looking thing). Although there are a lot of PCs out there that are still using monochrome (un-color) monitors, it's just easier to discuss things as if they're occurring in color.

The DOS Version on Your Computer

It really doesn't matter which version of DOS is loaded on your PC. They're basically all the same. One of the nice things about DOS is that it really hasn't changed a whole lot since it first appeared in the early 1980s. Most of the old DOS commands work the same way now that they did back then.

If you bought your PC recently, then you probably are using DOS 5. If you plan to buy a PC soon, or if you plan to upgrade to a new version of DOS, then you probably will be using DOS 5 or DOS 6. But even if you use an old version of DOS, this book can help you.

If you are planning to install DOS 6, now is as good a time as any. Go directly to Chapter 4 (after reading Chapter 0, of course!) to learn how to install DOS 6. Chapter 4 leads you though the process of safely getting DOS 6 onto your computer.

How This Book Is Put Together

This book is divided into seven parts, described as follows:

Part One: The Things You Really Have To Know

Just like the name implies, this part of the book tells you just what you need to know about your computer and DOS to get you started. There may be sections in the chapters in this part that you can jump over.

Part Two: What You Really Need To Know About Software

Software (also called *programs* or *applications*) is the stuff that makes your computer go. It's like the gas in your car or the charcoal in your backyard grill. Without it, you won't get very far. The chapters lead you through the maze of confusing terminology and the basic tasks you need to know so you can handle your software like a pro.

Part Three: PC Hardware and Other Cool Stuff To Know

Just as you don't need to know anything about how your car's engine works before you can drive somewhere, you don't have to know anything that's in this part of the book. But what happens if you have a problem with your computer's disk drives or monitor? How can you be sure that the guy at the computer store is telling you the truth when he says you need a new widget for your computer's hard disk. (And what is a hard disk anyway? Is it really "hard"?) Check out these chapters for all this and more!

Part Four: What To Do When Something Doesn't Work Right

Computer repairs rank right behind car repairs in terms of how much they cost and how badly the work is usually done. Often the guy at the computer store that you're trusting to set things right with your hard-working machine doesn't know much more about your computer than you do. I am not kidding! The chapters in Part Four help you understand what's gone wrong with your computer, help you fix the problem, and tell you when you really do need help.

Part Five: The Biggest and Best Things To Remember

Your computer is actually quite reliable. Most problems with computers and programs happen when some basic rule or idea has been overlooked. These chapters provide all the background you need to avoid the most common computing problems.

Part Six: Graduate-Level Topics

Here is where most computer books *start*. You'll learn the very few DOS commands that you'll use a lot. There's also a chapter to help you know where to go next. There are a tremendous number of resources available to help you out, if you know what they are and where they go.

Part Seven: Resources for Non-Nerds

The chapters here provide information that wouldn't fit anywhere else in this book. The glossary will "demystify" most of those nerdy terms you keep hearing. If you want to join a PC user group, there is a list of the biggest and the best in this part.

A Promise To Keep

As I said earlier, dear reader, *you are no dummy*. There are many, many things you are already good at. Maybe today, you just aren't that good at DOS. This book will help you change all of that. If you stick with it past the initial hump, you'll see that computers are pretty easy, and can even be fun.

This book will never treat you as if you are too stupid to understand some DOS concept or principle. If you will forgive my occasional attempts at humor and levity, I think you will find a lot of valuable information in *DOS for Non-Nerds*, and you'll never hear me talking down to you. The nice thing about all of this is that you don't have to become a nerd yourself in order to conquer your PC!

Conventions Used in This Book

Convention is a high-falutin' editor word meaning the rules we have for the format in the book. For example, you'll see these special typefaces:

`Special font`: This font is used for DOS "stuff": commands, files and directories, and things you see on the screen.

`Bold, special font:` This font is used for anything you are instructed to type.

You'll also see some other cool, helpful sections:

These nerdy, technical sections give you more stuff than you'll ever need to know about DOS so that you can intimidate your friends. You can avoid these if you don't want nerd contamination.

Even though it takes *a lot* to break or damage your computer (don't put it in the microwave—it has metal on it!), these sections warn you to stop and watch out.

These sections are for useful or entertaining DOS tricks that can simplify your life or make your computer do something really awesome.

SAVE THE DAY!

It's hero time (or goat city): sometimes catastrophes or holocausts happen. What to do? Don't end it—read these notes to get you out of hot water.

Isn't this fun? Time now to open Chapter 0 and enter the wonderful universe of DOS!

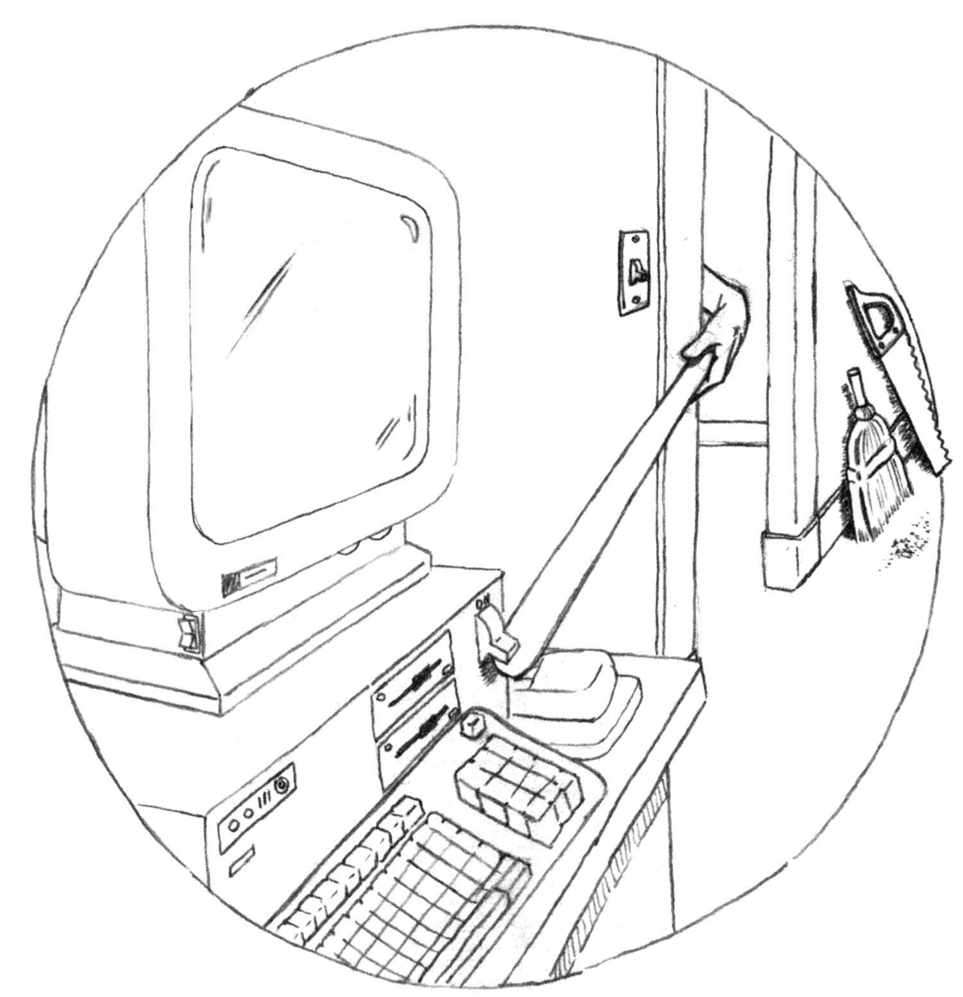

PERFORMING THE SMOKE TEST

Getting Comfortable with Your PC

First-time computer users often treat their computer the same way a first-time cook treats an old gas stove—with fear. Don't worry; your computer will do a lot of things you don't like, but it won't blow up. This chapter gets you cooking fast by showing you these things:

- How to turn your computer on and off the right way
- The most important computer terms and expressions
- The most important concepts to understand
- The most important rules to live by
- You can't really break a computer
- What to do if your computer doesn't act right

Computers are also nicer than gas stoves because you don't need those heavy oven mitts (they really make it hard to type). Now fire up that thing and get to work!

Fire It Up! (You're NOT Cooking with Gas)

Just like a stove, your computer has to be turned on before you can use it. If you haven't turned on your computer yet, the on/off switch could be in one of several places:

- Right on the front (a little push button or a toggle switch)
- On the right side, toward the back (a big paddle switch)
-  On the back, toward the right (a big paddle switch or toggle switch)

Being electric, your computer should not make a hissing sound or a strange smell when you turn it on. If it does, open a window to let the smoke out, then go to a neighbor's house and call the fire department.

NERDY DETAILS

> Nerds don't just "turn on" their computers. That would be too simple. Instead, they "power up the system unit."

Figure 0.1 shows normal spots for these critters.

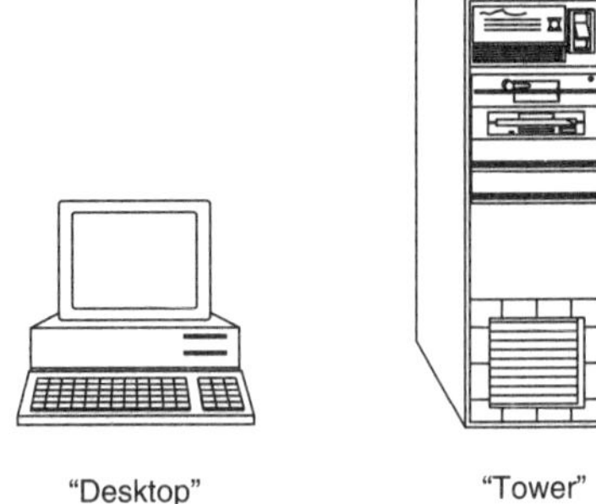

Figure 0.1
Typical locations for PC power switches.

If you don't see the switch right away, poke around a bit and experiment. If you find something that even remotely looks like a switch, flip it, push it, turn it, or do whatever else to make it go. The power switches on laptops and notebooks are notoriously difficult to find!

NERDY DETAILS

> Some computer power switches use goofy international symbols instead of just saying "on" and "off," like this:
>
> ¦ = On
>
> 0 = Off
>
> If you have trouble with goofy international symbols, just remember that a computer's on/off switch is like a light switch. Flip it one way to turn it on, and flip it the other way when you want to turn it off.

If you can't get the machine to start, go ahead and flip, poke, punch, turn, and twist everything that looks like a switch. If you still can't get the thing to run, you've got problems. ("No $#!+, Sherlock!" you might say.) Common-sense time. Make sure the computer box is plugged into an outlet that you know is working, or turn to Chapter 15 for more help.

If You Want To See What You're Doing, Turn On the Monitor!

When the computer is on (you'll hear a hum—not a hiss!), you may need to turn on the screen. Nerds call the screen a *monitor*. The screen's power switch can be just about anywhere, as you can see in figure 0.2. In fact, it may be hidden behind a little door.

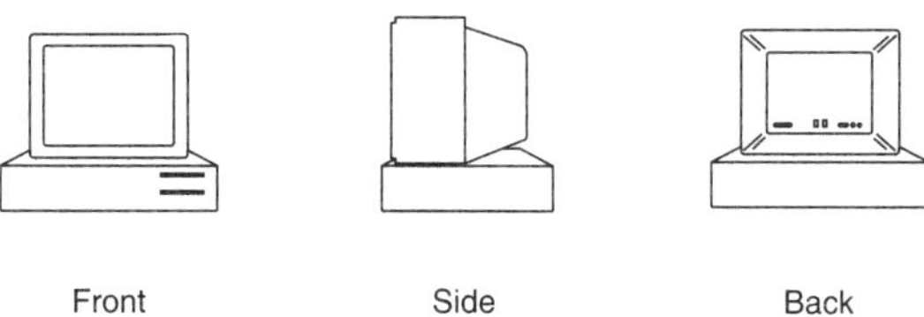

Figure 0.2

Typical locations for monitor power switches.

Most laptops and notebooks don't have separate switches for the screen, so don't spend time looking for one!

NERDY DETAILS

Some computers have screen savers that make the screen go blank if you don't type anything for a few minutes.

If you go away from your computer and return to find the screen blank, don't panic. Try pressing the spacebar or another harmless key such as the one labeled "Shift." If a screen saver is at work, the monitor should come back to life.

What Next?

Were you successful? Is it running? To find out, look at your computer now and answer the following questions:

1. Is the computer just sitting there, no different in any way than it was before you started throwing switches and pressing buttons?
2. Is the computer's box humming (like the sound of a fan), and are letters and numbers skating across the screen?
3. Did it blow up like an old gas stove?

If you answered "yes" to question 1, you failed. Try again. If you answered "yes" to question 2, you did just fine. If you answered "yes" to question 3, go to a neighbor's house and call the Fire Department. (And I take back what I said before about computers not being able to blow up.)

By the way, if you answered "yes" to question 2, and your computer is running fine, don't worry about the letters and numbers that are skating across the screen. They are only important to computer nerds. After the skating's over, your screen can look one of several different ways. Most computers, however, start out by displaying the DOS prompt.

The Dreaded DOS Prompt (I Bet You'll Hate This...)

When a computer is turned on, the first and most common thing to appear on the screen is the soon-to-be familiar DOS *prompt*:

```
C:\>
```

NERDY DETAILS

Okay, so what's a *prompt*? It is not something that's compulsively on time; it's what DOS puts on the screen when it's ready for your next command. Although it doesn't look like it, `C:\>` *prompts* you to give DOS a new command.

TRICKS

Don't worry if your DOS prompt doesn't look exactly like the one shown here. The prompt can look any number of ways. Later in this book you'll learn how to set your prompt to suit your own personal style. For now, you've got other things to worry about.

If your screen is now displaying anything that looks like a DOS prompt, you are now experiencing first-hand the whole reason this book was written. That glowing little jumble of characters is one of the most intimidating things in all of computing. There's nothing helpful at all about the DOS prompt. Even its name isn't helpful; it really doesn't "prompt" you to do anything. It just sits there and glows at you.

SAVE THE DAY!

If, for some reason, the DOS prompt is not glowing at you right now, skip ahead to the end of this chapter to the section titled "What To Do If It Didn't Display the DOS Prompt." There, you will find instructions that can help you figure out where your machine has taken you.

Want To Find Out What's in Your Computer?

What do you do now? Well, your computer probably has some programs and other information stored inside, just waiting to be used. Maybe the best thing to do is find out what's in there.

Just type this:

```
DIR
```

That's all. Just type the three letters **DIR** and press the Enter (or Return) key. As you type them, you'll see them appear next to the DOS prompt. You can type **DIR** in capital letters or lowercase letters; DOS doesn't care. Don't put spaces, quotation marks, or any kind of punctuation around the word **DIR**; just type the letters.

Your screen should change now. It should be showing you some information (nerds call information *data*), in addition to the DOS prompt. Your screen should resemble figure 0.3:

Figure 0.3

You should see something like this after you type DIR.

```
C:\>DIR

 Volume in drive C has no label
 Volume Serial Number is 1AE6-0E27
 Directory of C:\

ACCESS       <DIR>       01-10-93  12:03a
BATCH        <DIR>       11-10-93  12:04a
DOS          <DIR>       11-10-93  11:57p
HYPEROID     <DIR>       01-17-93  11:57p
LOTUS123     <DIR>       01-12-93  12:03a
NETWORK      <DIR>       01-18-93  12:04a
NORTON       <DIR>       01-18-93  12:03a
PARADOX      <DIR>       01-18-93  12:04a
PCPLUS       <DIR>       01-10-93  12:03a
WEP          <DIR>       01-17-93  11:57p
WINDOWS      <DIR>       02-17-93  11:57p
WINWORD      <DIR>       11-07-92  11:57p
COMMAND  COM      53405 12-06-92   6:00a
CONFIG   SYS        804 01-17-93  10:48a
MOUSE    SYS      55160 02-12-92  12:48p
       15 file(s)      109369 bytes
                     11308672 bytes free

C:\>
```

"OK," you may ask, "so what is DIR, what does it mean, and what's all this stuff on my screen?" To DOS, the word DIR is a *command*, which says a lot about your relationship with the computer. You give it a command, and it does exactly what the command tells it to do.

As a command, DIR means *directory*; it tells the computer to give you a list (like a phone directory) of everything that's stored in the computer. You'll learn more about DIR and other commands as you go through this book. As for all the other stuff on your screen, don't worry about it for now.

If At First You Don't Succeed...

You may see something on the screen that looks different from the information I just described. You may even see an *error message*, like this:

```
Bad command or file name
```

Don't panic—you are not being yelled at. You probably typed the DIR command wrong. Just try it again. Type **DIR** (remember not to use quotation marks or punctuation), and press Enter.

If you see something like figure 0.3, you did it right—DOS is showing you the directory, or contents, of your disk.

Now Reward Yourself!

Congratulations! You've just conquered DOS and made it do something for you. No matter what you do later on in this book, the principle remains the same:

1. Type a command.
2. Press the Enter key.
3. DOS does your bidding.

DOS is no harder than that. The secret is knowing *what* to type and *when* to type it. That's what the rest of this book is about.

You're well on your way to learning DOS—without turning into a computer nerd! You'll only have to learn five or six commands to become DOS-proficient. Leave it up to the truly nerdy to learn the more than 150 other DOS commands that no one really uses!

Some Really Important Terms To Know

Some people like to think that they learned everything they would ever need to know in kindergarten. Well, those people are wrong. They don't teach you how to use DOS in kindergarten. (This would give a kid a complex for life.) But they do teach you lots of new words in kindergarten.

This book's going to teach you lots of new words, too—but it won't smack you with a ruler if you forget them, or make you stand with your nose in the corner, or skip recess.... In this book, when you find a new word, it will be carefully described and probably illustrated with a picture.

Meanwhile, the following section defines words that you've got to know before we can go much further. It's a lot easier on us both if I put them all together here instead of scattering them throughout the chapters that follow.

Don't forget the glossary at the end of the book!

Computer Program

By itself, a computer is incredibly dumb. It's no more than a collection of electrical parts and a few boxes that hold the parts together. Unless it is told what to do, a computer can do *nothing* at all.

Who tells the computer what to do? You, for one. But a *computer program* also can tell a computer what to do. A computer program (also called *software* or an *application*) is just a set of instructions that tells the computer how to perform specific tasks. The computer program is written in a format that the computer can understand. (And it's not English!)

Your computer comes with a number of programs built right in. For example, when you turn on the computer, a very important little program helps get the machinery into gear. This program wakes up the rest of the computer and gets the machine ready for you to use. When all of the computer's parts (the keyboard, disk drives, and others) are ready to go to work, the little "genie" program turns the machine over to DOS, and goes back to sleep.

DOS

DOS is the thing that makes your computer go. That's all it is. The word *DOS* stands for *disk operating system*, which means that it's the magical thing inside your computer that controls all the computer components.

Here's a tip for your DOS Survival Guide, if you're keeping one: unless you want to sound like a goof, *always* pronounce DOS like "DAAHS," not "DOSE." Few people have pronounced DOS as "DOSE" and then survived all the ribbing they had to take from nearby computer nerds.

You work with DOS by typing commands at the keyboard. When you press the Enter key (some computers are equipped with a key labeled "Return" rather than "Enter"), DOS reads the command and tries to carry it out.

Error Message

An *error message* is just DOS' way of telling you that you made a mistake. If you're a beginner, you'll probably see this message a lot:

```
Bad command or file name
```

If you see this message, don't worry; nothing is broken. It's just that DOS is really stupid and doesn't understand what you're trying to tell it. In fact, DOS is so stupid that there's an entire section later in this chapter, which describes just how dumb DOS can be.

There are a few variations on the basic DOS package. One of these is "DR DOS," which is produced by Digital Research (hence, the "DR"). Unless you want people to think you're a dope, pronounce DR DOS like this: "Dee Are DAAS," not "Doctor DOS."

Disks

So, DOS stands for *disk operating system*, eh? So, what's a disk? *Disks* are things on which you store computer programs, documents, and other things you produce on your computer.

Computer disks are a lot like the recording tape found in audio cassettes. As the name implies, a computer disk is a round, flat thing that spins around real fast. Its surface is covered with a magnetic coating, like an audiotape.

The computer records and writes information on the disk's surface, like a tape player records and plays music on the surface of a cassette tape. The information can be a program, a letter you write on the computer, a drawing, or many other things.

You'll learn a lot more about disks in Chapter 2.

Floppy Disks

The disks you'll come in contact with most often are called *floppy disks*. They're flat, square things (see fig. 0.4) that you insert into a *disk drive* on the computer so your computer can read them or write new stuff on them.

Figure 0.4

Typical floppy disks.

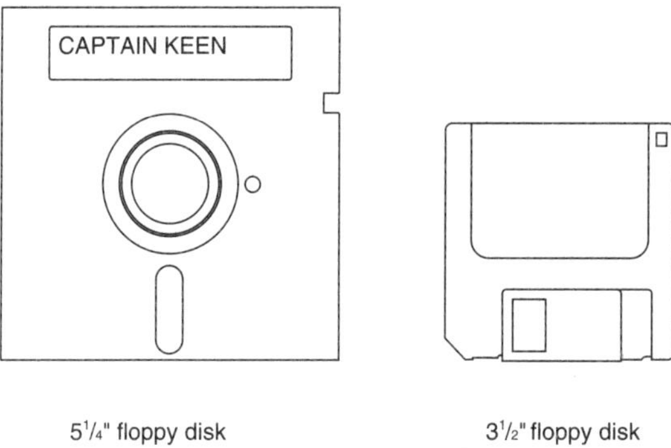

Floppy disks come in two sizes. The bigger ones measure 5 1/4-inches square. The smaller ones are just about 3 1/2-inches square. Floppy disks, therefore, must be a nerd creation because only a nerd would come up with such odd sizes.

By the way, the small kind of floppy disk can hold more information than the large-size floppy disk. More proof that they were created by nerds. Don't worry; you'll get more information about floppies and the amount of information they hold later in this book.

NERDY DETAILS

Lots of people have trouble with the name "floppy disk." First of all, these disks aren't floppy. The large-size floppy disks can bend, but you shouldn't bend them because you can hurt them. The little floppy disks are in a hard case, so if you try to "flop" them, you'll break them.

Computer nerds have a special term for floppy disks. Nerds call them *diskettes*.

Hard Disks

The other kind of computer disk is called a *hard disk*. A hard disk usually is permanently installed inside the computer's big box. You can't see it or touch it, but you can hear it whirling inside your computer. Some computers make a gurgling sound when they are reading the hard disk. (Mine sounds sort of like a toilet!)

There's no picture of a hard disk here because you normally can't see one. It's buried inside of your computer, and can only be seen if you take the cover off. You didn't need to see a picture of a car's engine to learn how to drive, did you?

Compared to floppy disks, a hard disk holds an incredible amount of information. DOS and your programs are normally installed on your hard disk and, until you start running out of space on your hard disk, you rarely have to even think about it. For now, think of your hard disk as a big filing cabinet inside your computer for storing things.

Command

A *command* is an instruction that DOS carries out for you. Just as you tell your kids to clean up their rooms, you instruct the computer by typing *commands* at the keyboard. The biggest difference between DOS and your kids is that DOS will instantly obey your every command (if you've spelled it right!). Each DOS command is a very special word with very specific spelling.

The `DIR` command (which you typed earlier in this chapter) is by far the most common DOS command you will use. It tells DOS to list the contents of your disk. (Remember? The disk is the filing cabinet inside your computer.) When you use `DIR`, it's like opening a file drawer and looking in. Chapter 2 explains the DOS filing cabinet in detail.

TRICKS

> The first trick to mastering DOS is to learn only the commands you need to know. There are dozens of commands, but you only have to know five or six of them to use your computer like a pro. The second trick is to learn when to use those commands. Chapters 20 and 21 will teach you every command you need, in detail.

File

A computer *file* is like a piece of paper stored in the filing cabinet. You'll learn everything you need to know about files and how to use them in Chapter 2.

If you think of your computer as a busy office and the disk inside your computer as a special kind of filing cabinet, DOS serves as a little file clerk cheerfully shuffling the pieces of paper (the files) you've got stored in there.

You'll read a lot more about files in Chapter 2.

The Most Important Concepts To Understand

In fact, you can sum everything up in one sentence:

> *DOS is a computer program that responds to your commands to manipulate the files on your disk.*

Now that you understand those "high-tech" words, you need to learn some very important concepts about the computer. I don't believe that there's another computer book anywhere that explains this stuff to you. Some of it is so basic that maybe it doesn't even deserve to be mentioned. Even so, bear with me as you read through this section.

You Are in Control, Not the Stupid Computer!

And I mean the *stupid* computer! Without the computer programs described earlier, the computer is nothing more than a bunch of metal and plastic (OK, exotic and expensive metal and plastic) that's not too different from your microwave oven or car. A microwave oven is computerized, but it won't do anything unless you tell it to. Without gas to make it go, your car is a dumb, heavy thing that can't do much, right?

Remember that *you* are in command of your car, and you make it go where you want to go. Once they learn to drive, most people quickly forget the thrill of controlling a car for the first time.

Compared to your car, DOS is a wimp! It weighs nothing! You can't slam its doors, turn up its radio really loud, or squeal the tires. And DOS is really stupid! It understands only the precise commands you type in at the keyboard.

When you sit in front of your computer, you're much more in control than when you drive your car to work. At least you don't have to worry about some other confused, frustrated DOS user running you off the road! (Unless you're on a network, but that's a topic for another book....)

Computer Programs Are Magic

Computer programs are the magic that makes your computer into a wizard that can help you compose a letter, draw pictures, or add numbers. And programs perform these tasks *incredibly fast.*

Programs are magic because they transform computer parts into an intelligent, obedient servant that is eager to do your bidding.

The Reset Button Always Wins!

Some people like to say, "Computers don't make mistakes. People make mistakes." Those people are morons. Sooner or later, your computer is going to screw up. It may lose your information, lock up, refuse to carry out a command, or just sit and stare at you.

When that happens, you always have the option of getting even instead of getting mad. The best way to get even is to turn the stupid thing off. Or, if your computer has one, you can press the Reset button. Either approach gets the same results.

SAVE THE DAY!

> If your computer doesn't have a Reset button, try this instead: locate the keys labeled "Ctrl," "Alt," and "Del." The Ctrl and Alt keys are somewhere on the *left* side of the keyboard; the Del key is normally near the lower *right* corner of the keyboard. While holding the Alt and Ctrl keys down with your left hand, press the Del key with your right index finger. Poof! Away goes DOS!

The Most Important Rules To Live By

These indeed are the golden rules of personal computing. If you follow these rules at all, you'll be well on your way to happier computing.

Don't Panic!

Without a doubt, panicking is the worst thing you can do. And there usually is no good reason to lose your cool with the computer. Sure, it's going to screw up, but don't let it get you down. If you plan for the worst and understand that things are going to go wrong from time to time, you'll be OK.

There are very few things you can do to really mess things up. The only way you can "break" a computer is by dropping it out a window or pouring water into it. The only way to "hurt" a program is to delete part or all of it. You can't screw anything up just by misspelling a command. And most commands are safe and won't damage anything.

If something goes wrong, you can usually get back where you were before the spit hit the fan. This book will help you out. If you find yourself getting overly frustrated with something, reset the machine and go for a walk.

If all else fails, turn to Part Four of this book and follow the troubleshooting advice you'll find there. Believe it or not, you can fix the most common problems you're likely to experience—without help from a computer store or your neighborhood computer nerd.

SAVE THE DAY!

This is a true story that happened while writing this very chapter late one night, my computer suddenly shut off. All by itself, its little lights went out, the disk stopped turning, and it went dead. Following my own advice (which can be found in Chapter 15), I checked the power cord leading into the back of the computer. Somehow, for no good reason, the power cord had come loose and worked its way out of its socket. All I had to do was push the cord back into its socket and the machine woke back up and ran fine. Things like this happen a lot with computers. You just have to get used to it.

Give Yourself a Break

After all, you're just starting out! How many people really hit a homer their first time at bat? Were you really that good when you first tried to ride a bike? I don't think so. After five years of trying, I still haven't mastered the fine art of hitting a golf ball straight and true. I'm not even sure I want to, although it's fun to try it.

Give yourself a break. You're only human!

It's Not the Computer's Fault (Well, Not Always)

When something goes wrong, it's not necessarily your computer's fault, even though the computer is pretty dumb. In fact, it may not even be your fault. Stuff happens from time to time. There's a Murphy's chip in every PC. It's the law!

The best way to avoid disaster is just to expect one, and learn how to prepare for it. Sooner or later, it will happen. Just when you absolutely need to use your computer to prepare a report or recalculate a spreadsheet, it'll die on you. Maybe it's just your machine's turn to go to that big scrap heap in the sky, maybe not. In any case, bad stuff will happen from time to time. Get used to it.

Chapter 7 tells you all about "backing up" your files for safe keeping.

Check Your Spelling, Please!

Most mistakes you'll make at the computer will be simple spelling mistakes. For instance, it's easy to mistake a 0 for an O. DOS doesn't know the difference.

When you get an error message from DOS, particularly `Bad command or file name`, check your spelling or type the command again. That's all there is to it.

Know When To Quit

Some people like to say "Quitters never win and winners never quit." True enough, but it's still better to quit than to get mad and bash your keyboard in with a potted plant.

Sometimes it doesn't make sense to keep banging your head against the wall. Turn the thing off and go get a cold drink or something. Unless you're working under a tight deadline or you just want to torture yourself, give it up now and then.

Confidence Booster: Reset It!

If you've been following along in this chapter, your machine will still be at the dreaded `C:\>` prompt. If so (or even if not), it's time for another quick confidence booster: reset your machine. You can do it in one of two ways:

1. Press the Reset button on the front of the big box.
2. Press the Alt, Ctrl, and Del keys simultaneously.

Now, sit back and let your machine wake itself back up and come to attention. You'll soon be back where you were when you first turned on the machine at the beginning of this chapter.

If your computer displays the `C:\>` prompt when you start it up or reset it, skip over the next section entirely, which is for machines that are set up to normally display something other than the `C:\>` prompt.

What To Do If It Doesn't Display the DOS Prompt

If your computer starts up normally and the `C:\>` prompt appears on the screen, you don't have to read this section at all. Consider yourself lucky.

But if your machine took you someplace unfamiliar, quickly look at the pictures in this section to see if any of them are similar to the stuff on your screen.

It Went to a Complicated Screen I Don't Understand

If the DOS prompt doesn't appear when you start your computer, your screen may look something like figure 0.5. This is called the *DOS Shell* because it's supposed to provide a nice, consistent "cover" over the ugly DOS prompt and commands.

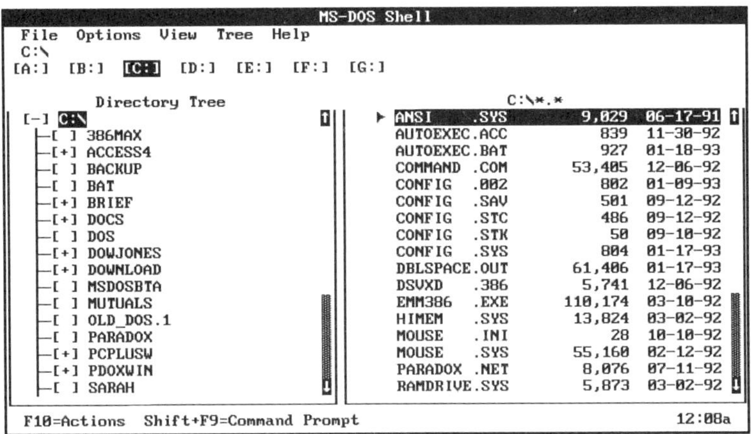

Figure 0.5

The DOS Shell: prettier than the prompt, but not much friendlier.

> It's easy to tell if the DOS Shell is running on your computer. Just look at the colored bar that stretches across the top of the screen. If the DOS Shell is active, the words `MS-DOS Shell` appear in that bar. (See how simple DOS can be?)

The DOS Shell is a nicer connection between you and your computer. But it's so complicated that there's a whole chapter devoted to it later in this book. The really nice thing about the DOS Shell is that you don't have to use it unless you want to. (Most people don't.) It's actually just another computer program.

If you have the DOS Shell on the screen, you can "kill" it by pressing the Alt key and the F4 key simultaneously. (F4 will be along the top or left side of your keyboard. You may have to use two hands to do this the first few times. The important thing is to press both keys (Alt and F4) *at the same time*. The DOS Shell should disappear and be replaced by the DOS prompt.

If the DOS Shell *doesn't* go away, you haven't succeeded in doing the Alt-F4 key combination thing properly. If it goes away but comes back, it means somebody has been fooling around with your computer and has set it up to keep the DOS Shell running. You should go find this person and make him give you a DOS prompt!

If you succeed in killing the DOS Shell, congratulations! You're on your way to taking control of your computer, and have just succeeded in putting DOS in its place!

I Think I'm in OZ Now

Oh, you lucky person. If your screen looks anything at all like figure 0.6, your machine is set up to automatically load Microsoft Windows. It probably took a long time (15 or 20 seconds) to get here. Although Windows is a wonderful thing to have, it is not the subject of this book. (You should go out and get *Windows for Non-Nerds* to get the lowdown on Windows.)

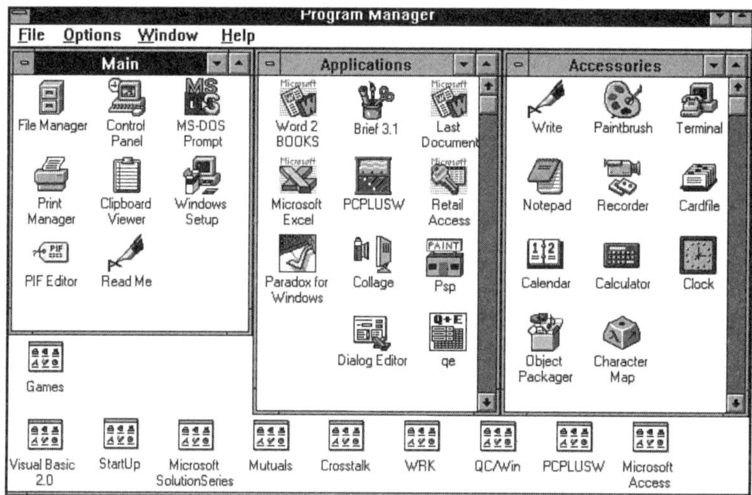

Figure 0.6

Microsoft Windows, otherwise known as The Land of OZ.

A lot of new computers come equipped with Windows. Many of these machines are set to automatically load Windows when the machine is turned on. If you want to use Windows every day, this is fine. Unfortunately, you can't do everything you need to do from "inside" Windows, so you'll still end up having to learn at least a little bit about DOS.

Because we're not going to study Windows in this book, go ahead and kill it by pressing the Alt and F4 keys (F4 is near the top or left side of your keyboard). A little box should appear on the screen warning you that `This will end your Windows session`. Kill Windows by pressing Enter.

You should be left at the DOS prompt. It's time to go back to the section labeled "Want to find out what's in your computer?"

The Machine Went Somewhere Else

Some people hate DOS so much that they'll do anything to avoid it. They cram their computers full of *utility* programs, which do the same thing as

DOS, but which also take up a lot of space and require you to learn a whole new way of doing things. If someone else has set up your computer, or if you bought a used computer, a menuing program may appear on the screen when you start the machine. Good luck if this happens to you. Figure 0.7 shows a typical DOS menuing program.

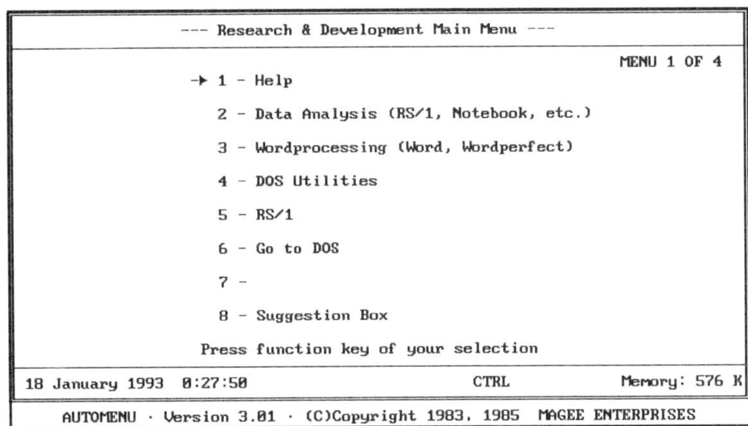

--- Research & Development Main Menu ---
MENU 1 OF 4
1 - Help
2 - Data Analysis (RS/1, Notebook, etc.)
3 - Wordprocessing (Word, Wordperfect)
4 - DOS Utilities
5 - RS/1
6 - Go to DOS
7 -
8 - Suggestion Box
Press function key of your selection
18 January 1993 8:27:50
CTRL
Memory: 576 K
AUTOMENU · Version 3.01 · (C)Copyright 1983, 1985 MAGEE ENTERPRISES

Figure 0.7

A typical DOS menuing program.

There are literally dozens of different DOS menuing programs available, so I can't begin to tell you how to get out of all of them here. Look at the screen and try to find an option named `Exit to DOS`, `DOS Prompt`, `Exit`, or something like that. If you don't see such an option, you might need help from somebody who understands the program.

Before you wake up your local nerd to ask for help, try this: hold down the key labeled Ctrl (it may also be labeled Control), and press the C key at the same time. The Ctrl key will probably be near the lower left corner of the keyboard. Pressing the C key while holding down the Ctrl key is called a *Control-C* as in "do a Control-C." The Ctrl-C combination is frequently used to *stop* something (like a runaway program that won't behave or a program that suddenly stops running because of some error).

You might also try the Esc (Escape) key (it'll be near the upper left hand corner of your keyboard).

Finally, you can try Ctrl-C's big brother, Ctrl-Break. The Break key is usually embedded somewhere in the right half of the keyboard.

PART 1

The Things You Really Have To Know

1. *Really Basic Computer Science*
2. *Playing Those Filing Clerk Blues*
3. *All About Files*

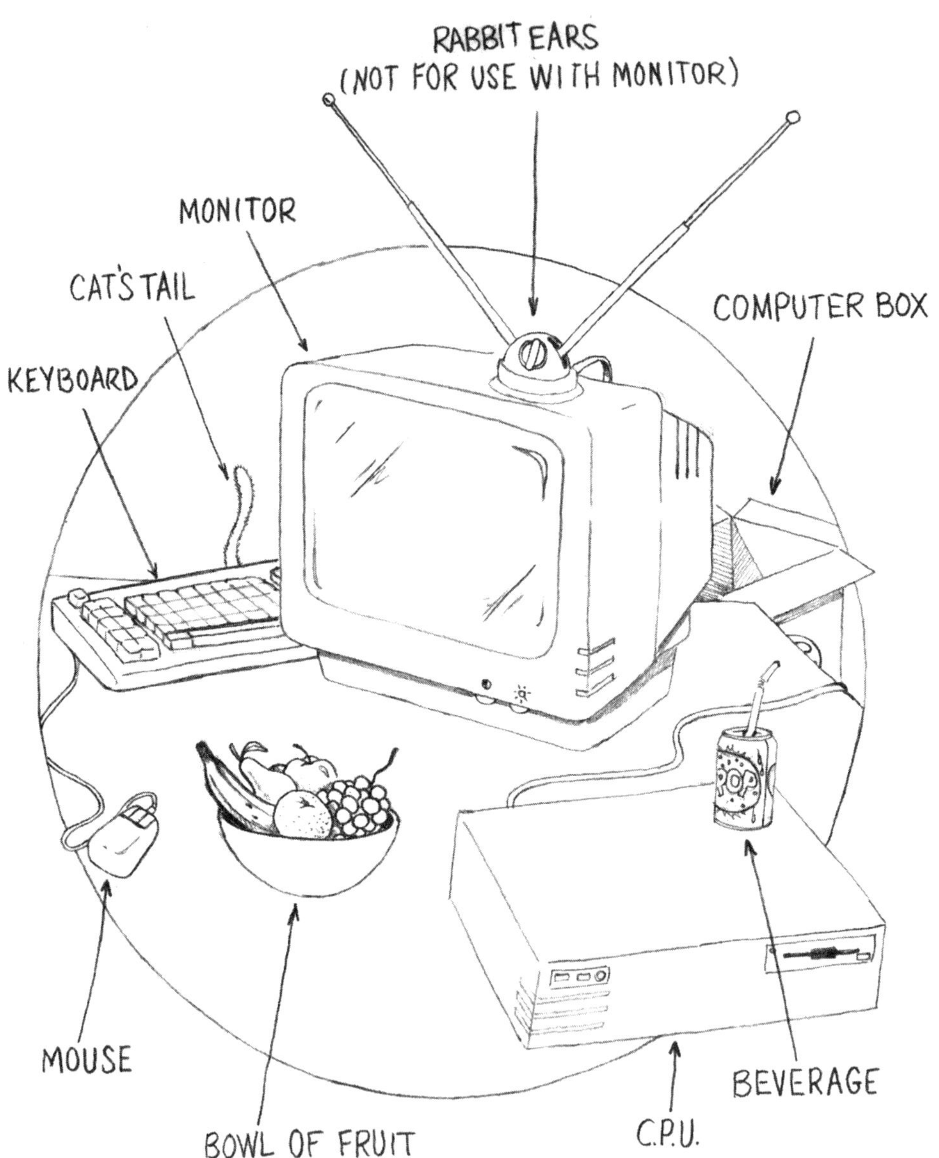
RABBIT EARS
(NOT FOR USE WITH MONITOR)
MONITOR
CAT'S TAIL
COMPUTER BOX
KEYBOARD
POP
MOUSE
BOWL OF FRUIT
C.P.U.
BEVERAGE

Really Basic Computer Science

"Computer science? That's for nerds!" Yeah, I can hear you saying it. But remember: you'll only be a nerd if you soak up too much computer science (and actually start to enjoy it). If you want to learn how to use DOS, you just need a little computer science. It's more like computer basics.

This chapter covers the following basics, which will help you become a straight-A DOS user (but not a computer nerd):

- Getting more information on hardware
- The DOS command line
- Software, programs, and applications
- Everything you need to know about disks
- Turning off your computer

But First, a Word About Hardware

By leaping into all this stuff about DOS, commands, disks, and such, I'm assuming something about you. I'm assuming that your computer is already set up, all of its cables are plugged in, it's turned on, and you're ready to start learning about DOS.

If I'm right about this, then you are lucky indeed. Either a computer-wise friend (or the guy you bought it from) helped you set up your PC, or the office geek did it for you. Either way, you're ready to go.

If not, then you may need to take some extra steps before you read the rest of this chapter.

If Your PC Is Already Set Up

If your computer is set up, but you want to learn more about the hardware before you start working with DOS, turn to this book's Table of Contents. This book has several chapters that talk about different types of hardware. They can help you understand the pieces of your PC before you start using it. You can read those chapters first, if you like.

If Your PC Is Not Set Up

If your PC is not set up, then you need to back up and get the thing put together. Fear not; it's easier than setting up a typical home stereo.

If you're confused about what to do (and the directions don't help), you should start by calling the store or person that sold you the computer. They can walk you through setting up in less than 10 minutes (knock on wood!), right over the phone.

SAVE THE DAY!

If you don't trust the person you bought the computer from, or if he won't help you set it up, then take the thing back and demand a refund. PCs are too expensive for you to have to deal with a bunch of jerks. If you hate confrontation, then you'll need to take some time to figure it out. It's best to have a friend who knows something about computers—and a helpful book or two.

Time for a Shameless Plug

If your PC is still in the box and you've never put one together, I suggest that you run out and buy a copy of *PCs for Non-Nerds*, from New Riders Publishing.

It explains everything you'll ever need to know about computers—buying one, installing it, or upgrading it.

You're the Boss: DOS Commands

In Chapter 0, you got a little practice typing things at the keyboard. Each time you type a command and press Enter, you complete a *command line*. DOS reads the command line and thinks of it as an instruction that must be completed.

Here are some of the most popular DOS commands; all are discussed in this book:

```
DIR

COPY

DEL

CD

MD

RD
```

The DOS command line sometimes contains more than just a simple DOS command. You may need to add other information that DOS needs to complete the task. Computer nerds call this extra information "parameters." Sadly, you may need to learn about some parameters and switches before you can get the most from some DOS commands.

Parameters Are Easier Than They Sound

The word "parameter" may sound pretty high-tech, but it isn't. To show you how easy it is to add parameters to a DOS command, here's one quick example.

The TYPE command tells DOS to display the contents of a file on the screen so that you can read it. For this command to work properly, DOS needs to know which file to display. Therefore, you have to provide the name of the file when you enter the TYPE command.

Suppose that you want to read the contents of a file named AUTOEXEC.BAT. Enter the command like this:

```
TYPE AUTOEXEC.BAT
```

In this example, the file name (AUTOEXEC.BAT) is a *parameter* to the TYPE command.

The results of this command are shown in figure 1.1. The stuff that you see on the screen, starting on the line after the TYPE command, are the contents of the AUTOEXEC.BAT file on a computer in my office. The contents of your AUTOEXEC.BAT file probably will look very different from mine.

Figure 1.1

The results of the TYPE AUTOEXEC.BAT command.

```
G:\>TYPE AUTOEXEC.BAT

LH /L:1,41824 C:\DOS\SMARTDRV.EXE /L
set prompt=$t$h$h$h$h$h$h $p$g
PATH C:\DOS;F:\BAT;C:\WINDOWS;C:\PDOXWIN;E:\EXCEL4;C:\;E:\PUBDOM;C:\BRIEF
REM C:\WIN31\SMARTDRV.EXE /L
LH /L:1,13984 C:\DOS\share /L:200
LH /L:1,6400 C:\DOS\doskey
REM
REM Setup Brief variables
REM
set bpath=;c:\brief\macros
set bhelp=c:\brief\help
set bfile=c:\brief\state.rst
set bbackup=c:\brief\backup
set bflags=-i120k1l256Mrtu50 -mMG -mrestore
set btmp=.

G:\>
```

THANKS FOR TRYING
GRABBER™
800 242-4PSL

AUTOEXEC.BAT is a very special file on your computer system. AUTOEXEC.BAT tells DOS how you want it to start up, and provides a lot of information that the computer needs to do its job.

Don't forget that DOS doesn't care whether you type the command in capital letters or lowercase letters. DOS is not *case-sensitive*. To DOS, **TYPE AUTOEXEC.BAT** is the same as **type autoexec.bat**. I just put the commands in capital letters to make them easier to see.

Programs, Software, Applications, and Other Words That Mean the Same Thing

So far, so good. But the reason you have a computer is to get work done, right? Although your computer comes with a certain number of different computer programs installed (DOS, after all, is not much more than a collection of different little programs), it really isn't very useful without some major programs that help you get your job done.

Another word you'll hear a lot is "software," which is a very general expression that includes all kinds of computer programs. That's all it means. The term doesn't make any distinction between computer programs—just about every program that runs on computers (games, database programs, DOS itself) is covered by the word "software." Think of *software* to mean the universe of computer programs. All computer programs are part of the software universe (see fig. 1.2).

Different Kinds of Software

Your computer already has a certain amount of software installed on it. *Remember that DOS is software!* Your machine probably has other software installed, as well. See? You are already part of the software universe, and you may not have even known it. You just need to figure out what kind of software you have.

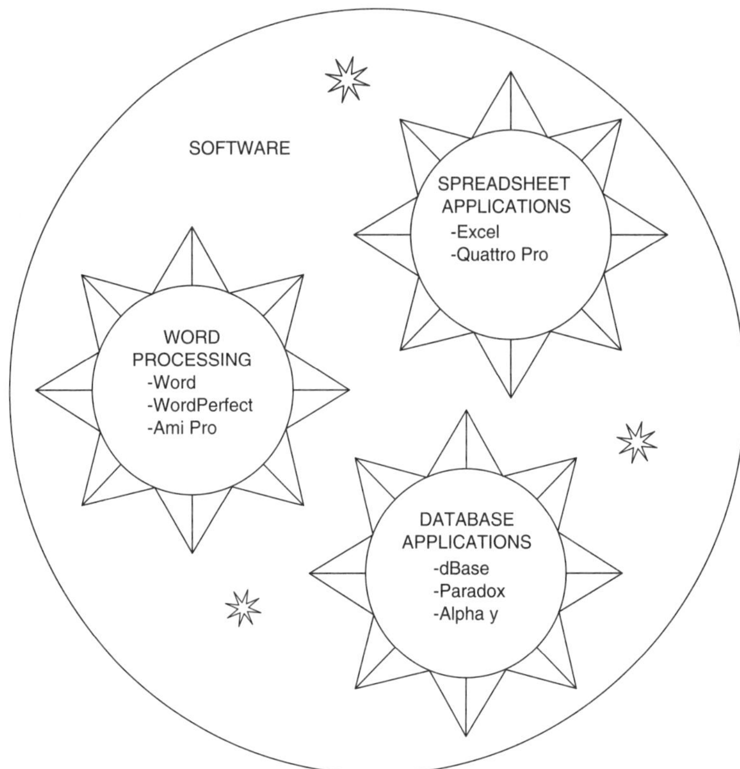

Figure 1.2

The software universe.

Here are what the most popular kinds of software can do:

 **Word processors.** When you use your computer to write letters, reports, or other correspondence, you use a *word processing application.*

 **Spreadsheets.** If you're entering financial or other numeric data into a spreadsheet, you are using a *spreadsheet application.*

 **Databases.** If you keep rows and columns of information, such as lists of names and addresses, or parts and part numbers, you are using a *database application.*

 **CAD.** If you want to use your computer to create architectural or engineering drawings, or other drawings that need a lot of precision, then you probably are using a *CAD application.* "CAD" stands for "Computer-Aided Design."

Graphics. If you need to draw free-hand illustrations, do "painting," and create other kinds of graphics, you can use a *graphics application.*

There are zillions of other kinds of software applications. These are just the most popular kinds. The following chapters will show you how to look at the contents of your computer's disks and figure out what kind of programs (if any) are already there.

NERDY DETAILS

An *application* is a program that performs a certain type of task. For instance, Excel, Lotus 1-2-3, and Quattro Pro are all *spreadsheet applications*. Word, Ami Pro, and WordPerfect are all *word processing applications*.

The word "application," therefore, refers to a computer program that performs a certain kind of task: spreadsheet, word processing, database, communications, and so on.

What's in a Program?

Good question. But the answer can be confusing, so here's the simplest way to think of it. A program (or application, if you like that word better) contains lines and lines of computer "code," or instructions that are written in a language your computer can understand. These instructions tell the computer to perform certain kinds of tasks.

Remember that most programs don't just start working and take control of your computer. Instead, they make the computer work for you. By selecting commands from a menu or typing them on a line (as in DOS), you tell the program that you want to make the computer do a certain task. The program then takes care of the hard work, and gives the computer all the real instructions.

DOS is a program. Actually, DOS is a collection of little programs, all put together into one big program that can make your computer do hundreds of things for you. In DOS, each program has a name, and that name is the command you use to run the program.

Table 1.1 shows you some examples of these little programs and their command names in DOS.

Table 1.1
Some DOS Commands, the Programs They Run, and What They Do

Command	Program Name	What It Does
DIR	DIR.EXE	Shows you a list of the files in a directory.
COPY	COPY.EXE	Lets you copy a file from one place on a disk to another place—or to another disk.
DEL	DEL.EXE	Lets you erase an unwanted file from a disk.
MD	MD.EXE	Lets you create a new directory to hold certain files.
FORMAT	FORMAT.EXE	Lets you prepare a disk so that it can hold information.
REN	REN.EXE	Lets you give a file a new name.

You used the `DIR` command a little bit in Chapter 0. You'll use it again in the next chapter, and in lots of other places in this book. You'll also learn how to use dozens of other DOS commands, and how to control the little programs they run.

Disks, Floppy and Otherwise

Your computer stores information (or "data," as geeks call it) on disks. You will learn a lot about disks later in this book; here I'll just introduce the basics.

Computers can use several kinds of disks:

- Floppy disks
- Hard disks
-  Optical disks

-  CD-ROM disks
-  RAM disks

RAM disks are exclusively for nerds (in fact, they aren't really disks), so we won't bother with them here. Optical disks and CD-ROMs are expensive and pretty high-tech, so you shouldn't worry about them until you've got some more experience.

Just about every PC can use floppy disks, and just about every PC has a hard disk built into it. So let's look at floppy disks and hard disks.

Floppy Disks

Floppy disks are really common. Just about any computer user has dozens of them stacked all over the place, stuffed in little disk holders, hidden in drawers, lost in books and album covers, stashed in closets, and so on. You'll have the same problem some day.

Most software programs come on floppy disks, and you'll be using floppies to store things from your computer from time to time. A *floppy disk* is a small, round, flat platter (hence the name "disk") that's coated with a magnetic substance. That substance is a lot like the stuff on the surface of a cassette tape.

The disk is enclosed in a plastic sleeve, which protects it. They come in two sizes: 5 1/4-inch and 3 1/2 -inch. Figure 1.3 shows you what typical floppy disks look like.

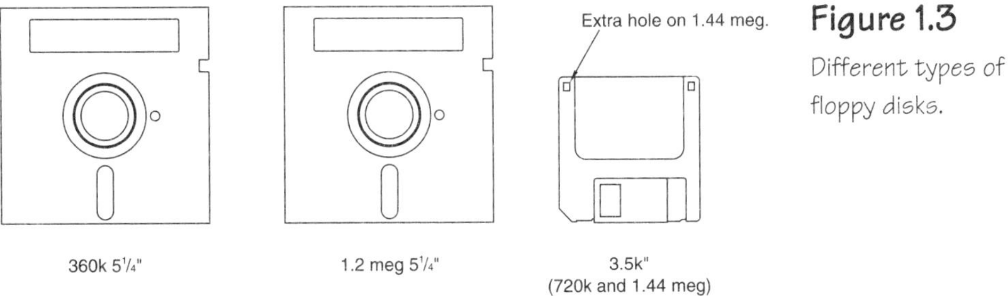

Figure 1.3
Different types of floppy disks.

In short, there are four kinds of floppy disks for PCs. Table 1.2 describes them.

Table 1.2
Common PC Floppy Disks

Size	Capacity	Distinguishing Characteristics
5 1/4"	360K	Has a "hub ring," which is a plastic ring that lines the hole at the center of the disk.
5 1/4"	1.2M	Looks just like a 360K disk, but doesn't have a hub ring.
3 1/2"	720K	Has one square hole at the top.
3 1/2"	1.44M	Has two square holes at the top.

Storage Capacity: Watch Your Ks and Ms

A disk's *capacity* is the amount of information it can hold. This is true for both floppy disks and hard disks. Capacity is measured in bytes. A *byte* is just a tiny piece of information in magnetic form. A letter of the alphabet, for example, might be a byte's worth of information.

When you read about disks, you see the letters "K" and "M" used a lot. Simply put, "K" means 1,000 and "M" means 1,000,000. A 360K floppy disk holds about 360,000 bytes of information; a 1.2M disk holds roughly 1,200,000 bytes.

Nerds call 1,000 bytes of information a *kilobyte*. They call 1,000,000 bytes of information a *megabyte*.

Protect Your Floppies!

That's about all you need to know right now about floppy disks. But there are a few rules about floppy disks you should remember:

 Don't stick your floppy disk to your refrigerator with a magnet. You'll erase it. Also, some desk gizmos, like paper clip holders, sometimes contain magnets, which are almost always fatal to floppy disks.

 Never, ever touch the brown part of the floppy disk that is visible through the slot. This is hard to do on 3 1/2-inch floppies because the brown part is protected by a sliding metal door. It's still possible to touch it if you try. Don't do this!

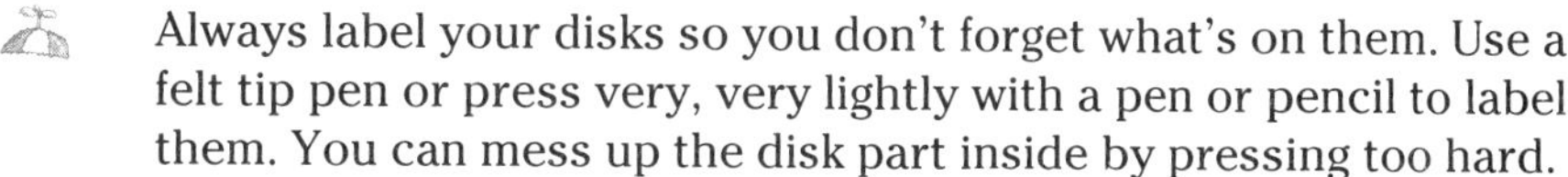

- Always label your disks so you don't forget what's on them. Use a felt tip pen or press very, very lightly with a pen or pencil to label them. You can mess up the disk part inside by pressing too hard.

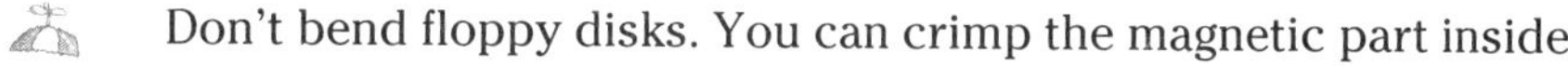

- Don't bend floppy disks. You can crimp the magnetic part inside.
- Keep your 5 1/4-inch disks in their envelopes when you're not using them. The magnetic part that shows can get damaged if you aren't careful with the disks.
- Some people say not to smoke near floppy disks. I think this is overkill when you consider how much dust even very well-maintained disks are exposed to.

Hard Disks

For simplicity's sake, you can think of a *hard disk* as being the same kind of thing as a floppy disk. The big difference is that hard disks can hold tons more information than a floppy disk can.

These days, the smallest hard disk you will find can hold about 20M of information. (That's about 20,000,000 bytes.) Some PCs have 500M hard disks. (That's about 500,000,000 bytes!) But a disk that big is really expensive.

NERDY DETAILS

> Your computer's hard disk is hidden inside the computer box. You only know it's there when the disk light on the front of the computer flashes. Some hard disks make a gurgling sound when they are active. (Lub dub, lub dub...)

You probably will store all your programs directly on your computer's hard disk. This makes them a lot easier to run, and they will run faster from the hard disk than they can run from a floppy disk.

You also will store lots of your files (letters, reports, and so on) on the hard disk. Most people do this. Later in this book, however, you will learn some tricks that will help you protect this information—just in case something goes wrong with your hard disk.

Drives

Your computer uses *disk drives* to turn all those disks. The PC should have a separate drive for 5 1/4-inch floppies, for 3 1/2-inch floppies, and for your hard disk.

To use the floppy disk drives, you put the floppy disk into a slot on the front of the computer, flip a latch, and that's that. Your hard disk is always in its own drive, so you don't have to do anything with it.

Later in this book, you'll find complete instructions for using floppy disks and floppy disk drives, and for managing your hard disk.

Quittin' Time!

There's not much to know about turning off the computer. Just make sure that you aren't running a program when you turn off the power. A lot of applications will end if you press the F4 key while holding down the Alt key (this is called "doing an Alt-F4"); others will end if you press Alt-X (hold down the Alt key while you press the X key).

If neither of these work, you'll have to read the program's manual or ask someone how to turn it off.

When you get back to the `C:\>` prompt, or if you're already there, it's okay to turn off your computer. Don't forget to turn off the monitor if it doesn't go off automatically with the big box.

To Shut Down or Not To Shut Down?

Some people say you should leave your computer on all the time. I think this is a bad idea for a number of reasons.

1. You will wear out certain parts of your computer (like the fan and hard disk) sooner than you will by turning it off when you're not using it.
2. All the time the computer is running, the fan is drawing air from the room and blowing it through your computer system to keep it cool. It also fills the computer with dust, hair, bugs, and anything else that can get inside.

3. Electricity isn't perfect. Spikes, surges, brownouts, and other electrical boogers can come through your power cord and toast part or all of your PC. You reduce this risk by turning off the machine when you won't be using it for several hours.

If, for some reason, you need to leave your computer on *all the time*, you should buy an air filter and a good power-line conditioner that will really protect your machine from these hazards. Auxiliary filters are relatively cheap (a kit should cost you less than $20). Power-line conditioners are quite a bit more expensive (like $100 or more). It's your choice.

Finally, if you don't use your computer constantly during the day, but you do use it frequently for short amounts of time, you should probably leave it on between sessions. It'll be more gentle to the components in your machine if the computer is left on for an hour or so at a stretch than if it is turned off and on multiple times during the day. I suggest that you don't leave it on overnight or over weekends, however. Too many bad things can happen to it while you're not there.

"I HATE IT WHEN THEY EAT JUST BEFORE THEY COME IN. THIS ONE JUST HAD A WHOLE BAG OF CHIPS."

Playing Those Filing Clerk Blues

This chapter shows you how DOS stores files on your computer's disks. You have to know the stuff in this chapter so you can easily find the files on your disks. It's just too bad that there are so many new terms to learn and understand!

The good news is that once you learn the things in this chapter, you'll be able to organize the files on your disk in a logical, easy-to-remember way that actually *helps* you find things! In this chapter you learn:

 How disks work

 What files are

 What directories are

 How to tell what's on a disk and in its directories

Get on a First-Name Basis with Your Disks

All computers use disks to store information. A *disk* is just a flat, round thing that spins real fast.

A disk's surface is covered with the same stuff as a cassette tape (the tape itself, not the little box). The computer "records" information onto a disk and "reads" information from a disk, just like a tape player records and plays sounds on a tape. (Actually, computers and tape players work in very different ways, but only nerds care about such stuff.)

Your computer uses a *disk drive* to make the disk spin and to record and read information on it. Most computers have three disk drives, although yours may just have two. Table 2.1 shows you how disk drives usually are named.

Table 2.1
Disk Drive Names

Drive Name	Which Drive Is It?
A:	The big floppy disk drive on the front of the computer
B:	The small floppy disk drive on the front of the computer
C:	The "hard disk," which is hidden inside the computer

Notice the colon (:) after the letter. Always use the colon when you type the drive's name; this tells DOS that you are talking about the disk drive and not something else.

A computer can have more drives than just A:, B:, and C:. If you're interested in finding out more about this, see the following "Nerdy Detail." If you don't want to have more drives than fingers, you can skip it.

NERDY DETAILS

Even though your computer probably has only one hard disk, that disk can be divided up, so the computer treats the drive like it has more than one disk in it. Nerds call this "partitioning," because you divide the disk (with partitions, get it?) into chunks. Each chunk gets treated like it's a separate disk. If your hard disk is partitioned, it may contain drive C:, drive D:, drive E:, and so on. If your hard disk is partitioned, however, it probably was set up that way by a nerd, and it probably only goes up to drive D: or E:. Even nerds get confused if a hard disk is divided up too many ways.

If you're one of those unlucky souls whose computer is tied to a network, then you may have access to several disk drives that aren't even part of your computer! DOS lets you name drives up to drive Z:, which means you could have as many as 26 drives. By playing some nerdy tricks on your computer, you could come up with even more, but that's almost never necessary.

If you're using a laptop computer, you probably have only one floppy disk drive, and it will always be drive A: (unless some nerd has messed around inside your computer). Some desktop computers only have one floppy disk drive, too. The following note gives you all the gory details on how this works.

NERDY DETAILS

Here's a real mystery. If your computer has only one floppy drive, its name is "A:." The hard disk in such a computer is still drive "C:," not "B:," as you might expect. Where did drive B: go? Well, just to be confusing, it's still there; you just can't see it. Your one floppy drive serves as both the A: and B: drives. If you ever try to do a **DIR** on drive B: on a computer equipped with only one floppy drive, DOS comes back with this message:

```
Insert disk in drive B: and press return
```

DOS is not too helpful because it doesn't tell you to stick the disk in drive A:. Once DOS reads the disk in the "phantom" drive B:, it "pretends" that drive A: is now drive B:.

What's a "File"?

Whenever you work on a computer, you work with a file. To understand what a *file* is, just think of a filing cabinet full of folders. Each folder is a file. A file, then, is just a thing that holds some information.

Imagine that you don't have a computer; you only have a typewriter and a file cabinet. Here's how you would create a file:

1. You'd type something—say, a list of ways to kill your neighbor's dog, which barks all night.
2. You'd put the list in a folder.
3. You'd write something on the folder's tab (like "Ways to Kill Bob's Dog"); that is, you'd give the file a name.
4. You'd put the file in a drawer, so you'd always know where the list was.
5. You'd make sure that the drawer had a good name, so you'd know what kind of files were in it. In this case, you might label the drawer "Dog-Related Stuff."

A simple process, right? Well, it's even simpler if you use a computer. And you can use your PC to do exactly the same things. Just think of the keyboard as a typewriter (without the little bell), the screen as your paper (you never need to erase!), and the disk as your filing cabinet. What does that make DOS? Your own personal file clerk. Figure 2.1 illustrates the DOS filing cabinet.

A file can contain any kind of information that you can create on your computer. You may have files that contain letters, drawings, tax information, recipes, maps, charts, and so on. Just remember that each letter or drawing is stored in its own file.

If you're in a hurry to start making files, turn to Chapter 3, which gives you an overview of the way the DOS filing system works. Chapter 3 tells you everything you'll ever need to know about making, copying, moving, and erasing files on your PC.

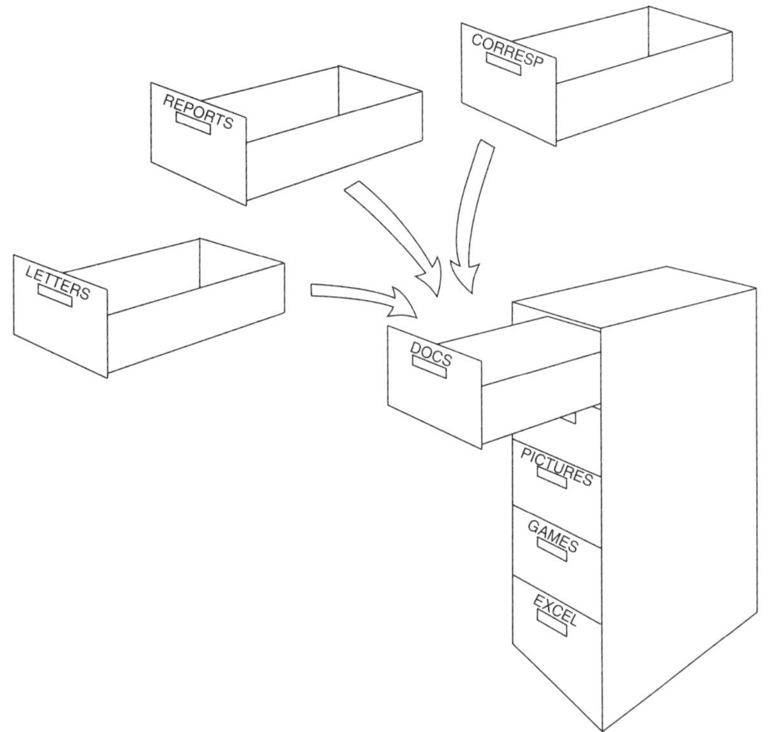

Figure 2.1

The DOS filing cabinet.

Your PC's File Drawers: Directories

Most filing cabinets have a number of drawers in which folders and papers are kept. DOS has its own kind of drawer, which is called a *directory* in nerd-speak. A directory is just a place on a disk where you can keep things together.

You can have a separate directory (drawer) for each kind of file you create. For instance, you can have separate directories for:

- Letters
- Taxes
- Drawings
- Recipes

Just to name a few. You can give any directory a unique name, and that name can have up to eight letters. If you have a directory that just holds letters, you can name it LETTERS. Chapter 13 tells you all about creating and naming directories.

DOS is the ultimate file cabinet because you can add as many drawers as you need. You can even add drawers inside drawers! (And drawers inside those drawers, and so on....) Nerds call these sub-drawers *subdirectories*. Unfortunately, that's what I call them in this book, and that's what you should call them, too.

NERDY DETAILS

Any directory can hold both files and other subdirectories. Any subdirectory can hold both files and sub-subdirectories. And so on, and so on....

Subdirectories let you be very precise in your filing. Figure 2.2 shows how you might set up some directories and subdirectories on your computer.

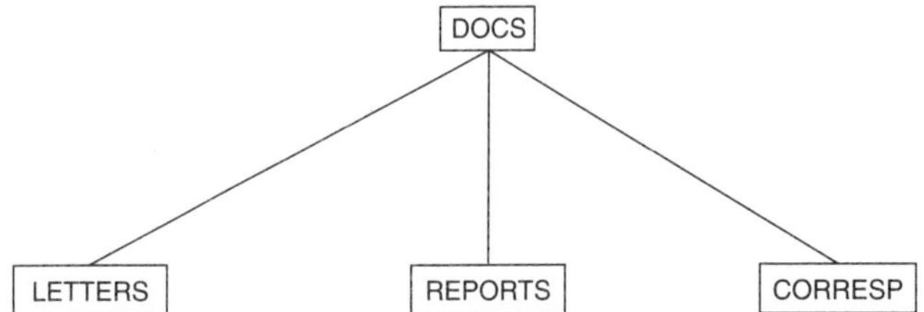

Figure 2.2
An arrangement of directories.

Just like your sock drawer or silverware drawer, your DOS drawers (directories) can be arranged any way you like. If you decide you don't like them arranged the way they are now, you can change them at any time. (Chapter 13 teaches you all the commands you need to know to control and change your directories.)

Where Do All These Drawers Fit?

Where do you put all this stuff? Well, DOS provides one big, main directory to hold all the directories and subdirectories you create. You can think of this main directory as the frame around the filing cabinet; it holds all the drawers in place. But it can hold other files, too, as well as directories and subdirectories.

NERDY DETAILS

Nerds call this main directory the **root** directory. They claim that when you draw a picture of a computer's directories and then turn it upside-down (as in fig. 2.3), the directories and subdirectories look like a tree branching up and out. Because the main directory is at the bottom of all this mess, some nerd decided to call it the **root**. Charming, huh?

Figure 2.3

A typical DOS directory map.

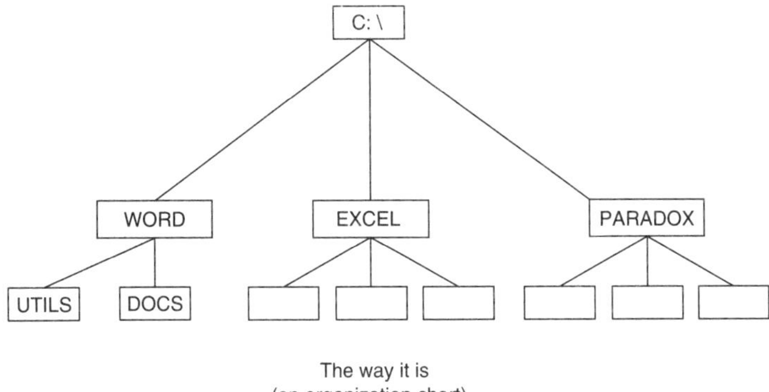

The way it is
(an organization chart).

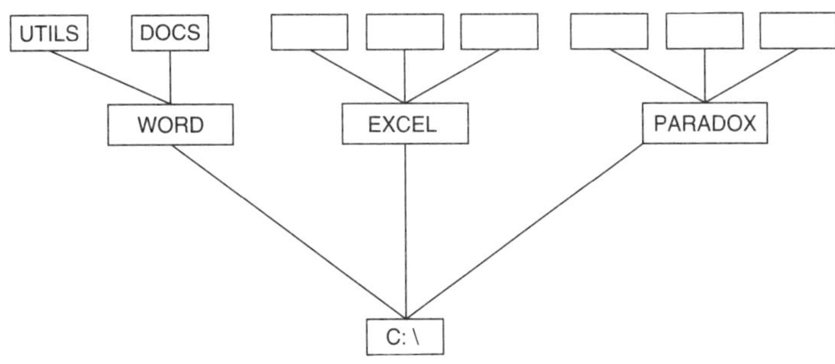

The way nerds see it
(a tree).

One of the things that makes the concept of a `root` directory so hard to grasp is that you don't use its name to reference it. The name of the root directory isn't `root`, it's "\"(a *backslash*). Isn't that stupid?

SAVE THE DAY!

> Do not confuse the *backslash* (\) with the *forward slash* (/). You should locate both of these keys on your keyboard now, because you'll be using them both a lot as you use DOS.
>
> If you want to put a file in the root directory (named \) of your hard disk (named C:), you identify it this way:
>
> `C:\`

What's in Those Drawers?

Remember the `DIR` command? You used it in Chapter 1. `DIR` tells DOS to show you a list of what's inside a directory. Using the `DIR` command is like opening a file drawer and looking inside. You can see the names of all the files inside the directory. You also can see the names of any subdirectories that are stored inside the directory.

If your computer is running, type this at the DOS prompt:

```
CD\
```

Then press Enter. This tells DOS that you want to work in the root directory of drive C:. Now type the `DIR` command, like this:

```
DIR
```

And press Enter. You should see a display that resembles figure 2.4.

SAVE THE DAY!

> Don't worry if your screen doesn't look exactly like figure 2.4. In fact, it probably won't. That's because you and I have different files and subdirectories in our root directory.

Each line of the display in figure 2.4 is the name of a thing that is stored in the open drawer of the DOS filing cabinet. Although you might be able to open more than one drawer in a filing cabinet at a time, you can only open one DOS drawer at a time (the open drawer is called the *current directory*, but more on that later).

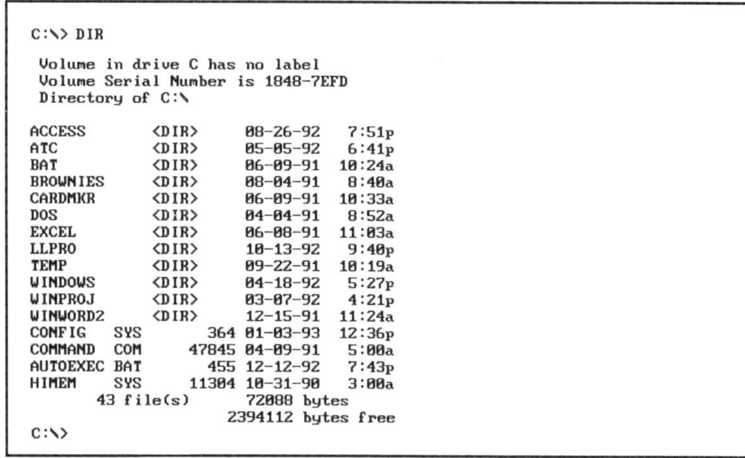

```
C:\> DIR

 Volume in drive C has no label
 Volume Serial Number is 1848-7EFD
 Directory of C:\

ACCESS       <DIR>      08-26-92   7:51p
ATC          <DIR>      05-05-92   6:41p
BAT          <DIR>      06-09-91  10:24a
BROWNIES     <DIR>      08-04-91   8:40a
CARDMKR      <DIR>      06-09-91  10:33a
DOS          <DIR>      04-04-91   8:52a
EXCEL        <DIR>      06-08-91  11:03a
LLPRO        <DIR>      10-13-92   9:40p
TEMP         <DIR>      09-22-91  10:19a
WINDOWS      <DIR>      04-18-92   5:27p
WINPROJ      <DIR>      03-07-92   4:21p
WINWORD2     <DIR>      12-15-91  11:24a
CONFIG   SYS        364 01-03-93  12:36p
COMMAND  COM      47845 04-09-91   5:00a
AUTOEXEC BAT        455 12-12-92   7:43p
HIMEM    SYS      11304 10-31-90   3:00a
       43 file(s)      72088 bytes
                     2394112 bytes free
C:\>
```

Figure 2.4

The results of the `DIR` command.

The display in figure 2.4 shows two different kinds of things in the root directory: files and directories (remember, directories can contain other directories).

Telling the Socks from the Underwear

In figure 2.4, look at the line that starts with the word ACCESS. DOS is giving you all this information about it:

The <DIR> to the right of the word ACCESS tells you that the thing named ACCESS is a directory.

ACCESS is a subdirectory that is under the current directory (this means that ACCESS is a filing cabinet drawer that is *inside* the drawer that is currently open).

The numbers to the right of the <DIR> are the date and time that the directory was created.

Each thing in this display followed by <DIR> is the name of a directory contained within the current directory. So, what are the other lines in this display?

Disks Aren't the Only Things with Names

Near the bottom of the display in figure 2.4 are the names of four files that are kept in the currently open directory.

There are two parts to each file name you see in figure 2.4. The first part (CONFIG, COMMAND, AUTOEXEC, and HIMEM) is the proper name of the file. The second part of each file name in figure 2.4 (SYS, COM, BAT, and SYS) is called the file-name *extension* (think of the extension as the file's last name).

NERDY DETAILS

A file's first name cannot be more than eight letters long. It also can't contain spaces or certain other punctuation. This is a real pain because it means that you can't be real descriptive when you give your files names. A file's last name—its extension—can have up to three letters. File names don't have to have extensions, but it's a good idea to add them. Some programs automatically add the proper extensions when they save files for you.

Although the DIR command does not display it, there is a period (.) between the file's name and its extension. For instance, if you ever want to refer DOS to your AUTOEXEC file, you must enter the full name of the file (**AUTOEXEC.BAT**). Although DOS doesn't put the period between the first and last names of your files, you have to do it when you talk to DOS.

Chapter 3 explains everything you need to know about files and their names. It also provides some clues for you to tell what kind of file you're dealing with. Chapter 3 also tells you how to do some pretty neat things with your files.

NOTE
DATA
A-Z

All About Files

Files, files, files. Files. Files and more files. They're everywhere. Just about every page in this book has the word "file" on it. Your computer is crammed with them. Stores are overflowing with them. You can buy them out of catalogs. Millions of people swap them across the phone lines and transmit them through the airwaves every day. Get the picture? If you want to use a computer, you have to know about files. This chapter is where you get the real poop on files:

- The different kinds of files
- How to recognize what kind of files you have
- The `DIR` command (slight reprise)
- How to duplicate files
- How to move files around on your disks
- How to rename a file
- How to remove files from your disks
- How to retrieve a file that was removed

This chapter will be the most important one you read when it comes to managing your files. You'll be able to use this information right away, and you'll need to understand it before going on to another chapter.

Create a New file

It's time to create your own simple file and put it into your DOS filing cabinet. It's not important for you to understand exactly what's happening or why you type what you're about to type. The objective of this exercise is to practice some simple DOS commands on a little file you create.

1. Type this command at the DOS prompt:

   ```
   ECHO HELLO, WORLD! > \HELLO.TXT
   ```

   Don't forget the right-pointing arrow (it's the "greater than" sign) or the backslash (\) in front of HELLO.TXT.

2. DOS comes back with a "plain" command line; that is, it has no prompt.

3. You're done! (There is no step 3...)

Now Just Look at What You've Done!

You've just created a simple file that contains the words HELLO, WORLD! in it. To prove it, use the TYPE command:

```
TYPE \HELLO.TXT
```

Don't forget the \ in front of HELLO.TXT. You should see this on your screen:

```
HELLO, WORLD!
```

Time To Play "Name That File!"

If you don't put names on any of the folders in your file cabinet, you can't tell one folder from another. The same is true of the files in your PC. Whenever you create a file, you should give it a name. Remember, too, that you won't create many files by yourself in DOS. Instead, you'll use a program to create new files. Most programs won't even save a new file onto a disk unless you provide a name for the file.

DOS is pretty picky when it comes to letting you name your files. Here are some points to remember:

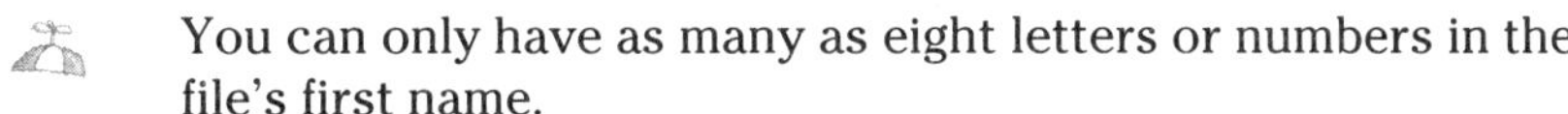

- You can only have as many as eight letters or numbers in the file's first name.
- You can only have up to three letters or numbers in the file's last name.
- There's always a dot (a period) between the first and last names.
- File names are not case-sensitive. DOS converts them all to capital letters along the way.
- You can't use punctuation or spaces in either the first or last name. Figure 3.1 shows a typical file name.

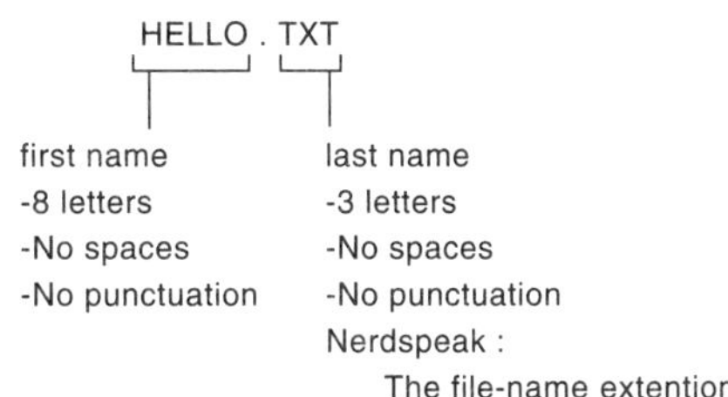

Figure 3.1

A DOS file name.

NERDY DETAILS

> Nerds use a technical-sounding word when they mean *letter* (as in "letter of the alphabet", not "Gee, I've got to mail this letter"). This nerd word is *character*. Some graduate-level nerds might even use the very nerdy word *byte* when they mean *character*, which, of course, means *letter*. They're all the same.

Whenever possible, you should use descriptive names for your files. Here are some examples:

`BUDGET92.XLS.`	A spreadsheet containing the 1992 budget
`XMASLIST.DOC.`	Your Christmas card list
`BROWNIES.TXT.`	A to-do list for a Brownie troop leader
`TOMOM.DOC.`	A letter you're writing to your mom

It's too bad that DOS only lets you use eight letters for a file's first name. But with a little imagination, those eight letters can go a long way. A little bit later in this chapter we'll look at the last names of some common types of files.

The last name of a file is usually referred to as its *extension*. You may hear computer nerds talk about a *file-name extension*. What they're talking about is the file's last name.

Sounds Like.... (Using Wild Cards in File Names)

From time to time, you will forget the exact name of a file. Try as you might, eight characters...er...letters really don't give you much to work with. You'd like to name your files something like `Household budget 1993`, but mean old DOS won't let you. You have to name it something like `BUDGET93.XLS`.

Or, you might be getting tired of having to type the entire name of a file when you use the `DIR` command to see how big it's getting. Typing **`DIR BUDGET93.XLS`** gets tiring after a while.

DOS has shortcuts for file names that are used for certain commands. If you want, you can substitute an asterisk (*) for any number of letters in the file name. Similarly, you can substitute a question mark (?) for any one letter in a file name.

Here's How Wild Cards Work

Suppose, for instance, that you use the Excel program. It creates files with the last name `XLS`. If you type the following command, DOS shows you all the XLS files in the directory you have open:

```
DIR *.XLS
```

Excel also creates other files with the letters `XL` in the extension. (Excel uses `XLS` for spreadsheets, `XLC` for charts, and so on.) If you want a list of all the files whose last names start with the letters `XL`, you can enter this command:

```
DIR *.XL?
```

DOS shows you all the Excel work files in the open drawer.

NERDY DETAILS

The *.* is a special wild card that indicates *all* files. (Some nerds refer to this combination as "stardotstar". The rest of us might say "star, dot, star".) You'll use *.* a lot—sometimes *too* much because some people accidentally remove all their files from time to time. Please be careful.

Super nerds call *.* by an even nerdier expression: "splat-dot-splat." Someday you can really impress some geek by casually using this expression.

From the annals of nerdlore, the over-all concept of using "wild cards" to find files was called "file masking." Hmmmm, I can see now why people aren't lining up to take continuing education courses in nerdisms.

Practice with Wild Cards

These shortcuts make it real easy to narrow down your search for a file. As an experiment, enter these:

```
DIR \*.TXT
```

or

```
DIR \HELLO.*
```

If you created the `HELLO.TXT` file earlier in this chapter, you'll find it in the `DIR` listing on your screen. Notice that wild cards help the `DIR` command narrow down the number of files you see on the screen.

STOP!

Unfortunately, you can't use the wild cards * and ? with just any DOS command. If you try to enter the command **TYPE *.TXT,** DOS will complain with an `Invalid filename or file not found` error message. With a little practice, you'll quickly learn when you can use wild cards and when you can't.

One last thing about the ? wild card. You can use several question marks in a row. Again, if you use Excel and have an Excel file named BUDGET, you can find all the related files by using this command:

```
DIR BUDGET.X??
```

This command will find these files:

```
BUDGET.XLS
BUDGET.XLT
BUDGET.XLM
```

STOP!

Be very, very careful using wild cards with some of the commands you read about in this chapter. DOS won't prevent you from making incredibly stupid mistakes. If you're not careful, you can wipe out a lot of stuff you didn't mean to lose.

It's usually safe to use wild cards to find your files. It is very dangerous, however, to use wild cards for deleting files. You can easily remove a valuable file from your disks if you aren't careful with wild cards.

If you're lucky enough to have DOS 6, it can help you repair the damage caused by some of these mistakes. You'll learn about DOS 6's capability to come to the rescue later in this book.

What Flavor Is This File?

There are many different kinds of files stored on your disks. Some of these files are "plain text" files, such as the HELLO.TXT file you just made. Others are much, much more complex.

What's in There?

Remember the TYPE command? It lets you see what's inside a file. (This is like opening the lid on a Tupperware container to get a look at what's inside. Except you don't have to hold your nose.)

Try this command:

```
TYPE \COMMAND.COM
```

Watch what happens. You should see a bunch of hieroglyphics rapidly stream across the screen, as shown in figure 3.2. It is hopeless to try to make sense of this display; only DOS can read the file named COMMAND.COM. (If you don't think you'll be able to sleep tonight unless you know more about COMMAND.COM, see the following Nerdy Detail.)

All files with last names of COM or EXE are *executable*, or computer program files, for DOS to run. An executable file tells the computer to do something.

```
C:\>TYPE \COMMAND.COM

θ]§`x§  π*  u♫  à↕                                        √δd ▲♫.  .♦☺√δY ▲♫.  ☺√δN ▲♫.
 .♀☺√δC ▲♫.  .►☺δ9 ▲♫.  .¶☺δ/ ▲♫.  .↑☺δ% ▲♫.  .∟☺δ← ▲♫.  .  ☺δ◄ ▲♫.  .$☺δ ▲♫.  .(☺£.Ç>4☺
 δ♀ s♥δ

C:\>
```

Figure 3.2

What happens when you enter TYPE \COMMAND.COM.

You may hear your computer beep as the contents of COMMAND.COM are displayed. Not to worry! It's just that some of the stuff in COMMAND.COM makes your computer beep as it gets displayed on the screen.

NERDY DETAILS

Although it's not obvious, COMMAND.COM is running all the time you use your computer. It's the program that DOS uses to read what you type at the keyboard. Nerds like to call COMMAND.COM a *command-line interpreter.*

File Names: A Real Alphabet Soup

You don't always need to look at a file's contents to tell what kind of file it is. You often can tell just by looking at the file's last name. Table 3.1 lists common last names for files, and tells you what type of files they are.

Table 3.1
Common Last Names for Files

Last Name	Meaning
BAT	A special kind of executable file. You'll make a BAT file or two later in this book.
COM	Another common kind of executable file.
DB, DBF	Common last names for database files.
DOC	A common last name for word processing files.
EXE	The most common kind of executable file.
INI	An "initialization" file for some applications.
PCX, BMP, GIF	Different kinds of picture files.
SYS	A special *system* file for DOS to use.
TXT	A text file in plain English.

There are a lot of different files that can be produced by applications on your disk. My hard disk has files with last names such as `C`, `DB`, `DBF`, `DLL`, `IDX`, `MDB`, `NDW`, `NCD`, and on and on.

And Now: Everything You'll Ever Need To Know About DIR

The `DIR` command is by far the most common instruction you will give DOS. `DIR` can reveal all of the contents of your DOS filing cabinet, even things that are "hidden" from view.

Table 3.2 describes all the different ways you can use `DIR`.

Table 3.2
Variations on the DIR Command

Command	Result
`DIR /P`	Causes the display to stop every time the screen fills up. This is useful when stuff would otherwise scroll (roll) off the screen.
`DIR /W`	Shows the directory listing in "wide" format. This puts five columns of file names across the screen without the file size, or date and time information. In this display, directory names have little brackets around them, and file names look like they ought to (they have the dot in the name). See figure 3.3 for an example.
`DIR /O-D`	Shows the disk contents in date order, with the oldest files first. If you want to see the newest files first, use `DIR /O-D`. The `/OD` parameter can help you find your old, unused files.
`DIR /S`	Searches all directories below the one you've got open. This is like searching through the many drawers in your file cabinet that are contained within the drawer you've got open, and then all of the drawers in those drawers, and so on.

```
C:\>DIR/W

 Volume in drive C is 10SEPT92
 Volume Serial Number is 1A30-AE96
 Directory of C:\

[386MAX]        [ACCESS4]       [BACKUP]        [BAT]           [NDW]
[BRIEF]         [DOCS]          [DOS]           [DOWJONES]      [DOWNLOAD]
[MSDOSBTA]      [MUTUALS]       [OLD_DOS.1]     [PARADOX]       [PCPLUSW]
[PDOXWIN]       [SARAH]         [TEMP]          [VBWIN1]        [WIN31]
[WINDOWS]       [ZIPMGR]        AUTOEXEC.BAT    AUTOEXEC.NDW    ANSI.SYS
AUTOEXEC.ACC    CONFIG.NDW      AUTOEXEC.ND0    CONFIG.ND0      TREEINFO.NCD
COMMAND.COM     CONFIG.SYS      CONFIG.STK      CONFIG.STC      CONFIG.SAV
CONFIG.002      TREEINFO.DT     DBLSPACE.OUT    DSVXD.386       EMM386.EXE
HIMEM.SYS       MOUSE.SYS       MOUSE.INI       PARADOX.NET     RAMDRIVE.SYS
SMARTDRV.EXE    HELLO.TXT       VI.EXE          WINA20.386      JUNK
       50 file(s)     426423 bytes
                    34107392 bytes free

C:\>
```

Figure 3.3
The wide display you see after using `DIR /W`.

You can combine parameters with DIR. For example:

```
DIR /O-D/P
```

This command displays a list of all the files in the open directory, with newest files first, and pauses after each full screen of information.

The Computer Lost and Found

Computers are supposed to make your life easier, but things can get out of hand. The DOS filing cabinet can have so many drawers and layers of drawers that it becomes nearly impossible to find something if it's gone into the wrong directory. (One of the hard disks in my home computer contains more than 7,400 files in almost 500 directories.) Imagine finding one white sock in 7,400!

You can use DIR to find things you've lost on your disk. This is helpful, for example, if you've saved a file from your word processor and you can't find it later.

Finding a Lost File with DIR

DIR can find every file on your disk, so you can find any file that's on the disk. As long as you have an idea of the file's first or last name, DOS can dig it out of the filing cabinet.

Suppose you think there should be a file named MYFILE.TXT somewhere on your computer, but you can't remember what directory you put it in. To find the missing file, type this:

```
DIR /S \MYFILE.TXT
```

The /S parameter tells DOS to look through all the subdirectories on your computer until it finds MYFILE.TXT. The backslash (\) that you attach to the file's name tells DOS to start its search at the root directory.

When I ran this command on my computer, figure 3.4 shows what I got back from DOS. This command took about 30 seconds to complete because DOS had to search a lot of directories to find MYFILE.TXT.

```
C:\>DIR /S \MYFILE.TXT

 Volume in drive C is 10SEPT92
 Volume Serial Number is 1A30-AE96

Directory of C:\DOWJONES\DJLOGS\1992

MYFILE   TXT     74195 01-01-93   2:27p
        1 file(s)      74195 bytes

Total files listed:
        1 file(s)      74195 bytes
                    34031616 bytes free

C:\>
```

Figure 3.4

Searching for a missing file with the `DIR /S` command.

This command tells me the following information about MYFILE.TXT:

 It's located in the directory `C:\DOWJONES\DJLOGS\1992`.

 It contains 74195 *bytes*, which are the same as *letters* or *characters*.

 It was last changed on 2:27 pm on January 1, 1993.

But I Can't Remember the Name!

If you can't remember the exact name of your file, or if you've forgotten the first name but you know that Excel always assigns `XLS` as the last name of an Excel spreadsheet file, you can use wild cards in the file name:

```
DIR /S \*.XLS /P
```

Use the `/P` parameter to make DOS show just one screenful of information at a time. Otherwise, the display will scroll off the screen if you have a lot of `XLS` files on your disk.

NERDY DETAILS

A couple of nerdy notes here for finding files:

You can enter the file name in lower- or uppercase. DOS doesn't care.

You can do the same search on a floppy disk as well: **DIR /S A:\MYFILE.TXT** (or **B:** if you want to search the B: floppy). It's much less likely you'll lose something on a floppy disk, however, because they hold so much less stuff than a hard disk.

Now That I Know Where Files Are, What Can I Do with Them?

Okay, so now you know the following things about files: how to make them, how to look at them, and how to find them on the disk. Now let's look at other things you can do with your files.

Copying Files

You often need to make a duplicate copy of a file you've been working on. Maybe you need to put the duplicate on a floppy disk so you can send it to someone, or put it on another computer. You use the COPY command to make a copy (not a *photo*copy, silly!) of your file.

COPY makes an exact duplicate of your file in the directory or on the disk you specify. There are lots of different ways to use COPY, and you'll be using this command a lot as you work with DOS.

Making a Copy with a Different Name

The COPY command is really simple to use for copying one file into another file. What's that mean? It means that you have the original file with its original name, and you want to make a copy of it and give the copy a different name. Here's an example:

```
COPY HELLO.TXT HITHERE.TXT
```

This action is illustrated in figure 3.5. Now you have the original HELLO.TXT, as you did before, but you also have a copy of the file's contents that is named HITHERE.TXT.

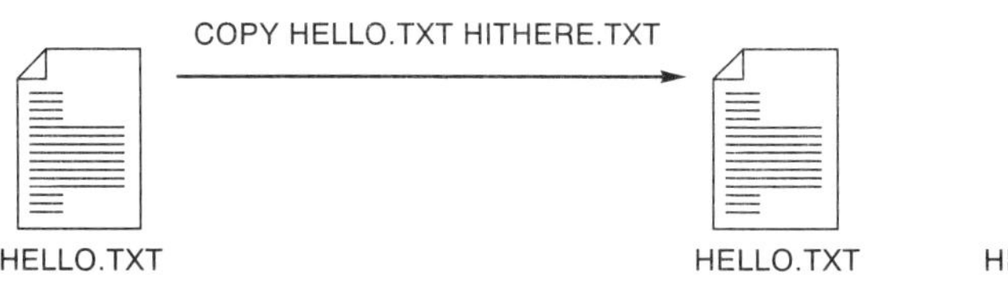

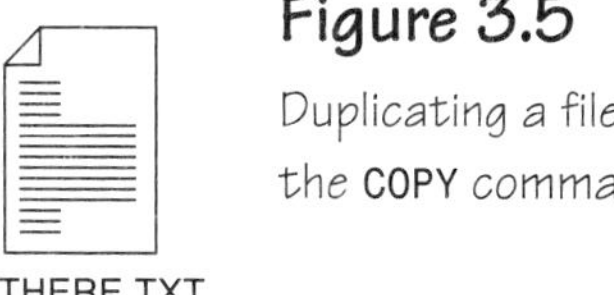

Figure 3.5

Duplicating a file with the `COPY` command.

Copying a File to Another Disk

Suppose that you have a file named `HELLO.TXT` in the `root` directory on your hard disk (drive C), and you want to put a copy of the file onto a floppy disk in drive A. Enter the following command:

```
COPY C:\HELLO.TXT A:
```

This command finds the file, and places a copy in the floppy disk's `root` directory. The copy has the same name as the original.

Copying a File to a Different Directory on the Same Disk

Suppose now that you have `HELLO.TXT` in your hard disk's `root` directory, and you want to put a copy in the `DOCS\LETTERS` subdirectory, which also is on your hard disk. To find out the name of the directory, enter this command:

```
COPY \HELLO.TXT \DOCS\LETTERS
```

This action is illustrated in figure 3.6.

In this example, the file **`HELLO.TXT`** has the name of the root directory (\) added to emphasize that a file is taken from the **`root`** directory and copied into another directory. You should probably only use directory names when necessary, though, to lessen the chance of making a spelling mistake or copying the wrong file.

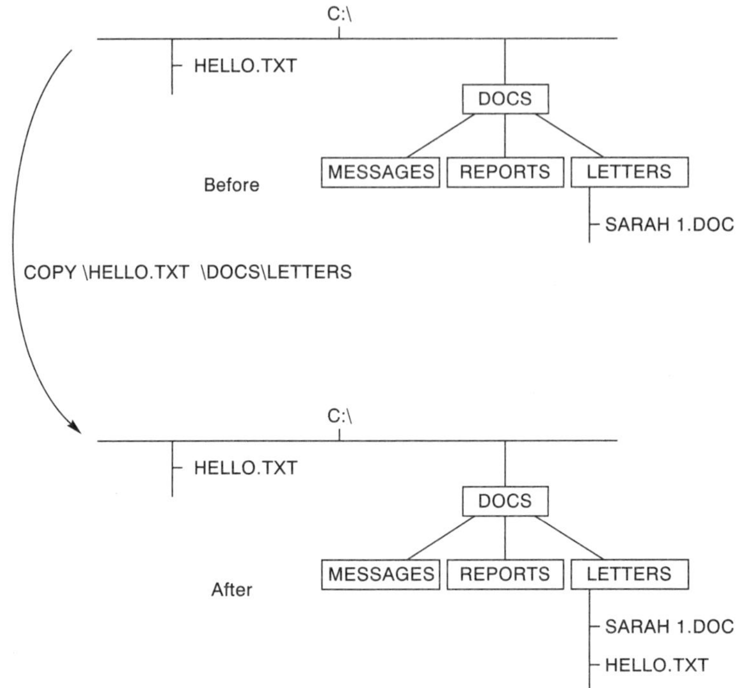

Figure 3.6

Putting a copy of a file into another directory.

Name-Calling (Keep It Clean!)

If you're copying to a directory, you don't have to specifically name the file at the receiving end. You might think of the COPY command as working this way:

```
COPY FROM-FILE TO-FILE
```

If you want to change the name of HELLO.TXT to HITHERE.TXT as it goes onto the floppy disk, enter this command:

```
COPY \HELLO.TXT A:HITHERE.TXT
```

This process is shown in figure 3.7.

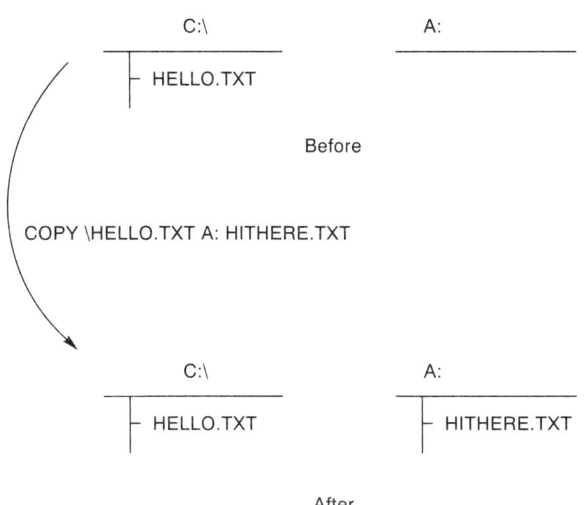

Figure 3.7

Putting a copy of a file onto a floppy disk.

The file named `HITHERE.TXT` is an exact duplicate of `HELLO.TXT` except that it has a different name, and it is on the floppy disk instead of the hard disk.

That's all there is to it. Just remember that the name of the file you've already got (`HELLO.TXT`) goes first; the name of the file where it's going comes next (`HITHERE.TXT`).

NERDY DETAILS

In nerd-speak, the file you're copying (`HELLO.TXT`) is called the source; the file you're copying to (`HITHERE.TXT`) is the destination.

The **COPY** command is really stupid. If you're copying **HELLO.TXT** onto a floppy disk, and there's already a file named **HELLO.TXT** on the floppy disk, DOS will copy right over the one on the floppy disk.

If this happens, you can't get back the original file. It's gone because DOS will lay the new one right over the old one.

This can be a real drag if you wanted to save the one on the floppy for some reason. Worse, imagine that you've got an older copy of a report on a floppy disk and the new version (which you've spent all day revising) on the hard disk. If you copy the file from the floppy disk to the hard disk by accident, you'll lose all your work.

There is no way you can get **COPY** to warn you before it overwrites an existing file, so please be careful. You should always do a **DIR** first on the drawer (directory or disk) where you're about to copy a file.

More Proof That DOS Isn't Perfect

Even if you think you're doing things right, all sorts of stuff can go wrong when you use the COPY command. As mentioned earlier, DOS won't always tell you when you make a mistake. That's because DOS can't tell that you don't mean to copy an old file over a new one.

Sometimes, though, DOS will show you a message to tell you that something's wrong when you try to copy a file. For example:

```
File cannot be copied onto itself
0 file(s) copied
```

This message means that you left out the name of the file you're copying to. DOS thinks you're trying to make a copy of the file right on top of the existing file. This can't happen; DOS will only copy a file from one place to a different place. You'll get this message, for example, if you enter the following command:

```
COPY HELLO.TXT
```

What's in a Name?

Because DOS only lets you use eight letters in your file names, it's easy to get confused and frustrated. I find myself debating all the time about how to name a file so that I'll know what's in it later. Sometimes, I'll decide that I need to give a new name to an existing file (usually because I want to give its name to another file). You'll probably do this a lot, too.

It's easy to change the name of your files in DOS. This is kind of like changing the label on a folder in your filing cabinet. Just use the REN command (short for "rename") this way:

```
REN OLD-NAME NEW-NAME
```

Practicing with REN

Suppose that you have a file called HELLO.TXT, and you want to change its name to HITHERE.TXT. Enter this command:

```
REN HELLO.TXT HITHERE.TXT
```

You can also rename a whole group of files at the same time by using wild cards:

```
REN *.DOC *.LTR
```

This command looks through the open directory and finds all the files with the last name DOC. Then DOS renames the files' file extension to LTR.

NERDY DETAILS

Just to be a little nerdy, you can rename a file this way:

```
REN HELLO.TXT *.LTR
```

Don't Expect Too Much from REN

There are two things you can't do with REN:

1. You can't use it to give a directory a new name.

2. If you try to rename a file to the name of a file that already exists, you'll see this error message:

```
Duplicate file name or file not found
```

This happens, for example, when you have a file named HITHERE.TXT, and you try to issue this command:

```
REN MYFILE.TXT HITHERE.TXT.
```

Moving Files Around (for the Lucky DOS 6 User)

If you're lucky enough to have DOS 6, you can easily move your files around on your disk. This way, you can rearrange your hard disk to make better use of your DOS filing cabinet. DOS 6 features a new MOVE command.

Older versions of DOS do not have a MOVE command. If you do not have DOS 6, you have to copy files to different directories if you want to move them, and then delete the original files.

NERDY DETAILS

If you're not sure what version of DOS you have, use the **VER** command at the DOS prompt. On my computer, I got the following message:

```
MS-DOS Version 6.00
```

This tells me that I'm using DOS 6, and that I'm a very lucky guy. The number reported by your computer may vary somewhat, but will probably be 3.*XX*, 4.*XX*, or 5.*XX* (*XX* is some two-digit number). If you are an unlucky user of anything older than DOS 3.31, please arrange somehow to upgrade to DOS 6. You'll *love* it! (This endorsement brought to you by the Bill Gates for President Committee.)

Practicing with MOVE

Using MOVE is simple. It's like the COPY command because it takes this general form:

```
MOVE FROM-PLACE TO-PLACE
```

Generally speaking, you will usually move a file from where it is to the place you want it to be. If you want to move HELLO.TXT from the open directory to a different directory (named \DOCS\LETTERS), use this command:

```
MOVE HELLO.TXT \DOCS\LETTERS
```

In this case, of course, LETTERS is a directory; you've just moved the HELLO.TXT file to the \DOCS\LETTERS directory. This process is shown in figure 3.8.

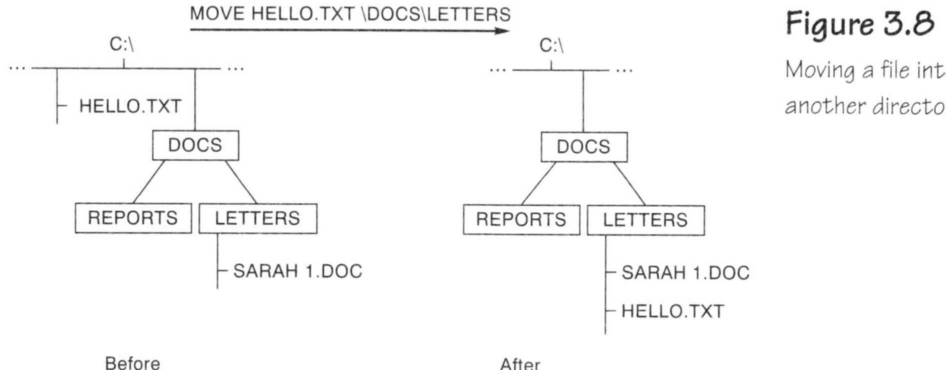

Figure 3.8

Moving a file into another directory.

A Moving Performance

But MOVE can do a lot more:

-  You can move a file from your hard disk to a floppy disk:

  ```
  MOVE HELLO.TXT A:
  ```

- You can move a file to a new name (this is the same as using the REN command):

  ```
  MOVE HELLO.TXT HITHERE.TXT
  ```

- You can move the contents of a directory into a new directory:

  ```
  MOVE \OLD_DOCS\LETTERS\*.* \DOCS\LETTERS
  ```

- You can rename a directory by moving it to a new name:

  ```
  MOVE \DOCS\LETTERS \DOCS\CORRESP
  ```

But You Can't Move Everything

But there are a few things you can't do with MOVE:

You can't move an entire directory and all its files from the hard disk to a floppy disk. The following *doesn't* work:

```
MOVE \DOCS\LETTERS A:\LETTERS
```

DOS shows you a nasty `Unable to open source` message. You have to move entire directories as a three-step process. First, create the new *destination* directory. Second, move all the files from the old directory to the new one. Third, delete the old directory. You learned about creating and deleting directories in Chapter 2.

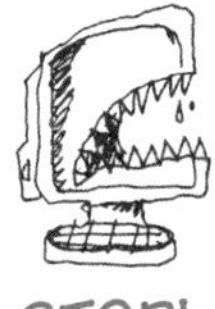

"DANGER, WILL ROBINSON," said the Robot. If you move a file from one place to another place, it will overwrite a file that's already at the destination with the same name. This is exactly the same antisocial behavior exhibited by **COPY** under the same circumstances. Be forewarned: you might accidentally **MOVE** right over something you care about.

Moving Files Around (for the Pre-DOS 6 User)

Don't bother reading this section if you know that you're a DOS 6 user, unless you have to use a pre-DOS 6 computer from time to time.

The only way to move files on pre-DOS 6 machines is by taking these steps:

1. Copy the file to its new name and location.
2. Delete the original file. Deleting files is covered in the next section.

The procedure is the same whether you're using this clumsy method to move files from your hard disk to a floppy disk, or just moving them around to a different directory on the hard disk.

Of course, if all you want to do is assign the file a new name, use the REN command.

Deleting Files

From time to time, you need to remove files from your hard disk. You read about the new DOS 6 MOVE command that you can use to move files from your hard disk to floppies. This is certainly one way to remove files from your hard disk.

A much simpler method of removing files from your disks is to just delete them by using the DEL (delete) command.

NERDY DETAILS

In nerd-speak, *delete* means "erase," "remove," or "get rid of."

DEL is easy to use. In fact, it's almost *too* easy:

 If you just want to delete one file named HELLO.TXT, use this command:

```
DEL HELLO.TXT
```

 If you want to delete a number of files with similar names, such as a group of files that all have the file extension TMP, use this command:

```
DEL *.TMP
```

 If you want to delete all the files in the open directory, use DEL like this:

```
DEL *.*
```

Watch It!

This last little number (DEL *.*) is a real scary thing to do, because you can easily wipe out files you didn't mean to erase. In fact, using wild cards with the DEL command is so dangerous that DOS will ask you:

```
All files in directory will be deleted!
Are you sure (Y/N)?
```

Read these warnings from DOS. You don't get too many of them because DOS assumes you know what you're doing most of the time.

Be Prepared for the Worst!

Remember that everyone makes mistakes. Even computer nerds. At some time, every computer user has deleted one or more important files. If you've spent hours and hours carefully writing an annual report, the worst thing that can happen is for that file to just disappear or be accidentally deleted.

DOS 6 provides you with a variety of protective measures against these disasters. Be careful when you use the DEL command, don't use pirated software (it could be infected with a computer *virus*), and consider the consequences if your hard disk with all its files and other important stuff suddenly quits working.

Keeping the Cabinet Cleaned Out

Each file on your disk has a purpose (or it *had* some purpose at one time). Each time you start a new letter in your word processor or make a new spreadsheet with your spreadsheet program, you are creating at least one new file on your disk.

Every now and then, you should check your DOS file cabinet to make sure you're not collecting a bunch of unused and unusable files. If a file is clearly outdated and not being used, you can throw it away with the DEL command. Or you can use COPY to copy the file to a floppy disk. Then you can store the floppy disk and delete the unwanted file from your hard disk.

Eventually, if you never take care of the files proliferating on your disk, the disk fills up and you don't have enough room to keep working or to install a new program. Many users let their computers get clogged up with old files from their word processor or spreadsheet programs.

If you recognize the name of a file as something you worked on a long time ago, copy the file onto a floppy disk, and delete the old file from your hard disk. You can get it back off your floppy disk later on if you need it.

Organizing Your Files

It's a good idea to keep your disk nicely organized. Just like your refrigerator, if you don't keep an eye on things from time to time, you'll lose files, and they'll get pushed farther and farther into the icebox, getting moldier and moldier until you won't be able to find or use them any more.

A big mistake many beginning computer users make is that they put too many files right in the `root` directory. As you saw in Chapter 2, it's easy to make new file drawers for your DOS filing cabinet. Because there's really no limit on the number of drawers you can have, why not make separate directories for each kind of file you have on your system?

Your programs usually create their own directory drawers when you install them the first time. If the applications on your computer were installed by someone else, it's probably been laid out in some logical manner (hope...hope...).

As you learn more about DOS, try to keep your disks organized. Put files into logically named directories (use `DOCS` or `REPORTS`, instead of `WORK`), at least as far as DOS allows you to be logical.

PART 2

What You Really Need To Know About Software

4. *Your Start-Up Files:* `AUTOEXEC.BAT` *and* `CONFIG.SYS`
5. *An Almost Likable DOS: The Shell*
6. *Batchman: The Caped Crusader*

Your Start-Up Files: AUTOEXEC.BAT and CONFIG.SYS

Your computer contains two start-up files, AUTOEXEC.BAT and CONFIG.SYS, which DOS uses to determine how it should behave on your specific computer. (If it doesn't have these files, or if it can't find them, DOS loads its default settings, without taking into account anything that could make it run better or more conveniently on your computer.)

In general, CONFIG.SYS handles the inside stuff—for example, how your computer copes with its memories, and how it communicates with the strange and myriad contraptions connected to it. These contraptions can include mice, joysticks, sound generators, scanners and many other devices.

Many peripherals require special *configurations*, which are changes to your computer's behavior, in order to work. In particular, they may require DOS to find and load a *device driver* (a program that helps DOS communicate with the device in question).

On the other hand, AUTOEXEC.BAT tends to handle the outside stuff, such as the list of external tasks you want your computer to perform before it announces: "I'm ready to get to work." For example, it might automatically load a program so you don't have to run the command yourself.

In this chapter, we'll walk you through some sample CONFIG.SYS and AUTOEXEC.BAT files, explain some commands that are often found in them, and then show you how to edit yours. You'll be able to answer these important questions:

- When should I change AUTOEXEC.BAT and CONFIG.SYS?
- What does my computer do when it wakes up?
- What is all that stuff in my start-up files?
- Why is the DOS 6 (and DOS 5) editor so downright handy?
- Should I scream? What do I do if it doesn't work?
- What if I don't have EDIT?

When Should I Change AUTOEXEC.BAT and CONFIG.SYS?

Much of the time, you won't have to worry about either AUTOEXEC.BAT or CONFIG.SYS.

But sometimes you will need to go under the hood yourself. For example, you might change AUTOEXEC.BAT to help DOS find one of your programs faster, or to always tell you which directory you have open. Or you might change CONFIG.SYS so that your arrow keys don't automatically turn into a calculator keypad when your computer is turned on.

Furthermore, there are certain tricks you can use to optimize your computer to make it run faster. (*Optimize* is nerd-speak for "make better.") Your computer can also do things for you to make your job a bit easier (how about the laundry?—Editor).

Often, the installation instructions for a new computer program recommend manual changes to AUTOEXEC.BAT and CONFIG.SYS. If you don't make these changes, the software may not run correctly, it may not start at all, or you may be whacked with a wet noodle.

You may see messages like: `Make sure the WHAMO directory is in the PATH statement in your AUTOEXEC.BAT file`, or `Set the FILES and BUFFERS lines in your CONFIG.SYS to no less than 30`. What do these guys mean? Are they joking or what?

Or, perhaps, the program's *own* installation program makes its own changes automatically — but messes things up in the process. (I've often wondered how many times software has been returned to the computer store because of an incorrectly-modified `AUTOEXEC.BAT` or `CONFIG.SYS` file. Must be in the millions!)

More experienced users, particularly nerds, mess with `CONFIG.SYS` and `AUTOEXEC.BAT` all the time, and the process has sometimes been mystified to the point of lunacy. But, as you'll see in this chapter, if you're reasonably careful, there's really not much to it.

Finally, knowing how to make these changes increases your independence as a computer user. No longer will you have to go get help from some eight-year-old Mario maven to make minor modifications to your system just to get a program to run.

If you are reading through this book from cover to cover, you can probably just jump over this chapter until you need to modify these files.

When Your Computer Wakes Up in the Morning...

Built right into your computer is a program that runs as soon as you turn on the computer. This program (nerds call it the "ROM BIOS" or just "the BIOS") controls your computer's most essential needs. It wakes up DOS and begins the process of loading DOS' most critical files (files that are so important that DOS hides them from you so you won't accidentally delete them).

These files, in turn, read `CONFIG.SYS` and `AUTOEXEC.BAT` to get the information DOS needs to prepare your computer for you. It's as if every day your mother had to give you directions on how to get to work, even if you take the same route every day.

What Is CONFIG.SYS, and Why Do I Want To Know About It?

Here's a typical CONFIG.SYS file for a reasonably high-powered computer (one with an 80386 or 80486 microprocessor chip under the hood). The lines on the *left* tell DOS what to do when it starts up. (Brush teeth, situps, shower...) The lines on the *right* are our notes, which tell you what DOS is doing.

This won't all be on the exam! We're showing it to you just to give you a feel for the kinds of things that CONFIG.SYS does. We'll explain most of this stuff in more detail later.

`DEVICE=C:\DOS\SETVER.EXE`	Loads a file that tells DOS 6 about some programs that must be tricked into running with it.
`DEVICE=C:\DOS\HIMEM.SYS` `DEVICE=C:\DOS\EMM386.EXE`	Together with the next line, helps you use all of this computer's memory.
`BUFFERS=10`	Sets aside chunks of memory to hold your information on its way to and from your disk.
`FILES=30`	Tells DOS how many files it can open at once.
`DOS=HIGH,UMB`	Tells DOS to load itself out of the way, so you can fit more programs into the memory that's best able to work with them.
`SHELL=C:\COMMAND.COM /P`	Tells DOS where to find one of its most critical programs, and to keep it around no matter what.
`DEVICE=C:\DOS\SMARTDRV.EXE`	Runs a program that makes your hard disk seem to work much faster.

Your CONFIG.SYS file will be different, and if you have an older, slower computer, it may be simpler.

You can display the contents of your own `CONFIG.SYS` file, if you have one, by entering **`TYPE CONFIG.SYS`**, and pressing Enter, at the DOS prompt.

TRICKS

Type **CD** and press Enter to get to the top of your DOS filing cabinet if you see a **File not found** message.

The important thing to understand is that `CONFIG.SYS` contains *configuration data* that DOS needs to properly get started. Every DOS computer should have a `CONFIG.SYS` file in the `root` directory. (In fact, DOS can find `CONFIG.SYS` only in the `root` directory!)

Final Housekeeping Tasks: AUTOEXEC.BAT

The second file read by DOS at start-up time is `AUTOEXEC.BAT`. This file contains a bunch of DOS commands that you want DOS to run before you go to work. Unlike `CONFIG.SYS`, these are all commands you could type at the DOS prompt. `AUTOEXEC.BAT` just automates the process for you, making sure everything runs before you start working. Here's a typical `AUTOEXEC.BAT` file:

`PATH=C:\;C:\DOS;C:\WP51;C:\PARADOX4`	Tells DOS where to find the programs it needs most often.
`PROMPT $P$G`	Tells DOS what the prompt should look like.
`SET TEMP=C:\TEMP`	Tells DOS where to stick the temporary files that it sometimes creates.
`C:\MOUSE\MOUSE`	Tells DOS to load a program that controls a mouse.

You'll learn more about `PATH` and `PROMPT` later. For now, just notice that `AUTOEXEC.BAT` is handling housekeeping tasks. Some are essential; some simply make your computer more convenient to use. (Now if only it would do the ironing!)

What Is All That Stuff in My Start-Up Files?

It would take me forever to explain all of the possible additions to the CONFIG.SYS and AUTOEXEC.BAT files. It seems that every application under the sun expects to have its own entries in these files. We'll look a little more closely at a few of the most common entries you'll find in these files, and explain what's going on in there.

Reading Between the Lines in CONFIG.SYS

Remember, CONFIG.SYS is the magic place where DOS gets instructions on how to configure your computer (normally, the very first tasks as it starts up). The CONFIG.SYS file shown starts with this line:

```
DEVICE=C:\DOS\SETVER.EXE
```

This loads a file containing a list of programs that *ought* to be compatible with DOS 6, but actually go looking for a specific, older version of MS-DOS. When they find DOS 6, they refuse to run. What SETVER does, quite simply, is to tell these programs what they want to hear: "I'm not DOS 6, I'm really DOS 3.3," or some such.

Next, there's:

```
DEVICE=C:\DOS\HIMEM.SYS
```

This line loads up a *memory manager*, which is a utility that makes some types of memory available to certain programs. Some programs (such as Windows) need memory managers to run. If this line is not in CONFIG.SYS, they won't run.

As you'll read in Chapter 12, no matter how much memory you've paid for, only 640K is really ideal for your programs. Sure, you can use more, and if you've bought your computer recently, you almost certainly do. But there are tradeoffs and complexities involved. Running programs like HIMEM.SYS is one of them.

(By the way, we're talking about memory on *chips* here. RAM—the working scratchpad your computer uses when it's running programs. You can have plenty of storage space on *disk*, and still run out of the chip-based memory you need to run a program.)

Another way to make more room for your programs is to move part of DOS somewhere else—to a rarely used location called the *High Memory Area*. It's like pushing your toaster and Mr. Coffee aside so you can brandish your butcher knife. That's what the next line does:

```
DOS=HIGH,UMB
```

Next. Any program, such as Word, Excel, or Lotus, uses one or more files stored in your DOS filing cabinet. Most programs need to use several files at once, but unless you tell DOS to make more files available, it can only open eight files at once. Of these, five are always used by DOS itself, leaving your programs only three to work with at any time. The following `FILES` statement in `CONFIG.SYS` tells DOS it can open as many as 30 files simultaneously.

```
FILES=30
```

When DOS reads data from a file, it can stick that data into a chunk of memory temporarily, until it actually needs it. (Kind of like a temporary post-it note.) The data is then available more quickly when DOS needs it. The `BUFFERS` line tells DOS how many post-it notes to keep handy. (We'll cover a related concept, disk-caching, a little later in this chapter.)

```
BUFFERS=10
```

Then there's this pretty strange line:

```
SHELL=C:\DOS\COMMAND.COM /E:512 /P
```

It's not obvious, but DOS needs some way to communicate with you. When you type on the keyboard, a program named `COMMAND.COM` reads what you type, and interprets your typing for DOS. In fact, `COMMAND.COM` is one of your most critical DOS programs. This line in `CONFIG.SYS` tells DOS where to find its `COMMAND.COM` program. Otherwise, DOS can't "hear" you or respond to your commands.

If you don't have a `SHELL=` line, DOS looks in your `root` directory—which is fine, assuming that's where `COMMAND.COM` is.

NERDY DETAILS

This particular statement does a couple of other things, too. With /E:512, it sets aside more space for something called the *environment* (a bunch of settings DOS needs to keep in memory). With /P, it makes sure that COMMAND.COM stays in memory even if you type EXIT, which might otherwise unload it, leaving you high and dry.

In DOS 6, you're also likely to find one or more additional statements that load specific device drivers. If you're running a reasonably powerful PC, one of them is likely to be:

```
DEVICE=C:\DOS\SMARTDRV.EXE
```

This is a very special command. DOS sometimes needs help to get information off of the hard disk quickly enough to get work done. Hard disks are still very slow, when compared to the speed of your computer programs when they gobble the data stored on them.

Loading SMARTDRV.EXE, better known as SmartDrive, gives DOS a place in memory to put data that it might need later on. It's like filling a bunch of post-it notes with information that you might ask for. If it's already on the post-it notes when you ask for it, DOS can give it to you much faster than reading it off of the hard disk.

Sounds like a buffer, right? Actually SmartDrive is smarter—hence the name. It figures out which information you're most likely to need, and that's the information it keeps around.

In a nutshell, these are some of the most common lines found in CONFIG.SYS files. If you are instructed to make changes to this file, most often it'll be to change either the FILES or the BUFFERS lines.

Reading Between the Lines in AUTOEXEC.BAT

In some ways, the lines in AUTOEXEC.BAT are simpler and easier to understand than those in CONFIG.SYS. Each line in AUTOEXEC.BAT is something you might type in at the DOS command prompt, though it's almost always more convenient to do it here. This AUTOEXEC.BAT file has the following lines:

```
PATH=C:\;C:\DOS;C:\WP51;C:\PARADOX4
```

This is simply a list of disk drive and directory names, each separated by a semicolon. It tells DOS where to look when it's trying to find the different commands you type in at the keyboard. DOS certainly knows its own internal commands (DIR is one of them), but it needs help to find other things you might want to use.

(WordPerfect and Paradox are examples of these, but so are "external commands" such as EDIT, which come with DOS but have to be loaded separately. That's why C:\DOS, DOS' own subdirectory, is included in the statement.)

In addition, some programs themselves use the PATH information to find their data files. For instance, if PARADOX4 is missing from the PATH on my computer, I can't get Paradox to run properly.

Next, there's the PROMPT statement:

```
PROMPT $P$G
```

$P makes the DOS prompt report the drive and directory you've got open; $G puts a > after that information. If you have DOS 6, this type of prompt is the default DOS prompt, which means it's the way DOS does things unless you tell it otherwise. So this line is not needed.

As your computer runs AUTOEXEC.BAT, you will often see messages indicating that DOS has either succeeded or failed in loading each line of the file. However, some people get nervous seeing all that technical stuff fly by when their computer starts. If you're one of them, you can "suppress" the messages by starting the AUTOEXEC.BAT file with the line:

```
@ECHO OFF
```

Remember that by the time you see the AUTOEXEC.BAT file being read by DOS, the CONFIG.SYS file has already been processed.

The DOS 6 (and DOS 5) Editor—Downright Handy

Every DOS 5 and 6 user has a nice little program that can be used to make changes to plain files like CONFIG.SYS and AUTOEXEC.BAT. This process, called *editing*, is much like working on a document in a word processor such as Word or WordPerfect, except you can't add formatting (boldface, italics, new column widths, and so on).

Simple files, such as CONFIG.SYS and AUTOEXEC.BAT, are often called *text files*. All they contain are words and letters that a human (or humanoid) can read. You may also see the nerdy expression *ASCII* (pronounced AS-KEY) applied to these files, as in "it's a plain ASCII file". What the nerd means is that the file is all words and numbers—no bizarre formatting or program code.

The 1990s may be full of war, crime, and pestilence, but we do have the EDIT command as partial compensation. Older versions of DOS only had a crummy editor called EDLIN, which was even uglier to use than it sounds.

I'll describe the process of editing the CONFIG.SYS file we've been discussing as *if* you were doing it on your computer. But remember, the CONFIG.SYS file on your computer is probably very different than what you see here. These are only sample changes—by no means should you make them in your CONFIG.SYS or AUTOEXEC.BAT files. Remember: This is a test...this is only a test...

Before making any changes to either of your start-up files, always make backup copies. Use the COPY command:

```
COPY AUTOEXEC.BAT AUTOEXEC.SAV
COPY CONFIG.SYS CONFIG.SAV
```

The SAV files will always be there, in case you have to change things back again. After you are sure that your changes are successful (think positively!), you can repeat the COPY commands to make sure your SAV files are up-to-date (in case—God forbid—something happens to your start-up files).

If you do make a mistake that crashes your computer, DOS 6 lets you bypass your start-up files and get into DOS, where you can re-edit them back the way they started. If you aren't using DOS 6, however, make yourself an emergency boot disk right now. Place a blank disk in Drive A, and type:

```
FORMAT A: /S
```

Press Enter. The disk will be formatted to include the bare minimum files DOS needs to operate. Later, we'll tell you what to do with this disk in the event that you need it. (For a variety of other reasons, it's a good idea to make an emergency boot disk even if you are using DOS 6.)

Doing It

To edit the CONFIG.SYS file, type:

```
EDIT \CONFIG.SYS
```

Press Enter. The \ tells DOS that `CONFIG.SYS` is in your `root` directory drawer, where it's supposed to be. The screen should look something like figure 4.1.

File Edit Search Options
Help
CONFIG.SYS
DEVICE=C:\DOS\HIMMEM.SYS
DOS=HIGH,UMB
FILES=10
BUFFERS=10
SHELL=COMMAND.COM /E:512 /P
MS-DOS Editor <F1=Help> Press ALT to activate menus
00001:001

Figure 4.1

The screen display as the computer loads `EDIT \CONFIG.SYS.`

Notice that the `BUFFERS` line specifies only 10 buffers. Many programs require at least 20 buffers, so we're going to change the `10` to `20` in the `BUFFERS` line.

Your editor needs a file called QBASIC.EXE in order to load. If it's not there, EDIT says Cannot find file QBASIC.EXE, and refuses to start. In that case, someone might have deleted QBASIC from your computer. If you have your original DOS distribution disks handy, you should re-install DOS on your computer because there may be other things missing as well.

Moving the Cursor and Making the Changes

EDIT is very easy to use. Simply use the cursor keys to move the blinking or flashing underline cursor (it'll be in the upper left hand corner of the screen you see in figure 4.1). As you press the down-arrow key, the cursor moves down one line at a time; the right arrow key moves the cursor one character to the right. The End key moves the cursor to the rightmost character of the line; the Home key moves it to the very left of the screen. Experiment a bit to get the feel of how to move the cursor.

The *cursor keys* are the ones with the arrows on them. Chances are they're to the right of the typewriter keys on your keyboard... you may even have two sets of them. If your arrow keys type numbers instead of moving your cursor, then you've got your numeric keypad on—your computer thinks you want it to behave like an adding machine. Press Num Lock to turn these keys back into arrows again. Chapter 11 will tell you everything you need to know about keyboards.

Move the blinking cursor until it's right under the 1 in the BUFFERS=10 line, and then press the 2 key. It'll push the 1 to the right of the 2, so you end up with FILES=210, with the cursor still under the 1 (see fig. 4.2). Obviously, we didn't want 210 here, so press Del to delete the 1. The character that is underlined by the blinking cursor is the one that gets deleted by the Del key. Magic!

Saving the Changes

When you are satisfied with the changes you've made, press Alt (the words **Fi**le, **E**dit, **S**earch, and **O**ptions at the top of the screen will change their appearance, indicating that you're working up there at the top of the screen now). Press **F** to "drop down" the **F**ile menu.

Then press **S** to save the file. You can use the down arrow key to move the highlight bar to the Exit option, or just press **X** to instantly select the Exit option.

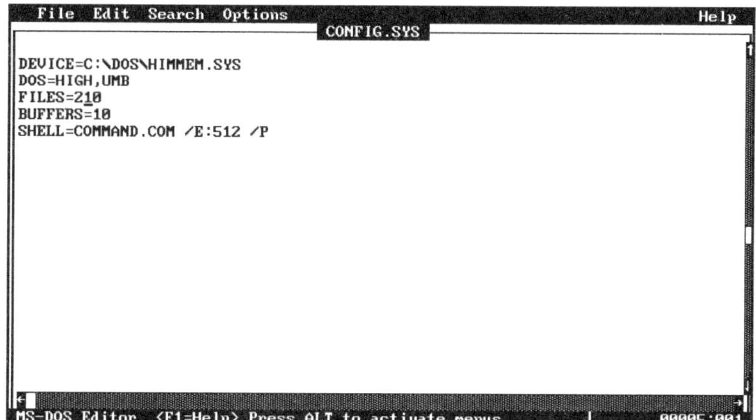
File Edit Search Options
Help
CONFIG.SYS
DEVICE=C:\DOS\HIMMEM.SYS
DOS=HIGH,UMB
FILES=210
BUFFERS=10
SHELL=COMMAND.COM /E:512 /P
MS-DOS Editor <F1=Help> Press ALT to activate menus
00005:001

Figure 4.2

The editing process.

GEEK
NERDY DETAILS

Each of those things at the top of the screen (**F**ile, **E**dit, **S**earch, and **O**ptions) has its own *drop-down menu* associated with it. As you become familiar with the DOS 5 and DOS 6 `EDIT` command, you will use these menus more often. Experiment with `EDIT` on a file that you really don't care about; it's well worth the time getting acquainted with `EDIT`.

Should You Scream? What To Do If It Doesn't Work

So, just what can you do if DOS refuses to start up after you've made changes on your computer? It's really scary, but you might see a message like `Bad or missing command interpreter` just before DOS goes off into never-never land, or else you get the message `Starting MS-DOS...` and then absolutely nothing happens.

Before DOS 6, this meant big trouble because you just absolutely had to have an emergency start-up disk to get your computer under way again.

NERDY DETAILS

That's why we told you pre-DOS 6 users to make an emergency boot disk with `FORMAT A: /S` a little while ago! If you've crashed, here's how you can un-crash:

Insert the emergency boot disk in drive A, and press Ctrl, Alt, and Del to restart the computer. DOS will start and you will see an `A:>` prompt. (This won't work with drive B!) Next, type:

```
COPY C:\CONFIG.SAV C:\CONFIG.SYS
```

This will copy your original (pre-catastrophe) backup `CONFIG.SYS` file *over* the bad one. Now restart your computer again, and all should be as it was.

DOS 6 includes a wonderful way to completely bypass `CONFIG.SYS` and `AUTOEXEC.BAT` so you can start your computer, even if you have royally messed up your start-up files. As you become more familiar with DOS, you'll quickly learn your computer's normal start-up routine, and know when something's gone wrong, when it's feeling under the weather, and when it's time to resort to one of the tactics described here.

The first thing you see from DOS as it starts is the message `Starting MS-DOS....` DOS displays this message just before beginning to read `CONFIG.SYS` and `AUTOEXEC.BAT`. This is your chance to interrupt the start-up process.

Bypassing AUTOEXEC.BAT and CONFIG.SYS Completely

If you press F5 while the message `Starting MS-DOS...` is on the screen, DOS won't read the `CONFIG.SYS` or `AUTOEXEC.BAT` files at all. Instead, you'll see the display shown in figure 4.3.

Of course, some of your programs won't start or run properly because DOS hasn't read the `CONFIG.SYS` or `AUTOEXEC.BAT` files, and it may not be configured properly.

The good news is that many of your familiar DOS commands still work, including `COPY`. This gives you a chance to fix things up and repair whatever damage has been done to your start-up files. Type:

```
COPY C:\CONFIG.SAV C:\CONFIG.SYS
```

This copies the good file over the bad file. Restart again, and you're in business.

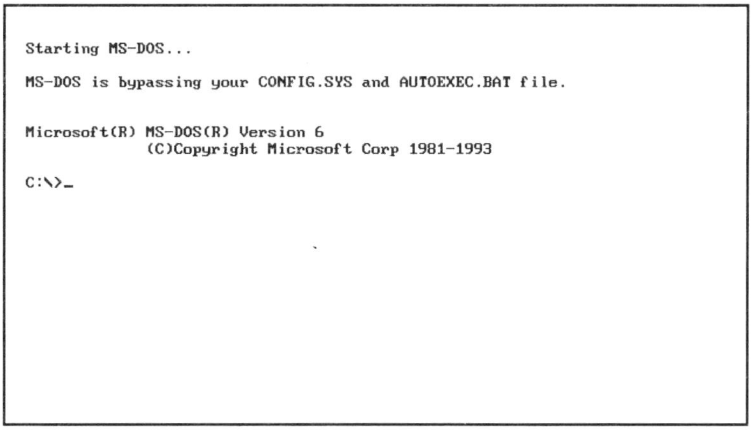

```
Starting MS-DOS...

MS-DOS is bypassing your CONFIG.SYS and AUTOEXEC.BAT file.


Microsoft(R) MS-DOS(R) Version 6
            (C)Copyright Microsoft Corp 1981-1993

C:\>_
```

Figure 4.3

Bypassing CONFIG.SYS and AUTOEXEC.BAT (DOS 6 only).

Stepping Through AUTOEXEC.BAT and CONFIG.SYS

Let's say you suspect there might be just one line in CONFIG.SYS or AUTOEXEC.BAT that's broken (maybe because you only changed one line in one of these files). In DOS 6, you can interrupt DOS' headlong processing of your start-up files by pressing F8 when you see the Starting MS-DOS... message.

After pressing F8, you'll see the display shown in figure 4.4. DOS tells you that it's going to work its way through CONFIG.SYS, one line at a time, asking you to confirm that you want it to process each line as it goes. When you come to the line you think might be causing the problem, enter **N** instead of **Y** to bypass the troublesome line.

In figure 4.4, the first two lines of CONFIG.SYS were accepted, and the user has stopped on the third line to consider whether he should allow it to be processed.

After DOS has processed each of the lines in CONFIG.SYS, it will ask you if you want it to process AUTOEXEC.BAT. If you've gotten this far, but your computer stops as it processes AUTOEXEC.BAT, it's a good guess that the problem is in AUTOEXEC.BAT, not in CONFIG.SYS.

Figure 4.4

Stepping through CONFIG.SYS and AUTOEXEC.BAT (DOS 6 only).

```
Starting MS-DOS...

MS-DOS will prompt you to confirm each CONFIG.SYS command.
DOS=HIGH,UMB [Y,N]?Y
DEVICE=C:\DOS\HIMEM.SYS [Y,N]?Y
FILES=20 [Y,N]?_
```

NERDY DETAILS

You can't process **AUTOEXEC.BAT** one line at a time like you can **CONFIG.SYS**. In fact, you don't have to. If there's a problem with **AUTOEXEC.BAT**, you can interrupt DOS's processing by pressing **C** while holding down the Ctrl key (this is called "doing a Control-C") as DOS reads through it.

If your computer starts up normally after bypassing the problem-causing line in CONFIG.SYS, you can use EDIT to either repair the offending line or to take it out entirely.

Once You've Gotten Under Way Again...

If you encounter problems after making changes to CONFIG.SYS or AUTOEXEC.BAT, you can always try EDIT again on these files to see if you can discover what went wrong.

What If I Don't Have EDIT?

Older versions of DOS (before version 5) only included an obsolete text editor named EDLIN. Until recently, the only good thing that could be said about EDLIN is that it was on every DOS computer ever built, unless someone purposefully deleted it. No more: as of DOS 6, you have to order it on a special Microsoft Supplemental Disk.

If your computer has an older version of DOS that includes EDLIN instead of EDIT, see if you can make a plain text file with your word processor (Word, WordPerfect, and all sophisticated word processing applications are able to save files as "Plain ASCII" or "Text" files).

YOU WIN
WILD
BUS TRIP TO Hawaii

An Almost Likable DOS: The Shell

Since version 4, DOS users have had an alternative to good ol' command-line DOS. Before DOS 4, you had to memorize a reasonable number of commands before you could consider yourself proficient with DOS. Beginning with DOS 4, users have had the option of using the *DOS Shell*, which is a program that provides a somewhat more friendly, less intimidating way to communicate with DOS. This chapter gives you the real skinny on the DOS Shell:

 What is the DOS Shell?

 Starting and stopping the DOS Shell.

 Performing basic file management with the DOS Shell:

- Copying files
- Renaming files
- Moving files
- Deleting files
- Finding lost files

 Running DOS commands and programs from within the Shell.

 Running more than one command at a time with the Shell.

 How to get the DOS Shell to start up automatically when you start your computer.

You can execute almost all DOS commands from within the Shell (I know it's kind of a weird concept, being *inside* a shell...).

Many computers that are sold nowadays have the DOS Shell installed as the default interface. When you turn on the computer, the first thing you see is the DOS Shell. Many successful DOS users have never encountered the infamous `C:\>` prompt. Instead, they've become proficient with the DOS Shell.

It's your choice whether to adopt the DOS command line or the DOS Shell. People who use the DOS Shell never learn many DOS commands, but they feel more secure in its friendly environment. If you have labored mightily to memorize DOS, you may prefer the speed and efficiency of typing commands at the DOS prompt.

A Better Interface to DOS?

The most common complaint about DOS is that the familiar `C:\>` prompt doesn't help the novice user very much. Even experienced DOS users often know only a few commands—just enough to get around on the disk and perform the basics of file management (copying, deleting, and moving files).

Oh Boy! Another TLA To Remember!

The DOS Shell provides a nice, *graphical* interface to DOS. This means that the various parts of your DOS file cabinet (disks, directories, files, etc.) are represented by little pictures or symbols indicating what each part is.

NERDY DETAILS

> A graphical program like the DOS Shell is often referred to as a *Graphical User Interface* or GUI (pronounced GOO-EE): yet another TLA (three-letter acronym) for you to remember.

Remember that the DOS Shell does not replace DOS—it's still there, hidden by the Shell. DOS is still just as dense as it is at the command line; the only difference is that the DOS Shell insulates you somewhat from DOS's uglier side. The DOS Shell lets you see commands, files, and directories on the screen, on which you can pick them instead of having to remember them and type them in.

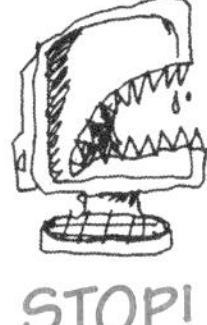

> One of the down sides to the DOS Shell is that, because of this insulating effect, you are somewhat removed from some of DOS's protection. For instance, the DOS Shell will allow you to remove even those files that are marked *Read Only* (see Chapter 3). Be very careful with the DOS Shell's power! (Think of those horror films where the old gypsy woman casts such warnings to the young and uninitiated; losing your files can be worse than turning into a werewolf.)

Entering and Leaving the DOS Shell

The DOS Shell is easy to start up. You start up the DOS Shell with the easily-misspelled `DOSSHELL` command. (Some initiates have taken to using the nickname DOS HELL.) After you type **`DOSSHELL`** and press Enter at the DOS prompt, DOS reads your disk information. You see the default DOS Shell display similar to that shown in figure 5.1.

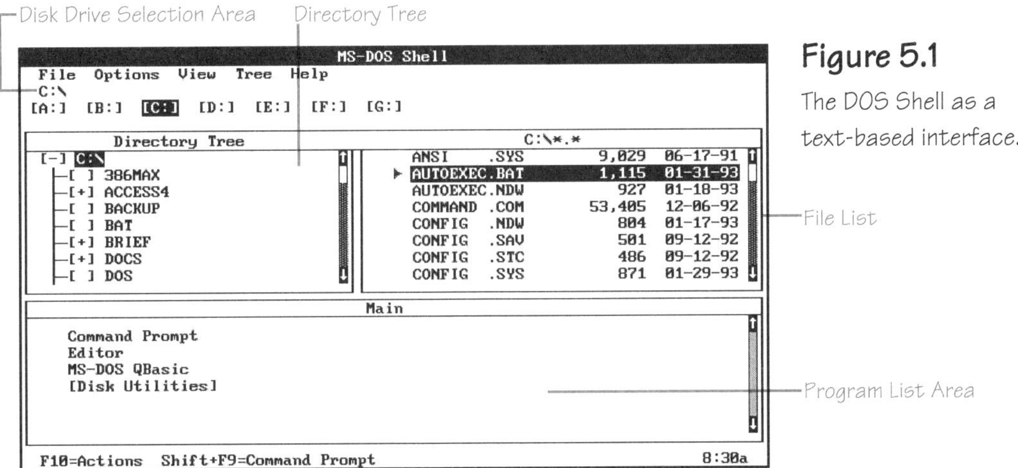

Figure 5.1

The DOS Shell as a text-based interface.

Leaving the DOS Shell is easy. Just press **F** key while holding down the Alt key (or you can press and release Alt, then press **F**). This will open the File *drop-down menu* near the top of the screen (each of the other words across the top of the screen—Options, View, Tree, and Help—also has its own drop-down menu). Now press **X** (you don't have to press Enter), and the DOS Shell will go away.

Navigating the DOS Shell

There are two basic ways to move around the DOS Shell: with your keyboard, or with your mouse. With the DOS Shell open, pressing the Tab key (near the left edge of your keyboard) will move you from one area of the screen to the next. You can work in only one area at a time—the area that's highlighted.

Depending on how the DOS Shell is set up, you can tell which area is highlighted in one of two ways. Either there's a stripe of a different color at the top of that area, or there's a small right-arrow somewhere inside it. (By the way, pressing the Tab key while holding down the Shift key moves you around the screen in the opposite order.)

Once you're in the portion of the screen you want (disk drive selection area, Directory Tree, file-list area, or program-list area), you can use the up- and down-arrow keys to highlight the specific item you're interested in. (If nothing happens when you use the arrow keys, tap Num Lock, then try again.)

If you have a mouse you can use it to choose the item you're interested in by *clicking on* it. Move the mouse around your desktop and notice the little rectangular mark (in text mode) or arrow (in graphics mode—the modes are explained later in this chapter) that moves when you move the mouse. Note, too, that like their furry brethren, computer mice can't fly—the cursor won't move unless you're scooting the mouse across a hard surface.

After you move the *cursor* onto one of the items on the screen (disk drive icon, file or directory icon, or program icon), pressing the left button on your mouse highlights it. If it's a disk or directory, you'll see the contents. If it's a program, another quick click on the left mouse button starts the program.

If there's a mouse attached to your computer but it doesn't seem to work, you may have to exit the DOS Shell (as described earlier in this chapter), and type **MOUSE** at the DOS prompt. If you're lucky, this will cause DOS to start up the mouse-tracking program. If you get a `Bad command or file name` error message, it means you don't have the MOUSE program where DOS can find it on your computer. You should go get help from someone who might have this program.

Text or Graphics?

One of the nicest features of the DOS Shell is that you have a choice of a text-based interface or a completely graphical appearance.

With the *text-based* display, the various components are built out of special characters that your PC uses to draw lines and boxes. Figure 5.1 shows the text-based DOS Shell.

In figure 5.1, the left side of the display shows you the directories on your hard disk; the right side shows the file in the directory that is highlighted on the left side. In this example, the `root` directory (`C:\`) is highlighted, so the files in the right side of the picture are all of those that are in the `root` directory on this computer. Notice that `AUTOEXEC.BAT` and `CONFIG.SYS` are in the `root` directory (you'll also notice a few files with the same first name as `AUTOEXEC.BAT` and `CONFIG.SYS`, but with different last names).

Figure 5.2 shows the same screen in *graphics* mode. This screen looks somewhat "busier" than figure 5.1. Each item in the lists at the left, right, and bottom of the screen has a little picture (called an *icon*) associated with it. The picture shows you what kind of "thing" the list item is.

A nerd might call the list items in figures 5.1 and 5.2 *objects*. These figures have objects that are *directories* (we've been calling them "drawers"), *files*, and *programs*. If you hear a nerd use the word *object*, he really means *a thing or item*.

Figure 5.2

The DOS Shell as a graphics interface.

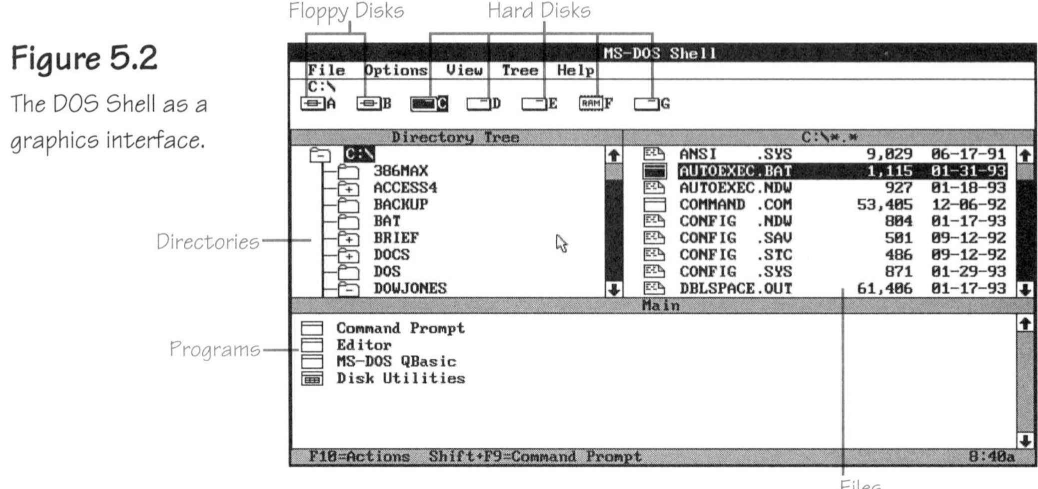

What You Can Do with DOSSHELL

The DOS Shell provides a graphical view of what's on your hard disk. Rather than having to repeat the DIR command to see what's on your disk, the left side of the DOS Shell continuously displays the currently opened directory's contents. You may have to *scroll* this window (move the display in it up and down) to see everything that's there.

Your active window contains a *scroll bar* for just these moments. It's that vertical bar on the right side of the window with the up and down arrows on it. To go to the top of the list, move the mouse to the up arrow, and hold down the left button until you can't go any further. The down arrow moves you to the bottom of the list.

It's easy to *launch* (start up) programs with the DOS Shell. The right side of the DOS Shell display shows you all of the files in the current DOS directory. You can start up a program (remember, files with last names of EXE, COM, and BAT are programs) by highlighting it and pressing the Enter key, or by double-clicking on it (quickly clicking the mouse button twice).

> The bottom of the screen in figures 5.1 and 5.2 shows you what the DOS Shell calls a *program list*. These lists are a quick way to start up a program. By highlighting the word **Editor** in the bottom part of the screen, and pressing the Enter key, you start up the DOS **EDIT** command you practiced using in Chapter 4. The program list saves you the trouble of having to search through the directories on your hard disk to find the program file you want to run.
>
> You can easily add your own programs to the DOS Shell program list at the bottom of the screen.

In figure 5.1. notice that the words `Disk Utilities` are surrounded with square brackets; in figure 5.2 the Disk Utilities list thing has a different icon than the Command Prompt, Editor, and MS-DOS Qbasic icons. This special treatment tells you that the Disk Utilities thing is actually another program list.

When you highlight the Disk Utilities item in the program list, and press Enter (or click twice with the mouse), you'll see something resembling figure 5.3.

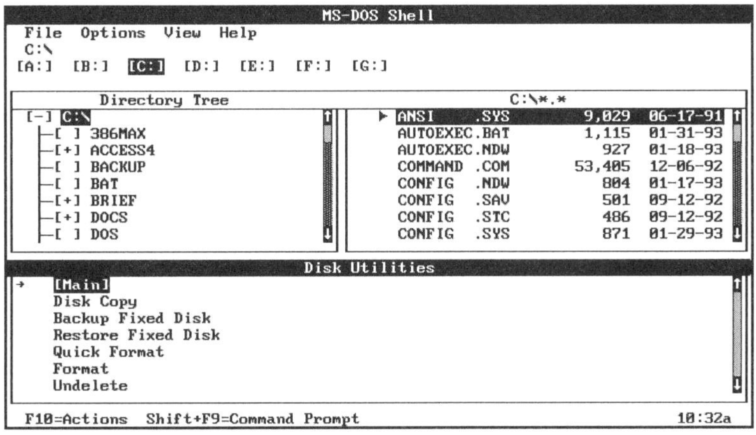

Figure 5.3

The Disk Utilities program list.

This list contains the essential disk-management tasks (each of these tasks are described in Chapter 13, so you don't need to know what they are at the moment).

Using DOSSHELL

You can do a lot of things from inside the DOS Shell. With a little practice, these tasks will become second nature to you. Trust me on this.

Starting and Stopping Programs

You've already read about starting a program file from the DOS Shell by using the basic DOS Shell navigation tricks (use Tab or Shift-Tab, plus the arrow keys, or click with a mouse) to move the highlight to the thing you want, and press Enter (or double-click with the mouse). The files that you can run as programs have the last names `EXE`, `COM`, or `BAT`.

> Don't run a program unless you know what it is, or else it might do something you will regret. (Ah, there's that gypsy woman's warning again. My, what big teeth you have... .)

You stop the program in whatever the normal manner is for that program. Many programs exit when you select `Exit` or `End` from a menu, press Esc, or press a certain sequence of keys. Whatever it takes to get out of your program, once you're out you'll be returned to the DOS Shell.

Copying Files with the DOS Shell

To copy a file, use the DOS Shell navigation techniques to highlight the file you want to copy, and press F8. Another way to do this is to use the Alt-F key sequence to open the File drop-down menu, then use the arrow keys or press **C** to select Copy in the file task list. Whichever technique you use, the Copy File *dialog box* will appear, as shown in figure 5.4.

> A *dialog box* provides you with a quick and easy way to communicate with your computer. When you see a dialog box, you can enter only the information it is asking for (in this case, the name of the file you want to copy to). Dialog boxes are one way the DOS Shell is easier to use than the DOS command line.

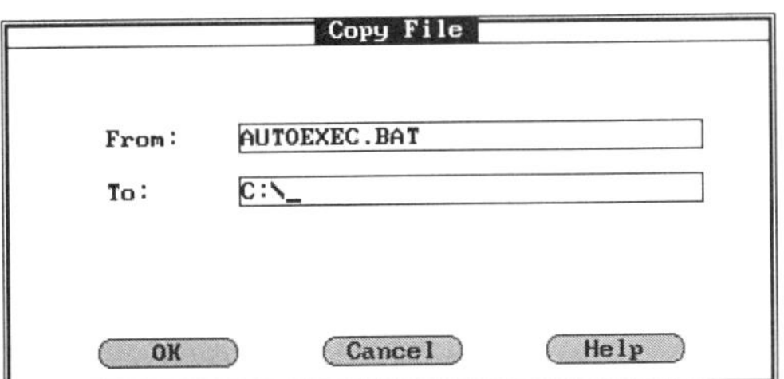

Figure 5.4

The File Copy dialog box.

The From: box shows the file name you highlighted and the To: box shows the current directory name. Obviously, it would not accomplish anything to choose OK yet because the file already exists in the current directory. You need to tell the computer where you want to send the new copy. Enter the name of the file, drive, or directory; and press Enter (or click on OK with your trusty mouse). If you change your mind, press Esc or use the Tab key to move the highlight to the Cancel button near the bottom of the dialog box (you can also click on the Cancel button with the mouse).

You may want to select more than one file at once. To select several consecutive files, select the first one and hold down the Shift key while you move the up arrow or down arrow to highlight the others. To select nonconsecutive files in a list, select the first one, then hold down the Ctrl key as you highlight each of the other files.

You can also select the Help button to get help with the Copy dialog box. The F1 key will also get you help. The DOS Shell is smart enough to give you the specific help it thinks you need, based on where you are when you ask. This is called *context-sensitive* help, invented by nerds for non-nerds.

Renaming Files with the DOS Shell

It's easy to rename a file with the DOS Shell. Simply highlight it as you did for copying a file, and select the Rename task from the File menu. Remember, you open the File menu by pressing **F** while holding down the Alt key (or right after pressing the Alt key), or by clicking on File with the mouse. The Rename File dialog box will appear (it is very similar to the File Copy dialog box in figure 5.4), asking you for the new name of the highlighted file.

Moving Files with the DOS Shell

You can move a file to a new name, drive, or directory (destination) with the DOS Shell. Highlight the file name, open the File menu with Alt-F, and select Move from the menu task list (or just press F7). You'll get the Move File dialog box (it looks a lot like the File Copy dialog box in figure 5.4) and enter the new destination for the file.

The destination can be another file (this is the same as renaming a file), another directory, another disk, or any combination of these. Moving files is a good way to clean files off of your disk and put them on floppy disks for safekeeping.

Deleting Files with the DOS Shell

Deleting a file with the DOS Shell is just like copying a file. Select the file you wish to delete by highlighting it. Then choose Delete from the drop-down File menu (or just press the Del key). You see the Delete File Confirmation dialog box shown in figure 5.5.

When you confirm the deletion by pressing Enter or clicking on the Yes button, your file will be deleted by DOS.

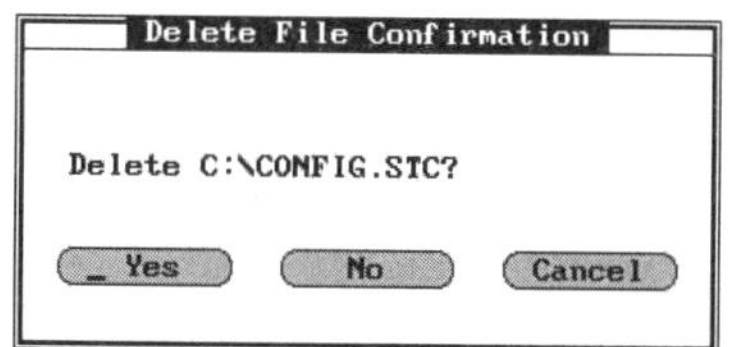

Figure 5.5

The Delete File Confirmation dialog box.

STOP!

BIG WARNING! The DOS Shell will let you remove just about any file from your disk, even those that are quite important to your system. Here are a few you should especially watch out for (these aren't the only ones!):

-  Anything in your DOS subdirectory.
-  AUTOEXEC.BAT, COMMAND.COM, or CONFIG.SYS.
-  Anything that starts with the letters DBLSPACE.

So be careful out there: the DOS Shell delete capability can get you in trouble, big time. (And don't venture out onto the moors without silver bullets and garlic, sayeth the gypsy lady.)

Finding Lost Files with the DOS Shell

The DOS Shell even provides a convenient way to find missing files. In contrast to the `DIR /S` trick you learned in Chapter 3, there is a specific Search task in the File drop-down menu. When you select this item from the File drop-down menu (you don't have to highlight a file first), you'll see the Search File dialog box shown in figure 5.6.

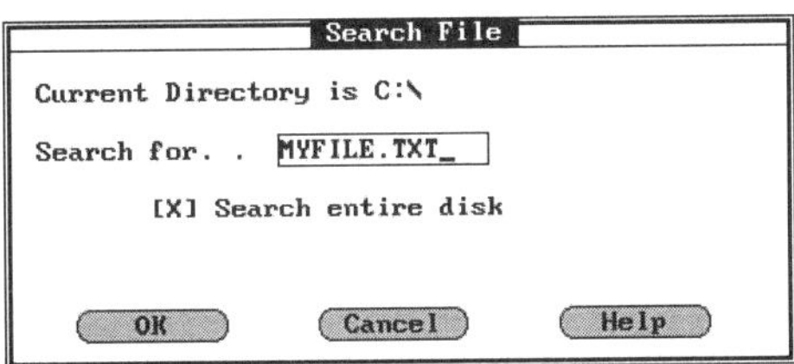

Figure 5.6

The Search File dialog box.

Enter the name of the file you want to find (wild cards are allowed, so you can search for `*.TXT`, `MYFILE.*`, or `REPORT.9?`). By default, the search task will only look through the currently open directory (in figure 5.6, the directory is `C:\`). If the `Search entire disk` option is checked (it's *checked* if there is an `X` between the square brackets), the whole disk will be searched. This can take quite a while on a large disk or slow computer.

TRICKS

You can check/uncheck the option by moving the highlight to the box formed by the square brackets and pressing the space bar, or by clicking on it with the mouse.

The result of a search is shown in figure 5.7. This display shows all of the files that match what you entered in the Search for.. box in the Search File dialog box.

You can press Esc to make the Search Results screen go away. If you are searching for a program file, you can run the program by highlighting the program file name, and press Enter (or double-click on it with your mouse).

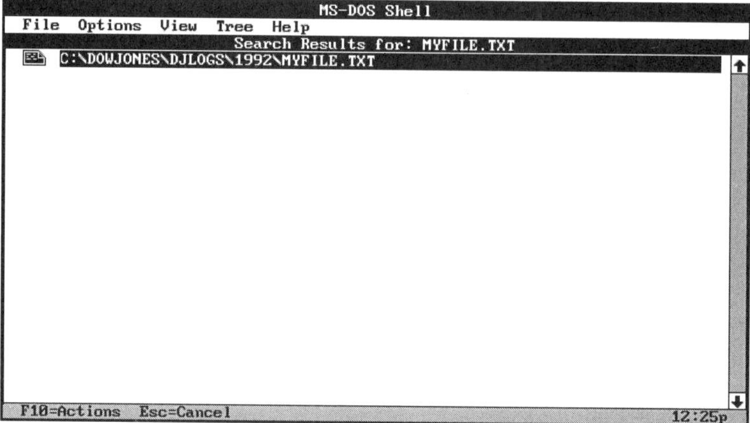

Figure 5.7

The Search Results screen.

Adding Programs to the DOS Shell Program List

The lower left hand corner of the DOS Shell screen contains a list of programs (called the Main Program Group) that are available for instant use. As mentioned earlier in this chapter, it is easy to add programs to this list:

- Highlight the Main Program Group by clicking on it with your mouse or by pressing Tab several times.
- Open the File drop-down menu (click on it with your mouse or press the Alt-F key combination) and select New from the File task list.
- The New Program Object dialog box will appear with Program Item already selected (the alternate selection is Program Group). Because you're adding a new program item, press Enter to accept this selection.
- The Add Program dialog box, shown in figure 5.8, appears. You must fill in the Program Title input box. The Program Title is the name of the item that will be added to the Main Program Group. `MS-DOS QBasic` is an example of a program title.
- You must know the exact commands that you would type at the DOS command-line prompt to start up the program. Use the Tab key to move to the Commands input box, and enter the command you use to start up your program.

Add Program

Program Title . . . . WordPerfect

Commands . . . . . . WP

Startup Directory . . C:\WORDPERF_

Application Shortcut Key

[X] Pause after exit   Password . .

OK   Cancel   Help   Advanced...

Figure 5.8

The Add Program dialog box.

For instance, to start WordPerfect, the DOS command is usually WP. If you are adding WordPerfect to the DOS Shell Main Program Group, enter **WP** in the Commands input box.

Finally, use the Tab key to move to the Startup Directory input box. This is the directory in which DOS will look for the program file and any accessory files that the program needs (such as font files or printer configuration files). Normally, the Startup Directory is the same directory where the program file is found. In the example in figure 5.8, the Startup Directory is WORDPERF.

When you press Enter to accept the changes you've made, the DOS Shell will add your new program item to the Main Program Group.

The DOS Shell does not check the information you've entered in the Add Program dialog box. For instance, if you've incorrectly entered the command you use to invoke your program, you'll just get a **Bad command or file name** error message from DOS when you try to use it. All the DOS Shell does with your information is pass it to DOS, which tries to run your program. If you enter bad information in the Add Program dialog box, it's the same as if you had entered bad information at the DOS command line. But once you get it right, you never have to retype it.

Deleting a Program from the Main Program Group

Deleting a program item from the Main Program Group is easy. Do this:

1. Move the highlight to the Main Program Group.
2. Use the mouse or arrow keys to highlight the program item for deletion.
3. Press the Del key.

The DOS Shell will ask you to confirm your intention to delete the program item. Answer OK to delete the item.

Running More Than One Program at a Time

Perhaps the best thing about the DOS Shell is that it provides a convenient way to "load up" more than one application at a time and quickly switch between them. This permits you to work with a spreadsheet in one screen, a word processor in another, and a communications program in yet another.

Although you can see only one program's screen at a time, you can move from one application screen to another as fast and as often as you want through the miracle of *task-swapping*. This is done with a simple keystroke combination, and it saves you from having to exit one application and then call up another and then exit that one and then call up another and then...well, you get the idea. It's a great time saver.

The DOS Shell maintains a list of programs that it has available for you to switch to. This list is called the *task list*.

Task-swapping with the DOS Shell is a rather advanced topic; many DOS books do not even discuss it. It's included here for a very simple reason: it is one of the most powerful features of DOS 6 (and DOS 5). When you have mastered task-swapping with the DOS Shell (assuming that your work requires you to work with more than one program every day), you will wonder how you ever got work done running only one program at a time.

Setting Up Task-Swapping

The first step is to activate the DOS Shell task swapper:

1. Open the Options drop-down menu by choosing it with your mouse or by pressing **O** while holding down the Alt key (or press **O** immediately after pressing the Alt key).
2. Select the Enable Task Swapper option by moving the highlight to it, and then press Enter or click on it with the mouse.

When the Options drop-down menu disappears, a new area named `Active Task List` will be added to the lower right hand corner of the DOS Shell window. This tells you that task-swapping is enabled. So swap to your heart's content!

Adding a Program to the Task List

To add a program to the Task list, follow these steps:

1. Using the DOS Shell navigation techniques outlined earlier in this chapter, highlight a program name you wish to add to the task list.
2. Press Enter while holding down the Shift key.

Your selection will instantly appear in the Active Task List in the lower right hand corner of the DOS Shell screen. See figure 5.9. After you add two or more programs to the task list, you can easily flip back and forth between them.

Figure 5.9

The DOS Shell with a program in the Active Task List.

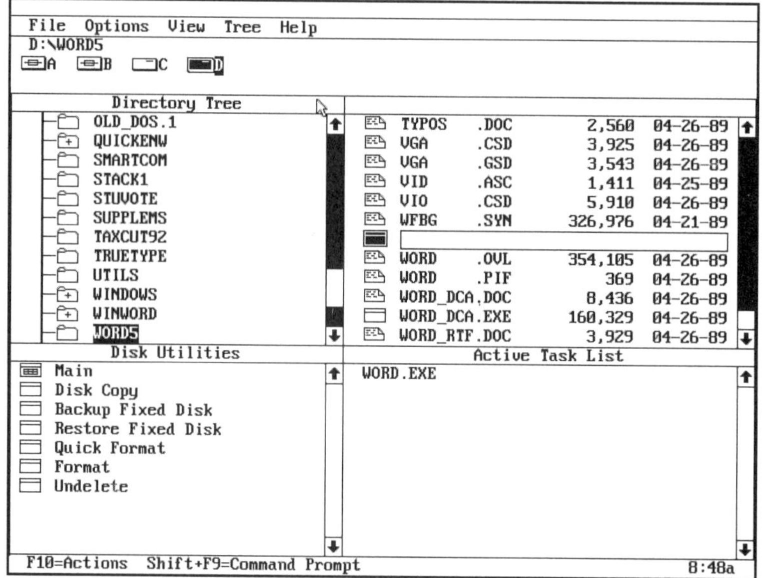

Moving between Programs in the Active Task List

Moving between programs in the Active Task List is easy:

1. Hold down the Alt key, and press the Tab key.

   The screen will "flip" to the first program in the Active Task List.

2. Press Alt-Tab some more to move through the programs in the Active Task List, activating each one.

   To simply see the name of the task without activating it, keep the Alt key pressed down after you press Tab.

Removing a Program from the Active Task List

Removing a program from the active task list is easy:

1. Switch to the program with the Alt-Tab keystroke combination.
2. Exit the program the way you usually do.

If you exit the program in its normal way, you'll never leave files half open or half closed on your disk.

Starting DOSSHELL Every Time You Start the Computer

If you decide you like the DOS Shell and want it to automatically start up every time you turn on your computer, follow these steps:

1. In Chapter 4, read the discussion about editing AUTOEXEC.BAT.
2. Make a backup copy of your AUTOEXEC.BAT file:

   ```
   COPY AUTOEXEC.BAT AUTOEXEC.SAV
   ```

3. Add **DOSSHELL** as the very last command in your AUTOEXEC.BAT file. It should appear on a line all by itself at the very bottom of the AUTOEXEC.BAT file.
4. The next time you start your computer, the DOS Shell should load and start automatically.
5. To test your changes to AUTOEXEC.BAT, restart your computer by pressing the Alt, Ctrl, and Del keys. Or press the Reset button (if you have one) on the front of your computer.

   When your computer restarts, the DOS Shell should start automatically.

If something bad happens (like the last thing you see when **AUTOEXEC.BAT** runs is a **Bad command or file name** error message from DOS), edit **AUTOEXEC.BAT** one more time to verify that you put **DOSSHELL** correctly at the bottom and spelled it right.

If everything looks right and the Shell still won't start properly, put back the original AUTOEXEC.BAT file. For some reason, it just won't start on your computer. (In Chapters 14 and 15, we'll discuss some of the things that can go wrong with your computer—these chapters might very well help you solve the problem.)

To put back your original AUTOEXEC.BAT file, enter the following DOS command:

```
COPY AUTOEXEC.SAV AUTOEXEC.BAT
```

Restart your computer, and you're done.

Why Shouldn't I Use the DOS Shell All the Time?

There are several reasons why you might *not* want to routinely use the DOS Shell:

- Once you learn a few DOS commands, you'll probably discover that using the DOS Shell is *much* slower than typing the commands at the DOS prompt. Generally speaking, experienced DOS users see the DOS Shell as an impediment, rather than as an aid.
- The DOS Shell itself requires some memory to run. On machines with limited memory (you'll read all about your computer's memory in Chapter 12), many things you run with the DOS Shell may run only very slowly, if at all.
- If it means anything to you, when you use the DOS Shell, you really don't become as proficient using DOS as the usual command-line person. This means you will remain dependent on having the DOS Shell because you won't know how to do a lot of things without it. It's like not learning how to drive a stick shift—someday you may need to!

THE FILES YOU NEED
TO BE FILED. OR NOT TO BE FILED
FILES AND MORE
FILES GALORE
FILES
FILES HERE
JUST FILES
F I L E S
STILL MORE FILES
FILES IN HERE SOME-WHERE
FILES THERE
JUST PLAIN OLD FILES
FILES, FILES, FILES
FILES
FILES AWAY
FILES EVERY-WHERE
MORE FILES
FILED AWAY

Batchman: The Caped Crusader

One of the nicest things you can do for yourself is to learn how to write *batch files*. A batch file is a collection of DOS commands that are all run at the same time when you type in the name of the batch file at the DOS prompt. Batch files are a way to automate things that take a lot of different DOS commands to perform (like saving a bunch of different files to a floppy disk). This chapter covers:

 How batch files make your computing life easier.

 How to reduce typing errors with batch files.

 How batch files let you be forgetful.

Although this chapter won't explain everything there is to know about batch files, it will provide you with enough background to start building and using your own batch files.

Save Yourself Some Time!

In the previous chapter, you learned about using the DOS Shell to make DOS easier to use. *Batch files* make DOS easier to use to automate tasks. A *batch file* is a plain text file containing one or more DOS commands exactly as you might type them in at the DOS prompt. Each line of a batch file is one command you would otherwise type in at the DOS command line.

They're called *batch* files because they can contain a batch of DOS commands that are run as if they were one command. I guess the nerds could have called them *bunch* files because they really contain a bunch of commands.

Batch files are good for a number of things:

 Automating repetitious tasks.

 Simplifying complex DOS commands.

 Making it easy to remember commands.

 Avoid typing paths and DOS commands.

 Customizing DOS to YOS (Your Operating System). This means you can make up your own YOS commands from one or more DOS commands.

Many times the work you do on your computer involves repetitious tasks. You may find yourself moving around your hard disk, deleting the same files or setting the same parameters over and over again.

Déjà Vu No More with Batch Files!

Other times, you've got to open a lot of drawers and shuffle through the stuff you find, looking for that program that you just ***know*** was there a few weeks ago. Batch files can help you find things by giving you a nice, simple, easy-to-remember command to use for almost anything.

Suppose you've been working on a file over a number of weeks, and each time you're done making changes to the file, you copy it to a floppy disk for safekeeping. After typing **COPY REPORT1.DOC A:** and **COPY SUMMARY.DOC** a few dozen times, you begin wishing you had some way to reduce the amount of typing it takes to complete this simple task. Creating a little batch file that contains just these two COPY commands requires very little effort, yet it can save you an incredible amount of typing in a very short time.

Batch files also protect you from the problem of mistyped commands. Because the most common mistake that most DOS users make is to misspell the command, a batch file can dramatically reduce typing errors.

A DOS To-Do List

Each line in a batch file is a different DOS command for DOS to carry out. When DOS processes a batch file, it reads each line of the batch file as if it were a command you typed at the DOS prompt. As a matter of fact, the last name of a batch file must be BAT, so that DOS knows how to treat the commands as the batch file.

Here is a very short batch file from my computer that starts the excellent game... er, simulation program called "Sim City" (the numbers at the left side of each line are not in the batch file):

```
(1)    C:
(2)    CD \MISC\GAMES\SIMCITY
(3)    SIMCITY
(4)    CD \
```

Line (1) makes sure I'm working from a directory on the C: drive, line (2) opens the SIMCITY drawer that's inside the MISC drawer, and line (3) actually starts SIMCITY. When I'm done with Sim City, line (4) takes me back to the root directory ("\").

See? With one simple command (SIMCITY) we get all four of those steps done at once! And we didn't have to remember the darn path to the SIMCITY directory, either! This little batch file is much easier to do than typing in all four lines as DOS commands, don't you think?

Automating DOS Paths

Remember the PATH that DOS uses to find programs (in Chapter 4)? Why not just add C:\MISC\SIMCITY to the PATH statement in my AUTOEXEC.BAT file? Then, every time I start the computer, DOS will read the PATH statement in AUTOEXEC.BAT, and find SIMCITY for me when I try to run it.

The answer is simple: DOS has a 128-letter limit on the PATH length. If I added the directories of all programs on my computer that I might ever want to run, the PATH would be several thousand letters long. Instead, I include the directory C:\BATCH in my computer's PATH statement. I put lots of different batch files (such as SIMCITY.BAT) into C:\BATCH. When I type **SIMCITY** at the C:\> prompt, DOS searches through the directories in the PATH statement, finds SIMCITY.BAT in the C:\BATCH directory, and runs it.

The SIMCITY.BAT file saves me from having to type the three or four commands that are necessary to run Sim City, as well as saving me the problem of having to remember where Sim City is installed on my computer. As long as DOS can find the SIMCITY.BAT file, I can run Sim City with just one simple command.

AUTOEXEC.BAT: A Special Batch File

Chapter 4 discussed AUTOEXEC.BAT in very general terms, calling it a to-do list for DOS. Every time you start up the computer, DOS reads the commands in AUTOEXEC.BAT and does whatever they say to do. What may be obvious to you now is that AUTOEXEC.BAT is just another batch file (it ends in BAT) with a special first name.

Normally only DOS runs AUTOEXEC.BAT. It contains things such as the PATH statement, a PROMPT statement, and anything else you might want to run automatically when your computer starts up. In Chapter 7, for instance, you'll read about computer viruses and how damaging they can be to your computer. It might make good sense to run the DOS 6 Anti-Virus program each time you start up your computer to search for and eradicate viruses that might be lurking in your files.

The only rule about AUTOEXEC.BAT is that it must live in your computer's root directory. Also, if you plan to make any changes to AUTOEXEC.BAT, you should always make a backup copy of it by copying it to another name (COPY AUTOEXEC.BAT AUTOEXEC.SAV) before making changes.

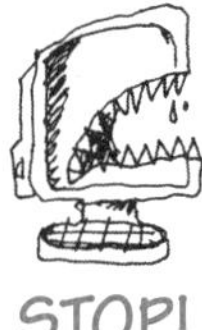
STOP!

> Even though AUTOEXEC.BAT is just another batch file, you shouldn't run it after DOS has started up because you might really mess things up. Sometimes AUTOEXEC.BAT starts up things that keep running after DOS is started or uses memory for this'n'that (like MSAV, the computer virus monitor). If you run AUTOEXEC.BAT after DOS is up and running, you might start up things a *second* time or cause AUTOEXEC.BAT to use a second set of memory for this'n'that.

Everything else you read in this chapter about batch files is also applicable to AUTOEXEC.BAT.

Batch Practice

Okay, let's make a quick 'n easy batch file. Rather than use the DOS `EDIT` command like we did in Chapter 4, we're going to do something rather special. Type this in at your keyboard:

```
ECHO DIR /P > D.BAT
```

Remember the `COPY` command? The first line makes DOS take the stuff you type on the keyboard and put it into a file called `D.BAT`. You did this back in Chapter 3.

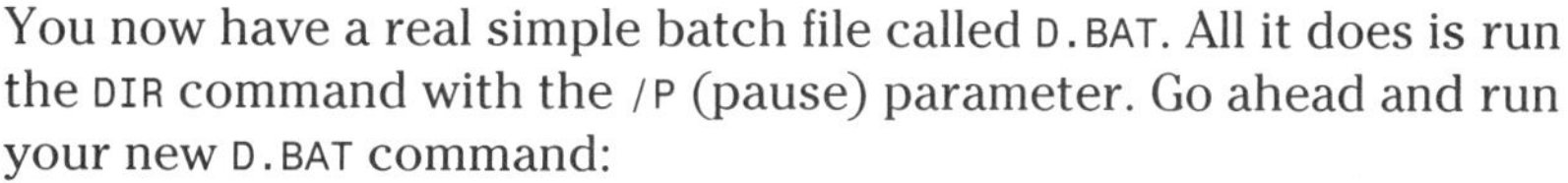

You now have a real simple batch file called `D.BAT`. All it does is run the `DIR` command with the `/P` (pause) parameter. Go ahead and run your new `D.BAT` command:

```
D
```

Easy. huh? When batch files get much more complicated than this, you won't want to use the `COMMAND > FILENAME.BAT` trick. Use `EDIT` instead (it's a lot easier).

Special Batch-File Commands

These "batch" commands have special functions when they appear in a batch file, and usually have no real purpose at the command line:

- **ECHO**. Use this to display `Hello!` as a message on the screen:

  ```
  ECHO Hello!
  ```

  Normally, when a batch file runs, you can see the lines in the file appear on the screen as if you typed them in. If this behavior gets in the way of seeing what's going on, you can turn it off with the command:

  ```
  ECHO OFF
  ```

- **REM**. This is how you insert notes to yourself in your batch files:

  ```
  REM This batch file starts up SimCity
  ```

- **PAUSE**. This stops your batch file and displays the message:

  ```
  Press any key to continue...
  ```

You can use `PAUSE` to give you a chance to put a floppy disk in the floppy drive, or for any other reason you might want to stop processing the commands in the batch file. You can use `ECHO` to display another message before the pause.

`GOTO`. This causes the execution of the batch file to jump to another place within the file. You can use this to jump over commands that you don't want DOS to run. The following `CHOICE` and `IF` commands can be used to help you decide where you want the batch file to go.

Obviously, if you use `GOTO` in your batch file, you've got to have some place to go to. You'll see how this works in a page or two.

`CHOICE`. In DOS 6, this lets your batch file check to see what you type in at the keyboard:

```
CHOICE Are you ready?
```

When this line is found in a batch file, DOS shows you this:

```
Are you ready [Y,N]?
```

Unless you tell it to display other choices, `CHOICE` askes you to type a **Y** (yes) or an **N** (no). The following sample batch file shows you how to make other choices. You can use the `GOTO` command and the following `IF` command, along with `CHOICE`, to help DOS decide what to do with a **Y** or with an **N**.

Unfortunately, `CHOICE` is only available to DOS 6 users. Incredible as it may seem, up until DOS 6 there was no way to get a batch file to stop and ask you a question (other than buying some program that provided this function).

`IF`. This gives a batch file the capability of making a decision. In a batch file, an `IF` command tests to see "if" one thing is equal to something else. See the example that follows to understand how this works.

A More Complex Batch File

Here is a much more complex example of a batch file. The numbers at the far left of each line are just to number the lines for the explanation that follows (they aren't part of the batch file):

```
1)    @ECHO OFF
2)    REM BATCH FILE TO SELECT A GAME
```

```
3)    CLS
4)    ECHO Select one of these games:
5)    ECHO 1) Sim City
6)    ECHO 2) Alien Force
7)    CHOICE  /C:12 "Select a game: "
8)    IF ERRORLEVEL 2 GOTO ALIEN
9)    IF ERRORLEVEL 1 GOTO SIM
10)   :SIM
11)   CD C:\GAMES\SIMCITY
12)   SIMCITY
13)   CD \
14)   GOTO END
15)   :ALIEN
16)   CD C:\GAMES\ALIEN
17)   ALIEN
18)   CD \
19)   :END
```

Figure 6.1 shows this batch file in action.

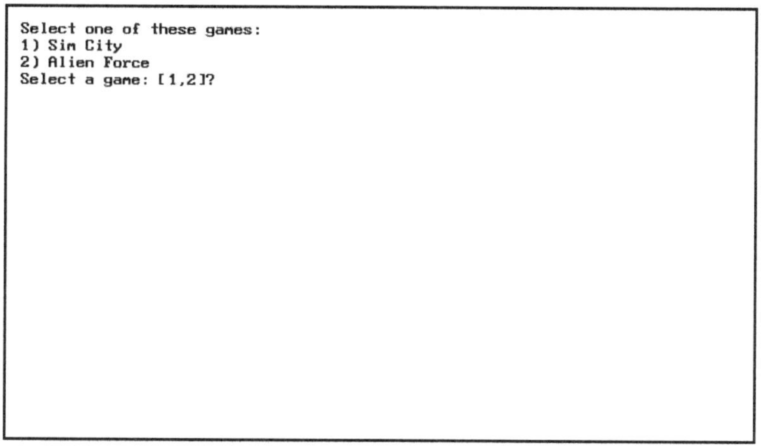

```
Select one of these games:
1) Sim City
2) Alien Force
Select a game: [1,2]?
```

Figure 6.1

The GAMES batch file in action.

Here's what's happening at each important line of this file:

1. @ECHO OFF starts off this batch file by turning off the ECHO behavior. Because this is a pretty complex batch file, we don't want the user to see all of the commands displayed on the screen. The @ sign in front of ECHO even turns off the display of the ECHO command itself.

If you're one of the two or three people out there using a really old version of DOS (like 2.01 or 2.1), the `@ECHO OFF` trick might not work.

2. `REM` makes this line a comment that does nothing except remind you about what this batch file does.

3. `CLS` clears the computer screen.

4,5,6. `ECHO` makes the next three lines (4, 5, and 6) display a list of games (Sim City or Alien Force) offered by this batch file. You can see this list in figure 6.1.

7. `CHOICE` lets you see what you type on the keyboard. The `CHOICE` command puts the text `Select a game: [1,2]?` on the screen, and gives you the choice of typing either **1** or **2**. These choices are the result of the weird `/C:12` parameter following the `CHOICE` command. It isn't really `12`, it's 1 and 2. If you want three choices (`[1,2,3]?`), use `/C:123`. Pretty nerdy, eh?

Remember *parameter*? Some DOS commands make you type something in along with the command so that DOS knows what you're trying to do. A good example is the ECHO command you saw a bit earlier in this chapter. Normally you use the ECHO command like this:

ECHO Hello there!

The "Hello there!" is the parameter for the ECHO command to work on.

Although the ECHO command is almost always used in batch files, you can type it in at the DOS command line. Go ahead and try this little example to see what happens.

The `CHOICE` command stops the batch file and waits until you type either **1** or **2** at the keyboard (you can't type anything else—just 1 or 2).

8,9. These two IF...GOTO lines test what you typed at the keyboard. If you typed a **2**, GOTO tells DOS to jump down to the line beginning with :ALIEN; typing a **1** takes DOS to the line starting with :SIM. Depending on what you type in when you see the Select a game: message, CHOICE sends a special message called ERRORLEVEL to DOS.

The ERRORLEVEL message depends on the things that come after the /C: on the CHOICE line. With /C:ABC, if you answer **A**, CHOICE will set ERRORLEVEL to 1, **B** to 2, and **C** to 3. If you don't use a /C: parameter, CHOICE sets ERRORLEVEL to either Y or N.

10,15. The :SIM and :ALIEN lines are nothing more than labels that give GOTO a place to jump. All lines between the IF...GOTO line and the label line that GOTO jumps to are ignored.

11-13, 16-18. Look at the commands right after :SIM (lines 11, 12, and 13) or :ALIEN (16, 17, and 18) in the file. They're what I would type in at my keyboard to start these games up. Instead of all that CD stuff, all I need to do is type **GAMES** and select 1 or 2 from the list displayed by this batch file.

14. GOTO END makes DOS skip the commands to start up the Alien Force game. If DOS doesn't skip these lines every time I run Sim City, Alien Force would run as well.

20. The :END label gives the GOTO on line 14 a place to jump to.

TRICKS

Here's a little trick you can use if you start writing your own batch files. Sometimes it's annoying to have applications start up until you're satisfied that the batch file is working correctly. It's a waste of time to start the application over and over as part of your batch-file testing. There's an easy way to disable the line that starts the application until you're ready for it.

Let's say your batch file changes directories and starts up an application such as Word. While you're testing the batch file, you might run the batch file five or ten times until you've got it working perfectly. If you don't want to start up Word every time you run the batch file during your testing, disable the line that starts Word by putting a colon (:) as the first letter on the line. DOS will just ignore the line, letting you run the batch file without actually starting up Word. Later, when you're done testing, remove the colon and run the batch file one last time to make sure it works like you want it to.

How Do I Use Batch Files?

You've probably got a number of programs installed on your own computer that you use quite a bit. If you find yourself typing the same long commands over and over again, it's easy to reduce them to very short one- or two-letter command names. Just tuck the DOS command line inside a batch file, and run the batch file when you need your program.

Or you can do something like the `GAMES.BAT` file, which offers you a choice of several different programs to run. You can add as many things to the `/C:` list as you want. Use all the letters of the alphabet, all the numbers from 0 to 9, and punctuation, if you want. Just be sure you count correctly and set the ERRORLEVEL test the right way.

A Final Suggestion

You might consider making "the ultimate batch file for your computer" that helps you remember the names of the batch files you've built for each of your programs. You can call this batch file `INDEX.BAT` because it tells you the names of your other batch files when you run it.

The design of INDEX.BAT goes something like this:

```
@ECHO OFF

CLS
REM INDEX.BAT - Because it's hard to remember this stuff
ECHO DOWP:     Starts up WordPerfect
ECHO DO123:    Starts up Lotus
ECHO DOPRO:    Starts up Procomm
ECHO DOWIN:    Starts up Windows
ECHO DOCOREL:  Starts up CorelDRAW!
ECHO GAMES:    All the games on my computer
ECHO.
```

With `INDEX.BAT`, all you have to remember is to type **`INDEX`** at the keyboard whenever you've forgotten the names of your batch files. Each of the batch files mentioned in `INDEX` (`DOWP`, `DO123`) contain all of the DOS commands you need to get the program (WordPerfect, Lotus 1-2-3, and so on) started up. Simple, isn't it?

When I run INDEX.BAT on my computer (by typing in just **INDEX**, of course), I see the display shown in figure 6.2.

```
DOWP:      Starts up WordPerfect
DO123:     Starts up Lotus
DOPRO:     Starts up Procomm
DOWIN:     Starts up Windows
DOCOREL:   Starts up CorelDRAW!
GAMES:     All the games on my computer

C:\
```

Figure 6.2

The INDEX batch file in action.

Of course, you have to keep INDEX.BAT up-to-date. As you add new batch files or remove old ones, make changes to INDEX.BAT so that its display is correct.

NERDY DETAILS

Did you notice that the last line of my **INDEX.BAT** files is simply **ECHO.**? Adding a period immediately after **ECHO** causes a blank line to be added to the screen display. Notice the blank line between the last line of the display and the **C:\>** prompt in figure 6.2.

PART 3

PC Hardware and Other Cool Stuff To Know

IMPROVED!
only $499.99
SUPER-PRO
V. 23.6
COMPU
RAMA
COMPUTER SALES STORE
SUPER-PRO
VERSION 2.1.6

Accidentally Deleted Files, Computer Viruses, and Other Scary Things

It's bound to happen! Someday you'll get an `Are you sure (Y/N)?` message when you've asked DOS to delete something. The "somethings" you're about to delete are all the files in a directory. If you ignore the message, DOS happily complies, and poof, baby, they're gone.

This chapter talks about how to make sure a simple slip of the fingers doesn't wipe out hours and hours of work, and how DOS 6 really is trying hard to keep you out of mischief. You'll learn about the following:

- Protecting yourself from stupid mistakes
- Using plain ol' `UNDELETE` to dig through the trash
- Meeting the Delete brothers: Tracker and Sentry
- Safe computing in the age of computer viruses
- How to treat a computer infected with a virus
- How to vaccinate your computer against social diseases
- How to make backups—your final line of protection

Oh, No! What Did I Just Delete?

If you're not careful, you can delete an entire directory of files. Let's say you type in **DEL REPORTS** (the name of the directory in which you store your report files) when you meant to type **DEL REPORT1** (the name of an old report). DOS will always come back to you with the message:

```
All files in directory will be deleted!
Are you sure (Y/N)?
```

If you ignore the warning and press **Y** without double-checking the directory name, DOS will delete all of the files in the REPORTS directory.

You'll get the same message if you ever make another easy error, such as entering the command:

```
DEL *.*
```

You meant to enter something like **DEL A*.*** (to delete all files beginning with an A). **DEL *.*** means, of course, delete everything in the currently open directory.

It's also very easy to use wild cards incorrectly. For example, you might think that DEL *ABC.DOC would delete only files with ABC in their names, such as QABC.DOC. But in fact, once DOS sees the wild card, it doesn't care what follows (up to the extension)! It'll zap everything in that directory.

The message is clear: be sure to read all of the messages DOS gives you. They're about your only protection against easy-to-make mistakes that can delete all of your hard work in an instant.

What To Do When You've Thrown Away the Wrong Thing

Normally, when you delete a file, DOS removes its listing from your directory by changing a single character in the file name. It also makes a note to itself that the space is now available to write a new file.

Until DOS uses the disk space for another file, it's possible to get the deleted file back. Unfortunately, DOS doesn't use all available blank disk space before overwriting the space of deleted files. No, it uses the most recently deleted file's space first, then uses other disk space. (You'd think a nerd could program a better way to handle disk space.)

UNDELETE and Older DOS Versions

In versions of DOS earlier than DOS 5, the fact that the information might still be there didn't do you much good. To retrieve deleted files, you had to purchase third-party utilities such as Symantec's Norton Utilities or Central Point's PC Tools.

DOS 5 introduced `UNDELETE`, which is a command that lists the files you've deleted, and gives you the chance to restore them...assuming that the data hasn't been overwritten yet. (Always use any UNDELETE command as soon as you realize you made the mistake!)

In DOS 5, you can go a step further—to have DOS track your deletions as you make them—by including the following statement in your `AUTOEXEC.BAT` file:

```
MIRROR /TC
```

By the way, this tracks only drive C. To track drives C and D, include:

```
MIRROR /TC /TD
```

DOS 6 makes some changes and adds some options to really extend the `UNDELETE` capability.

You still have the basic `UNDELETE` command. To use it, type **UNDELETE**, followed by the path and file name of the file you're looking for:

```
UNDELETE C:\FILES\DEADFILE.DOC
```

Press Enter. If the file's still there, DOS will undelete it.

Or, if you're not sure of the file name, type:

```
UNDELETE
```

Press Enter. (Pretty simple, eh?) DOS will search through the currently open directory drawer for files that can still be rescued (they've been deleted but not overwritten by new files). When it finds one, it'll show you something like the following:

```
UNDELETE - A delete protection facility
Copyright (C) 1987-1993 Central Point Software, Inc.
All rights reserved.

Directory: C:\
File Specifications: *.*

    Delete Sentry control file not found.

    Deletion-tracking file not found.

    MS-DOS directory contains   40 deleted files.
    Of those,    6 files may be recovered.

Using the MS-DOS directory method.

  ** ?IRTHDAY DOC   1978  1-26-93  8:53a  ...A  Undelete (Y/N)?
```

If you answer **Y** to the `Undelete (Y/N)?` question, DOS will ask you to provide the first letter of the file's first name:

```
Please type the first character for ?IRTHDAY.DOC:
```

When you type in a **B** (of course it's B!), DOS will neatly bring back the `BIRTHDAY.DOC` file.

If there are any other deleted files DOS can get back for you, it'll show you their names as well.

Sometimes you can't undelete a file. You'll get the very ugly message:

```
Starting cluster is unavailable. This file cannot be recovered
with the UNDELETE command. Press any key to continue.
```

That stuff about the "starting cluster" means that the file has been partially overwritten, so that you won't be able to get this file back.

Plain ol' UNDELETE is what you get by default when you install DOS 5 or 6, but it doesn't provide very much protection. Fortunately, starting with DOS 6, the nerdy DOS wizards at Microsoft took this business seriously (after all, they've had 10 years to think about it...).

UNDELETE's Bigger Brother: Delete Tracker

DOS 6 provides two additional layers of undelete protection. The next higher level of protection beyond UNDELETE is Delete Tracker, which is a lot bigger and meaner way of getting back files. (Hey, ol' D.T. doesn't GOTTA speak good—do ya want nice diction or lost data?)

Delete Tracker is similar to MIRROR in DOS 5, but you use it differently. There's no MIRROR command in DOS 6. Instead, there's Delete Tracker.

When Delete Tracker is started, it tries real hard to keep DOS from reusing the space left when you delete a file. Remember that "deleting" a file with the DOS DEL command just makes the space occupied by the file available for other files. Delete Tracker keeps telling DOS not to put files in the space left by a file that was deleted; that is, until there isn't any other disk space left, and Delete Tracker finally allows DOS to put files into the deleted file's space on the hard disk.

It's as if your disk were a crowded movie theater. When someone gets up to go get popcorn, Delete Tracker acts as an usher trying to keep his seat available for him when he comes back. If the person doesn't return in a reasonable amount of time and the theater is very full, Delete Tracker will let someone else take the empty seat.

Using Delete Tracker costs you very little, just a little memory and a little disk space to put the information needed to get your files back. In a few pages, you'll read how to turn on Delete Tracker.

The Biggest and Meanest of the Deletes: Delete Sentry

The junk yard dog UNDELETE protector is Delete Sentry. It keeps a complete copy of files that you've deleted in a secret directory called (oddly enough) SENTRY. After a specified period of time (seven days by default; later, we'll tell you how to change it to any number you want), DOS finally gets around to *really* throwing the files out. After the seventh day, you can't UNDELETE them anymore.

Delete Sentry works a lot like Delete Tracker, except that it needs a lot more disk space. Because it's keeping a complete copy of your deleted files, it can use up a lot of disk space.

Starting Up the Delete Brothers

Starting either Delete Tracker or Delete Sentry is easy. At the DOS command line, type:

```
UNDELETE C: /TC
```

and press Enter to start Delete Tracker, or type:

```
UNDELETE C: /SC
```

and press Enter to start Delete Sentry.

Better yet, include one of these lines in your AUTOEXEC.BAT file so that it loads automatically. (You can't run both at once.)

TRICKS

Remember that you can use the **EDIT** command to edit your AUTOEXEC.BAT file.

That's all there is to it. The Delete boys will automatically set up your computer's disk and go to work. They'll keep working silently in the background as long as they're active—forever if you've included them in AUTOEXEC.BAT.

Customizing Your Deletion Protection

One last thing. You can change how long deleted files are kept by using EDIT (or any text editor) to change a file named UNDELETE.INI that UNDELETE puts in your DOS directory. An example of this file is shown in figure 7.1.

```
C:\>TYPE \DOS\UNDELETE.INI
[configuration]
archive=FALSE
days=7
percentage=10
[sentry.drives]
C=
[mirror.drives]
[sentry.files]
s_files=*.* -*.tmp -*.vm? -*.woa -*.swp -*.spl -*.rmg -*.img -*.thm -*.dov
[defaults]
d.sentry=FALSE
d.tracker=TRUE

C:\>
```

Figure 7.1

An `UNDELETE.INI` file.

Change the number in the line that reads `days=7` to the number of days you want the deleted files to be kept on your hard disk. Don't worry about the other things in this file—they are a lot less important than how long you want the Delete boys to keep your files.

Of course, the `UNDELETE.INI` file applies only when you are using either Delete Tracker or Delete Sentry. Plain ol' `UNDELETE` doesn't need or use this file.

What the Heck Is a Virus?

A certain type of sociopathic nerd, obviously suffering from advanced Hitlerian emasculation-denial complex, enjoys writing devilish little computer programs called *viruses*.

Viruses have no function in life other than to mess up your computer. A computer virus is inserted into other programs (it *infects* the programs with the virus) by the megalomaniacal, altruistically impotent, chowderheaded ying-yang who wrote it. The virus is then passed from computer to computer by anyone who runs the infected program.

You don't go to the computer software store to buy a virus. Your computer becomes infected when you unwittingly run a game or utility on your computer that contains the virus. Often the game or utility is acquired from a friend or associate (who is not even aware of the problem on the disk that he or she hands you).

You'll be happy to know that a refreshing number of antisocial hacker nerds are busy splitting rocks in various jails and prisons around the country. The federal government and many state and local legal authorities have finally taken the threat from computer viruses seriously.

NERDY DETAILS

Occasionally too seriously. The FBI drove Steve Jackson Games into bankruptcy because the FBI thought Steve Jackson was a threat. All he was doing was writing a game about hackers. FBI agents seized the game and Steve's offices, and before they realized their mistake, Mr. Jackson was out of business!

Still, it's really nice to imagine real virus authors keeping busy punching license plates instead of computer keys.

NERDY DETAILS

From time to time, the news media picks up on a story about some terrible virus about to strike millions of computers across the country. In 1992 there was a great deal of hype about the "Michelangelo" virus, which was supposed to attack infected computers on March 6. While it's true a few hard disks were wiped out, the actual danger was much less than the media would have you believe. It's even rumored that a couple of anti-virus companies were prime movers behind the panic because anti-virus sales were beginning to soften.

When unleashed onto an unprotected computer, a virus may destroy all of the programs and data files on the hard disk (the hard disk itself is not physically damaged). Other viruses just cause the computer to crash or behave erratically. Games and utility programs are often infected with viruses because they are freely exchanged by PC users.

NERDY DETAILS

Computer viruses share some characteristics with their biological counterparts. Just like the flu virus, which lives inside you, a computer virus lives *inside* of another computer program. The computer virus is able to replicate itself and infect otherwise healthy programs. A computer virus may coexist with the files on your disk for months or years without causing damage, or it may suddenly erupt to systematically wipe out everything on your disk.

If you are one of the unfortunate few whose computer becomes "infected" by one of these programs, you may lose all of the programs and other files stored on your computer's hard disk. Happily, DOS 6 provides a reasonable amount of protection against the most common computer viruses.

If you haven't upgraded to DOS 6, third-party antivirus programs are still available.

Common Symptoms of Viruses

Just like a person infected by a biological virus, a computer infected by a virus will act sick or strange. My wife called me at the office one day to tell me that her computer needed servicing because the letters on the screen kept "breaking loose from the screen and falling to the bottom of the screen." Her computer had become infected with the "Stoned" virus, one of the most common varieties.

A virus-infected computer may exhibit any of the following symptoms:

- Unexpected messages are displayed on the screen. One of the more common viruses (called the "Cookie Monster") does little more than display "I want a cookie" on the screen.
- Files are randomly erased from your hard disk.
- Randomly changed data or information are contained within your files.
- Spontaneous and unpredictable *crashes* happen (the computer stops responding to your commands or typing).
- Data is erased from your hard disk and often replaced (or *over-written*) with random numbers and letters that prevent you from recovering what was lost.

At the very least, viruses are an annoyance and can disrupt your work. At the very worst, they can destroy weeks or months of hard work in an instant.

Because a virus can lay dormant for weeks or months, it is possible that your backups are also infected. If this is the case, your only recourse is to try to eradicate the virus with your DOS 6 tools, or completely wipe your disk free and start over by reinstalling all of your software. Yuck!

What To Do If You Think Your Computer Has a Virus

Fortunately, DOS 6 includes MSAV (Microsoft Anti-Virus), which is a rather efficient and effective virus fighter. MSAV is capable of recognizing over 1,000 different viruses, and will "scan" your computer's disks and memory, looking for telltale signs of viruses on your system.

If your computer exhibits any of the symptoms described a little earlier, or just plain starts acting weirdly, you should run MSAV without hesitation. The sooner you act, the less damage may occur. The steps for running MSAV are:

Type **MSAV**, and press Enter at the DOS prompt. The main MSAV screen (figure 7.2) appears after MSAV reads the current disk.

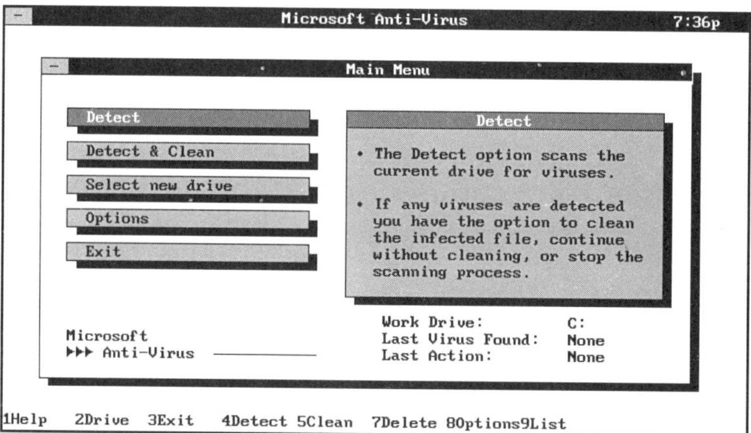

Figure 7.2

The main MSAV screen.

If you want to scan one of your floppy drives (for instance, if you've been given a game disk and you want to check it before running the game), press and hold Alt while you press **S**, or press the down arrow key twice to move the highlight down to the `Select new drive` option, and press Enter. A list of the drives on your computer will appear in the upper left hand corner of the screen. Use the arrow keys to highlight the drive you want to scan, and press Enter. (If the arrow keys don't do anything, press the Num Lock key and try again.)

If you have a large hard disk, it may take a while for MSAV to read the disk information. You can press Esc to stop it, and then use the arrow keys to select another drive.

MSAV offers two options to detect viruses: Detect only and Detect & Clean. Detect only (the default) scans for viruses but does not automatically kill them. With Detect & Clean, you can both scan and remove viruses in one step. Use the arrow keys to highlight either option, and press the Enter key.

MSAV will scan your hard disk for viruses (and will attempt to remove them if you select Detect & Clean). This can take awhile. On my 33MHz 486 with 16M of memory, scanning one of my 130M hard disks took more than half an hour.

MSAV always checks your computer's memory for viruses before looking at the disk. This ensures that there aren't any viruses lurking in memory that will write themselves to your disk as soon as the scan is complete.

While MSAV is checking your disk for viruses, you'll see a display like figure 7.3. The two horizontal bars in the Detect & Clean box indicate how much of the disk has been scanned; the lines under this box tell you how many viruses have been detected.

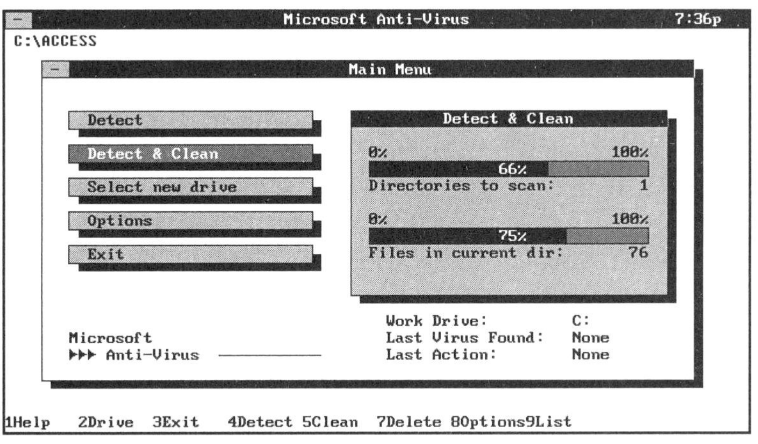

Figure 7.3

MSAV in action.

When the scan is complete, MSAV will display a report similar to figure 7.4.

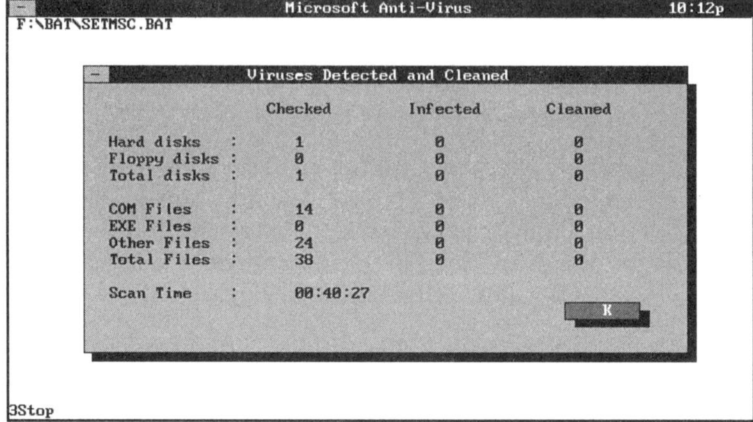

Microsoft Anti-Virus
10:12p
F:\BAT\SETMSC.BAT
Viruses Detected and Cleaned
Checked Infected Cleaned
Hard disks : 1 0 0
Floppy disks : 0 0 0
Total disks : 1 0 0
COM Files : 14 0 0
EXE Files : 0 0 0
Other Files : 24 0 0
Total Files : 38 0 0
Scan Time : 00:40:27
K
3Stop

Figure 7.4

The MSAV report screen.

If you do have a virus and MSAV is not able to restore the infected files, you may have to reinstall your programs or files from their original or backup disks (check them for viruses first).

> If MSAV discovers a virus, be sure to check all floppy disks that you've been using. It's possible that the virus has infected your floppy disks as well as your hard disk.

Preventing Viruses By Practicing Safe Computing

There are a few basic rules that will limit the chance that your computer might become infected by a virus:

Don't use pirated software! A favorite ploy of virus writers is to infect an otherwise perfectly working copy of legitimate software, and then pass it around. If you are using a pirated or otherwise illegally acquired copy of software, beware!

If you cannot vouch for the origin of a newly acquired "shareware" or public domain game or utility, you should run MSAV on the floppy disk before trying to run the program.

TRICKS

Shareware is software written by individuals who allow you to try it out free. If you like it, you send them a small amount of money. It's the honor system. There's lots of terrific, reasonably priced shareware. *Public domain software* is software that's simply free.

If you use a modem (see *PCs for Non-Nerds*, from New Riders, for a good section on modems), never, ever download a program, install it on your disk and run it before checking it for viruses. By far, the most common source of infection is from programs indiscriminately downloaded from a bulletin board system.

NERDY DETAILS

Downloading is the process of connecting to another computer through a *modem* (a computer-to-computer communicating device; it's kind of like a computer telephone). A *bulletin board system* (also called a *BBS*) is a computer that some nerd has set up in his or her home that is connected to the world through a phone connection. Nerds and computer hobbyists spend a great deal of time dialing into BBSs to exchange games and useful programs.

Inoculation Against Future Viruses

There are two things you can add to your AUTOEXEC.BAT file that will give your computer a high level of protection every time you start it up:

To automatically scan for viruses each time the computer is started, add the following line to AUTOEXEC.BAT:

```
MSAV /P
```

The only drawback is that scanning can take a considerable amount of time, particularly on a slow computer or one with a large hard disk.

To load a program that constantly watches for virus-like activity, add this line to AUTOEXEC.BAT:

```
VSAFE
```

VSAFE is a new DOS 6 utility that will instantly alert you if your computer has become infected.

Unfortunately, if you have a version of DOS before version 6, you do not have the built-in virus protection from MSAV and VSAFE. If you cannot think of any other reason to upgrade to DOS 6, this protection alone ought to be reason enough.

Protecting Your Files: Back 'em Up!

It's been said before, and it's true: sooner or later your hard disk will wear out and quit working. Or your computer may become infected with a virus that damages or wipes out a bunch of files. With any luck it'll be later, rather than sooner.

To protect your programs and the hard work contained in your files, make nice, pristine copies of important files onto floppy disks from time to time. DOS 6 provides the MSBACKUP command for this purpose.

Unlike some of the other commands we've discussed in this chapter, MSBACKUP is pretty complicated. We'll discuss the most important MSBACKUP options and how to go about making good, reliable backups of your system.

> The following discussion involves the DOS 6 **MSBACKUP** command. Earlier versions of DOS had a program called **BACKUP**, which was different in very significant ways. If you are using DOS version 5 or older, see "Backing Up with Earlier Versions of DOS" later in this chapter.

What Does MSBACKUP Do for Me?

MSBACKUP is a full-feature backup program. It lets you do all of the following with the files on your hard disk:

- Back up all of the files on your hard disk to floppy disks.
- Back up a select set of files or directories.
- Perform an *incremental* backup (only those files that have changed since the last time you did a backup).
- Restore files from a set of backup floppies. MSBACKUP keeps a "catalog" of all backups you've done and lets you select from a list of backup events before doing a Restore.
- Use a compression technique to squeeze more stuff onto a floppy than would normally fit.

How Do I Use MSBACKUP?

To back up your hard disk, perform the following steps:

1. Type **MSBACKUP**, and press Enter at the DOS prompt.
2. On the opening screen, press Enter to choose the Backup screen. The screen in figure 7.5 will appear.

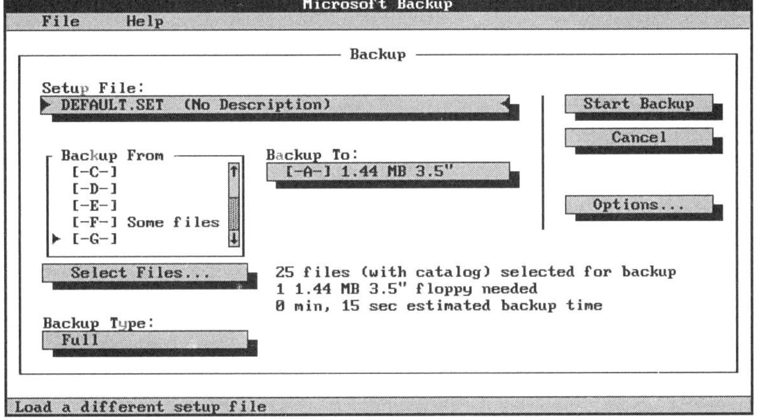

Figure 7.5

The Backup screen.

3. The first time you run MSBACKUP, you will be asked to allow MSBACKUP to "configure" your computer. This easy procedure simply checks what kind of floppy disk drives you have on your computer. All you need are two formatted floppy disks for one of your floppy disk drives.

4. The instructions on the screen are easy to follow. If all goes well, you should accept each of the choices by pressing Enter. If you need to make any other choices, use the Tab or arrow keys to highlight the choice, and then press Enter. To select a drive, use the up or down arrow keys, and then press the spacebar.

5. Normally, you won't want to back up your entire hard disk. Even with the MSBACKUP file compression, backing up a large hard disk may consume dozens of floppy disks and require hours of your time. Instead, use the Tab key to move the highlight in the Backup screen to the Select Files box, and press Enter. The Select Backup Files screen shown in figure 7.6 will appear, allowing you to select only those files or directories you wish to back up.

Figure 7.6

The MSBACKUP Select Backup Files screen.

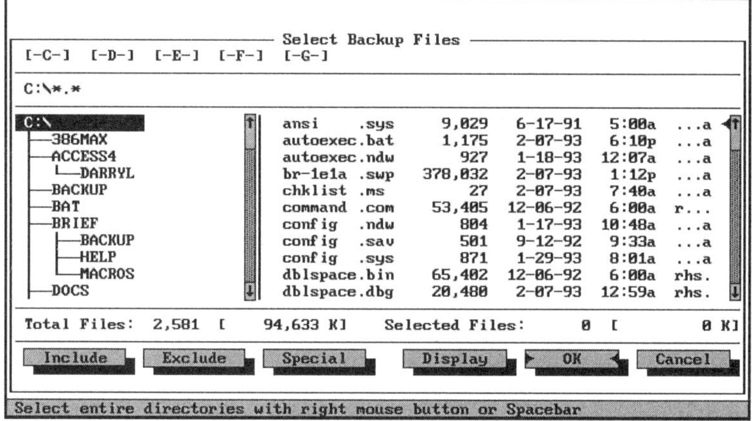

6. The left side of this screen allows you to pick the directory you want to back up; the right side lets you select individual files. If you use the arrow keys to move the highlight to a particular directory and press the spacebar, all of the files in that directory are selected for backup (a check mark will appear to the left of each selected file's name). Pressing the spacebar again deselects the files.

7. You can use the Tab key to move the highlight to the right side of this screen, and use the arrow keys and spacebar to highlight and select (or deselect) individual files.

8. When you are done selecting files for backup, press Enter to return to the Backup screen.

9. Using the Tab key, move the highlight to the Start Backup box, and press Enter. MSBACKUP prompts you for the disk(s) that are needed to do the backup. During the backup process, you'll see a screen that looks like figure 7.7.

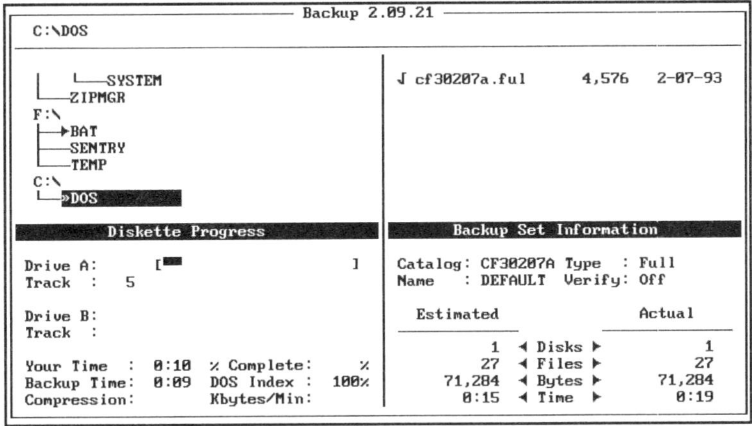

Figure 7.7

MSBACKUP in action.

The upper part of this screen shows you the files that are being backed up; the bottom half helps you follow what's going on.

Be prepared! A backup can take a long time and require a LOT of floppy disks! Even with file compression (this is used by default, by the way), a 40M hard disk will require between 20 and 30 1.44 megabyte floppy disks. Wow!

> Here's a good idea. When **MSBACKUP** prompts you for the disk, note that in the lower right hand of the screen is a weird number (in figure 7.7 it's **CF30207A**). This is the *catalog number* of your backup. Write this number on the floppy disks you use for your backup, and number the disks (1, 2, 3, and so on) to make it easy to *restore* the files later. You should probably also write what the backup is (**DOC FILES 2/8/93**), too.

One of the nice things about MSBACKUP is that it fills the entire floppy disk from end to end. If a file is too big to fit on the disk, MSBACKUP cuts the file into pieces that will conveniently fit on the disks you're using. This means you get the maximum use out of your floppies.

One of the crummy things about MSBACKUP is that it breaks your files into pieces. This means that you must use the Restore option if you need to take the files off the floppies and put them back on your hard disk.

Using RESTORE To Get Things Off of Your Backup Floppies

Let's assume that something has happened to some of your files, and you need the files that you backed up a while ago. How do you get 'em off the backup disks? Do this:

1. Start up MSBACKUP and select Restore on the main screen (use Tab to move the highlight to the Restore box).

   You'll see a screen like the one shown in figure 7.8.

Figure 7.8

The MSBACKUP Restore screen.

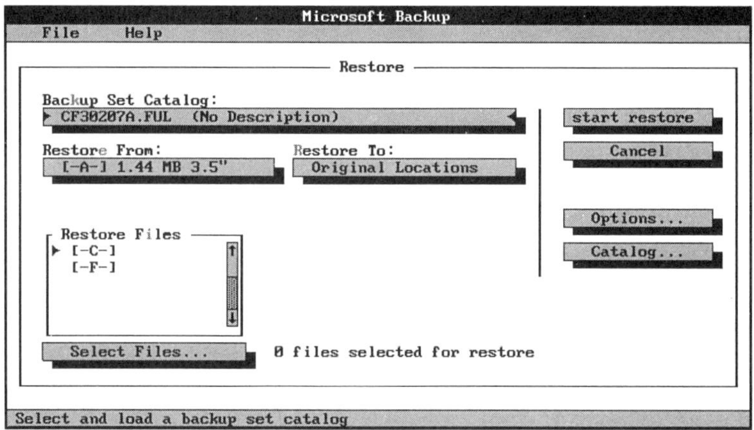

2. The Restore screen looks a lot like the Backup screen. The difference is that you have to first select the catalog you want to back up from. Select Catalog. You'll see a screen similar to that in figure 7.9.

3. Choose the catalog that matches the name you've written on your disk, and press Enter.

4. Return to the Restore screen. Now you have to tell MSBACKUP where your backed-up files are. Select Restor**e** From with your mouse or press **E**. You can either tell MSBACKUP that your files are on drive A, or you can specify a path of your own.

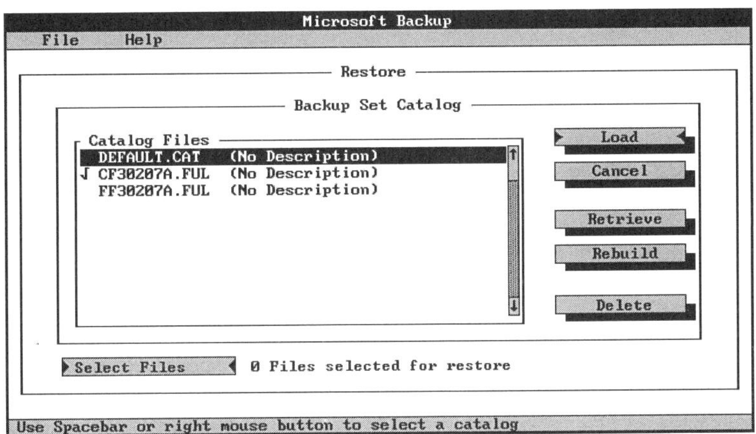

Figure 7.9

The Select Catalog screen.

5. Assuming that you want to restore all the files in the catalog, select Start Restore. Because your computer already knows what files are on the backup disks and where they belong, you don't have to worry about how to put them back in the right place.

Backing Up with Earlier Versions of DOS

If you are using DOS 3.3 or DOS 5, you have to contend with more primitive backup commands. To back up, use BACKUP instead of MSBACKUP.

NERDY DETAILS

> Versions of DOS prior to 3.3 have an even more Neanderthal, highly aggravating **BACKUP** command. Upgrade, or else get a third-party backup program.

Let's say you want to back up all files in the subdirectory C:\FILES and place them on a disk in drive A. Type:

```
BACKUP C:\FILES\*.* A:
```

You can tell DOS to back up only the files that have changed since your last backup by adding the `/M` option:

```
BACKUP C:\FILES\*.* A: /M
```

These commands only back up files in the subdirectory `C:\FILES`, not any files in subdirectories contained in `C:\FILES`. To also back up the contents of subdirectories within the directory you've chosen, use the `/S` option:

```
BACKUP C:\FILES\*.* A: /S
```

To restore files, you use an altogether different command, `RESTORE`. The idea is similar: you tell DOS where the backup files are, then where you want to put them (the *destination*). Your destination must be the same place where the files were originally located before you backed them up in the first place.

```
RESTORE A: C:\FILES\*.*
```

Some of the same options apply, but with a different twist. For example, adding `/M` restores only files that you modified since the last backup:

```
RESTORE A: C:\FILES\*.* /M
```

Adding `/S` restores the contents of subdirectories within subdirectories.

```
RESTORE A: C:\FILES\*.* /S
```

If you don't use `/S`, `RESTORE` will restore only the files within the current directory.

A Last Bit of Advice

Backups are important. You never know when your hard disk might quit working or when the files on your computer's hard disk will be damaged. Resign yourself to doing a complete backup of your entire system at least once. From then on, you should do incremental backups every month or so.

Remember, in the event of a disaster, you might lose everything that has changed since the last time you did a backup. If you only back up every six months, you could lose an entire half-year's work. When it comes to backing up, it pays to be like the nerds.

PEACEFUL PINES

Fun with Your Hardware

Although you don't have to know a lot about your computer's hardware to use the darn stuff, the more you know about the big and little boxes that make up your computer system, the less likely you'll get taken to the cleaners if they ever need repairs or upgrades. Also, there is a surprising number of common problems that you can fix without the help of a nerd.

This chapter will tell you all about the following things:

- Your computer's brain
- Disks—hard, floppy, and otherwise
- How to tell a megabyte from a troglodyte
- Getting in touch with your computer's keyboard
- Making the right connections

Most of the hardware things are explained in more detail in separate chapters later on. This chapter is an overview of the hardware universe.

Why You Should Care (Give a Darn?) About Computer Hardware

This chapter might seem out of place in a book about DOS. But without some computer hardware, you can't do much with DOS, eh? Also, DOS is closely related to your computer's hardware. When you print something, DOS handles the job of getting the letters out to the printer. If your printer quits working, there can be many things at fault, including DOS, the cable between your computer and the printer, or the printer itself. It's just hard to talk much about DOS without discussing hardware as well.

The more you know about your computer's hardware, the less likely you'll spend money when you don't need to. That's the honest truth. Sure, things will go wrong from time to time, and you will have to spend money to fix them. Or you may need to upgrade your machine with some zoomie add-on that'll set you back a few bucks.

The more you understand what's under the hood, the more prepared you're going to be when something goes BOOOIINNNGGG! late on a Sunday night when you're trying to get a big presentation ready for Monday morning.

Problem-Solving

Just like a car, the more you recognize your computer's moods, which are expressed as sounds from the big box and the things it might display on the screen, the sooner you'll notice something is going wrong.

Buyer's Guide

Let's face a simple fact: Computer hardware is darn expensive. Forget that you've been reading how cheap computers and peripherals have become. They're still awfully expensive when compared to watches, VCRs, television sets, CD players, or video games.

You'll probably want to add some of this cool stuff to your computer at some point. It'd be nice if you knew what to ask for when you go to the computer store and talk to the nerd there.

GADS! Avoiding Future Disappointments

The worst mistake you can make is paying good money for hardware that won't do what you need it to do. If what you need is a "super VGA" adapter, and you buy a "VGA card," you've got no one to blame but yourself when your programs don't run right.

The Big Box

The big box, which sometimes sits on the desktop or on the floor contains a lot of neat stuff. Inside this box is the real magic of a computer (CPU, memory, expansion cards, disk drives, and the power supply).

It used to be that there was only a single kind of PC computer box. The good ol' PC was a kind of tan color, had places for two disk drives, and the power switch was on the right side by the back. Nowadays, computer cases come in all kinds of styles: PC/XT style, AT, mini-AT, all different sizes of "towers" that sit on the floor or on top of your desk, and lots of "low-profile" cabinets that take up less room than "full-size" units. And that's before we even talk about lugables, notebooks, laptops, and palm-top computers. Jeez, sure gets confusing.

Whatever it looks like on the outside, almost all computers share a lot in common on the inside.

The PC Numbers Game

Looking at computer ads, you see a lot of numbers that supposedly describe what they're selling. You'll see a lot of references to "80486SX," "80386DX," and so on. Now, honestly, should you really care if you have a 80486SX or a 80286 in your computer? Darn right you ought to!

NERDY DETAILS

> The brain inside your computer is usually called a *processor*, which is short for *microprocessor* or *central processing unit*. Calling it a CPU is pretty nerdy; most people refer to their computer by the last three digits and any letters of the type of processor in their computer. I've got a "486" at home and a "486DX2" at work. Yep, pretty nerdy....

These numbers refer to the central processing unit, or CPU, that is the real "brain" of your computer. Generally speaking, higher numbers (80486 versus 80386 and 33 versus 25) mean a faster computer. And we all care very much how fast our computers are.

You may hear the expression *chip* a lot. Chip is nerd-slang for the nerd-formal *integrated circuit*. It refers to the tiny silicon wafer on which the integrated circuit is created. Integrated circuits contain many (sometimes several million) miniaturized transistors. There are lots of different kinds of chips in your computer. The CPU (brain) and RAM (memory) are some of the most important chips.

Also, the other problem is that some older computers can't run a lot of very popular programs. You just can't get an old PC or AT to run Microsoft Windows 3.1. So there's a certain justification in your learning a little bit about these things.

CPUs come in a lot of flavors. This list runs from the oldest to the newest:

- **8088**. The original PC/XT processor. You'd have to look long and hard for a new computer using this processor. The 8088 had a somewhat bigger brother called the **8086** that got used in a few popular computers back then.
- **80286**. A slightly more advanced processor than the 8088. Today, this processor is usually only found in small computers that you can hold in your hand or in inexpensive notebook-sized computers.
- **80386**. A family of fairly advanced processors. These were the first truly fast (and useful) desktop computer chips.
- **80386DX**. This is a full-fledged, normal, garden-variety "386" processor.
- **80386SX**. A stripped-down version of the 80386DX. It is cheaper to make, has less horsepower, and consumes less power, so it's often used in portable (laptop) computers. There's a special low-power version of the 386 (the 80386SL) that's used in a lot of laptops.
- **80486**. A more advanced version of the 80386. There are lots of different kinds of 486s.
- **80486DX**. A really, really fast computer chip. If you've got one of these, you've got a state-of-the-art computer.
- **80486SX**. Just like the 80386, it's a stripped-down version of the 80486. It is cheaper to make, uses less power, and is slower than a "full" 80486.

80486DX2. A very special version of the 80486. This guy runs really, really fast, and is considerably quicker than even a 80486DX. What's clever about the DX2 chips is that they are only running fast *inside* the chip. On the outside they're like any other 80486.

Whatever you do, please, please don't buy a computer with a 8088 or 80286 processor. You can certainly get by with a 80386 something-or-other, but an old 8088 or 286 will just be a drag, and it probably won't run the software you want.

NERDY DETAILS

Confused yet? It gets worse. Intel, the company that makes all these chips for PCs has decided to give chips *names* instead of numbers. So, in the future you'll be hearing things like *Pentium* and *P5*. At least with numbers, bigger numbers always meant bigger and better and faster computers. Now we're going to have to remember the darn *names* of the things and what the names mean. Jeez.

The Computer Screen

Chapter 9 deals with *video* (that's the TV part of your computer—it's usually called a *monitor* or *screen*). Although all monitors work more or less the same way, there are a lot of differences between them.

Chapter 9 describes all kinds of things about computer video. For now, understand that it takes two parts to make the picture on the screen: a *video card* (or adapter) that lives inside your computer's big box, and the *monitor* (or screen) that sits on top of your desk. These parts have to be made for each other in order for you to get the picture.

Disk Drives: Hard and Floppy

There are two basic types of disk drives on your computer. Somewhere inside is a hard disk drive; there are one or more floppy disk drives that you can get at from the outside. Chapter 13 explains what you need to do to take care of your disks and disk drives. But you'll learn the basics about your disks right here.

All About Hard Disks

Both hard disks and floppy disks are measured by their capacity (how much stuff they can hold). Hard disks hold millions and millions of letters and numbers. Your computer might have a 40-megabyte or a 120-megabyte hard disk (or some other size). The bigger and faster the hard disk, the more expensive it is.

NERDY DETAILS

> Just in case you were wondering, a *megabyte* is exactly 1,048,576 bytes. A *byte* is a complicated nerdy way of representing a single letter or character. The word megabyte is often abbreviated as a capital "M."

Almost without exception, the hard disk installed in any computer turns out to be too small. As you get more proficient with your computer, and you add more programs and stuff to it, you'll find the massive hard disk you bought getting smaller and smaller. A lot of popular programs require 10M of space or more (DOS 6 itself can take up 8M!), so when you're shopping for a computer, err on the side of buying too much hard disk rather than too little.

All About Floppy Disks

Even though they can contain the same files and programs that hard disks have, floppy disks hold a lot less stuff than hard disks do. Hard disks are measured in megabytes; floppy disks are measure in *kilobytes* (about 1/1000 of a megabyte, so it's a lot smaller!).

NERDY DETAILS

> Kilobyte is another of those darn nerdy terms you keep hearing. A kilobyte is exactly 1,024 bytes, and it is often abbreviated with a capital "K". You'll see floppy disks described as being "720K" or "360K" disks, although you will also see floppy disks described by megabytes ("1.2M" and "1.44M") as well.

Floppy disks are further complicated because they are either 3 1/2-inch or 5 1/4-inch drives. Jeez. Generally speaking, the 3 1/2-inch floppy disks hold more stuff than the 5 1/4-inch kind (just to be confusing).

NERDY DETAILS

Because the term megabyte is used to measure both memory and drive capacity, a lot of new computer users confuse the amount of memory on their computer with how big the hard disk is. Although it's true that memory and disks do pretty much the same thing (they hold programs and data), the memory in your computer only works while the power is turned on.

Your computer's CPU uses memory to hold things while the computer is working; the hard disk (and your floppy disks) are used for long-term storage. Whatever you put on a hard disk or floppy disk is there after the power is shut off. The stuff in memory simply vanishes.

The numbers used to describe memory and hard disk size are real different, too. A computer with 16 megabytes of memory has a lot of memory; a 40M hard disk is considered pretty small.

That's about all you need to know about your disks and disk drives. Chapter 13 explains how floppy disks are basically incompatible with each other—even though they may look alike, you have to be sure to use the right kind of floppy disk in your drive, or you'll run into trouble.

Puttin' It on Paper: Printer Principles

Because printers are so important, this book has an entire chapter (Chapter 10) devoted to them. In the meantime, remember that there are lots of different kinds of printers: dot-matrix, laser, inkjet, and color printers.

Carefully selecting a printer is important because you're likely to have it a long time. I've had the printer I'm using at home for almost 10 years, and it has outlasted four different computers. I wish I could replace it with something zoomier, but it does such a nice job that I'm going to keep it.

Chapter 10 will help you understand the differences between printer types and explains why the cost of printers varies so much.

Keyboard Capers

Of course, the keyboard is what you type on. With the exception of where some pretty important keys are placed, most PC keyboards are pretty much the same. Laptop and notebook computers don't count. They've got the weirdest key arrangements imaginable!

NERDY DETAILS

> A key, of course, is a button on the keyboard. I don't know why they're called keys, unless somebody in the far distant past thought that typewriter and computer keyboards were similar to the keyboards on pianos.

Old, very old PC keyboards only had 83-key keyboards. The function keys were arranged along the left side of the keyboard and the arrow keys were bunched in with the number keys.

NERDY DETAILS

> The function keys are labeled "F1" to "F12" (on old keyboards, they only go up to "F10"), and they have special meanings, depending on the programs you run.
>
> The arrow keys are used to move the cursor around the screen in some programs. Historically, the cursor indicated where you could type stuff in (like in a word processor), but the meaning has been expanded to include things like the *mouse cursor* (if you're using a mouse, of course), which shows you where the mouse is on the screen.

Newer computers have keyboards with 101 keys on them (some have even more). The function keys are arranged across the top of the keyboard, and there are a lot more special-purpose keys than on the older keyboards. Chapter 11 explains a lot more about keyboards.

Mouses (or Are They "Mice"?) and Trackballs

Chapter 11 also talks a lot about computer mice. A mouse is a clever little thing that you move around your desktop. As you move the mouse on the desktop, the mouse cursor moves on the screen, allowing you to move anywhere you need to go on the screen. All mice have buttons on them; when you move the mouse cursor over something and press a button on the mouse (usually the left button), you *click* on the thing on the screen.

Computer mice aren't used much in DOS applications. Usually, the arrow keys and other special-purpose keys are sufficient to get you where you need to go pretty quickly. But with certain programs (Windows, in particular) the mouse is very, very useful for moving you around the screen.

All the Connectors on the Back of the Box!

Without a doubt, just about the ugliest part of any computer is the back of the big box. Just like the back of your VCR, this area is normally a mess of tangled wires and cables.

All of those wires are used to connect the big box with the other parts of your computer. For the most part, you don't have to even think about the wires and connectors on the back of your computer (unless a wire has come unplugged). It's just when you have to reconnect something or are plugging something in back there that it's a problem.

TRICKS

Here's an idea: Once you've got all your stuff plugged into the correct plugs, connectors, and sockets on the back of your computer, why don't you label the cords and connectors with tape or labels? You don't have to put a name on every wire and connector; it'd be enough to just put an "A" on a wire and another "A" on the connector (or socket or plug) where that wire goes. Then you can get 'em back in where they belong if you have to move the computer or your kid pulls 'em out some day. It could save you a lot of time!

Ports-of-Call: Making the Right Connections

First of all, the connectors on the back of your computer are called *ports*, which is a really stupid nerdy word. Most computers have a lot of different ports. Although they mostly look alike, they are all very different from each other. This chapter discusses only the most common and important ones.

Ports look strange and complicated because most of the wires connecting your computer to the other parts of your computer system (the printer, monitor, and so on) have a lot of wires bundled up inside them. For instance, the wire between your printer and your computer's big box has a lot of different little wires in it! Each little wire carries a different bit of information between the big box and the printer. Wow.

There are two basic kinds of ports. The first kind has a bunch of holes where the electrical contacts are made when you plug a cable into this kind of port. This kind of port is called a *female connector*, for obvious reasons. The *male connector* has a bunch of prongs (usually called *pins*) in it that make electrical contact with the holes in the female connector.

NERDY DETAILS

You'll find ports on your other computer equipment as well. If you look at the back of your printer, you'll see some kind of connector (maybe more than one) back there. So, the word port applies to things other than those on the computer's big box.

Computer Cables and Correct Connections

If you look at the plug end of a computer cable, you see a male or female connector, so you should plug it into the opposite kind of connector on the computer or peripheral.

STOP!

The general rule concerning plugs and connectors is this: don't force a plug into its connector place. If it won't go in easily, maybe you've got the wrong connector picked out. If you succeed in forcing a plug into a connector it wasn't built for, you will probably ruin either the plug on the end of the wire or the connector you forced it into.

For instance, the wire coming out of your monitor that connects the monitor to the box probably has 15 prongs in it (it's a male connector, right?). You should look for a corresponding female connector with 15 holes in it on the back of the computer's big box. That's all there is to making the right connections.

NERDY DETAILS

Just to be confusing, the place where you plug in a joystick (it's a little controller thing that you use to play games like Wing Commander) is also a connector with 15 holes in it. The difference is that the 15 holes are arranged in 2 rows instead of 3 rows like your monitor's connector.

The Printer Connection

There is almost certainly a printer connector, er... port, on the back of your computer. It'll be a 25-hole female connector. You may have more than one of these; you can't really tell which it is from the outside. As you'll read in chapter 10, if you've got more than one 25-hole female connector, use the trial-and-error method to figure which printer port to plug into.

NERDY DETAILS

The 25-pin female connector is called the *parallel port*. All this means is that a lot of stuff flows out simultaneously through the little wires connected to this port to the printer. As you'll read later in this chapter, make sure you get the right kind of cable if you're buying a new one for your printer.

Serial Ports

You may also find one or more 25-pin male connectors on the back of your computer, or a combination of 25-pin and 9-pin male connectors back there. These are called *serial ports,* and they are the places where you plug in modems (boxes that let your computer communicate with another computer over telephone lines) and some kinds of computer mice.

NERDY DETAILS

Did you see the movie War Games a few years ago? Or have you read about "hackers" who have fun "breaking into" computers around the country? Or have you seen the ads on TV for CompuServe, Prodigy, America On-Line, or Genie? All of these things involve using a *modem* to connect a computer with another computer using normal phone lines as the link between the computer.

Modem is pronounced MOE-DEM, as when Curley says "Hey MOE! DEM are the ones we want!"

Special Ports

There may also be one or more special-purpose ports on your computer:

- **15-pin female**. This is where you plug in a "VGA" monitor. The holes in this connector are arranged in 3 rows.
- **9-pin female**. If your computer has a monochrome screen or a very old-fashioned, low-resolution color screen, this is where you'd plug it in.
- **15-pin female**. This means that your computer may be equipped for a joystick so you can play Wing Commander and other games that use joysticks. The holes in this connector are arranged in two rows.
- **Little, round weird port**. This is for a special kind of computer mouse (called a *bus mouse*), a hand-operated scanner, or another special piece of equipment.
- **Larger, round weird port**. Your keyboard plugs into a neat-looking, round connector that is usually recessed quite a ways into the computer cabinet.

Miscellaneous. You might find just about anything back there. Some computers have real specialized connectors for different kinds of equipment or for hooking up to networks. There are really too many other kinds to mention here.

If you're really excited by all this talk about computer hardware, you might want to pick up a copy of *PCs for Non-Nerds* the next time you're in the bookstore. It'll take you a few steps further into learning about your computer's innards without risking your non-nerd status.

All Those Cables!

Not to worry about cables. There may be a lot of them, but most of them are specialized; they will only plug into one or two different places on your computer. If the cable plugs in, it probably belongs there.

TRICKS

Put a piece of masking tape on the business end of the cable (where it plugs into the connector) and a another next to the connector on the PC's big box. It'll make it much easier the next time you have to replug something back there.

One cable that deserves special mention is the parallel printer cable. Most printers use the computer's parallel port. You can tell whether your printer has a parallel port by looking at the back of your printer where the cable plugs in. If you see kind of a "slot" instead of the connectors, you've got a parallel printer. If you see the 25-pin female connector, you've got a serial printer.

NERDY DETAILS

The nerds really messed this one up. The serial ports on the back of your computer are all male connectors (they've got pins instead of holes). On your peripheral equipment like printers and modems, the serial ports are female type. So, as with everything else with computers, there are no hard-and-fast rules for telling you what kind of port you have.

LAPTOPS ARE RELATIVE!

Your Video Display Is Not a Television!

This chapter will educate you about everything you should know about your computer's *monitor*, the part that looks like a TV:

- The two main parts of your computer's display.
- A lot more of the dreaded three-letter acronyms (TLAs).
- What is the difference between "VGA" and "SVGA"?
- What the heck does "640×480" or "1024×768" mean?
- The things to look out for if you're in the market for a new computer display.

There are lots of different names for the TV thing on your computer. Some people call it a *monitor* or *display*, others say it's a *screen*. Nerds often call it a *cathode ray tube (CRT)* because it sounds scary. Whatever it is, you'll spend a lot of time staring at the darn thing, so you may as well get familiar with it.

What It Takes To Get the Picture

Probably doesn't look like it, but there are actually two parts to your computer's TV screen. There's the obvious part you can see—it really does look like a high-tech TV, doesn't it? There's another part, called the *video adapter*, that you can't see inside your computer's big box. These two parts have to work together to get you the picture.

The picture on your computer screen (even if it's just words and letters) is made up of a bunch of really tiny dots. The video adapter inside your computer's box gets directions from your computer's CPU (remember him from Chapter 8?), and translates the CPU's directions into dots that shoot up the wire connecting your monitor to the big box.

NERDY DETAILS

If you're using a laptop, the adapter and the screen are probably contained as a single unit.

Each dot on the monitor's screen is called a pixel (pronounced PICKS-EL). On a color screen, the colors are made by blending colored dots together.

NERDY DETAILS

You may have noticed how often DOS things have more than one name. Some nerdy people call the dots on your screen *pels*, a kind of shortened version of *pixel*. If it wasn't bad enough to give a simple thing like the dots on your screen more than one name, why did they make 'em sound so much alike? (I think they should have called them *dotels*.)

Your computer's monitor is one of the most expensive parts of your computer system. Monitors are so expensive that the prices advertised for computers by a lot of stores are low only because they don't include the monitor. The type and quality of your computer's monitor also determines whether your text and graphics are nice and clear, or dull and blurry (which becomes very important the more hours you spend staring at it).

If you're not happy with what you see, it may not be your computer's fault! It may just be a poor match between your computer's video system components.

Lots and Lots of TLAs

Almost all computers sold today have color monitors, and almost all of them are the type called VGA (Video Graphics Array), another TLA (three-letter acronym) for you to remember. I don't know why they call it that; probably just because they're nerds. ("VGA" is pronounced VEE-GEE-AY, not VEE-GA.)

NERDY DETAILS

> Some nerds will tell you that the "G" in VGA stands for "Gate" and that VGA means Video Gate Array. Now, I ask you, does it really make a difference?

Unlike most things about PCs, VGA has been around for a few years, and hasn't yet been replaced by something better. The monitors that were first used on PCs were so bad that they were quickly replaced by newer kinds. The biggest difference between VGA and the older kinds of color monitors is that the dots are bigger on the older types of monitors, and they can't show as many colors.

NERDY DETAILS

> You might see obsolete types of monitors from time to time. Older computers might have EGA (Enhanced Graphics Adapter), CGA (Color Graphics Adapter) or even a HGA (Hercules Graphics Adapter. I'm not kidding. Hercules, like the big strong guy back in old Greece).
>
> Funny, isn't it, how the "A" in both EGA and CGA means "adapter," yet the "A" in VGA stands for "array"? Here's another example of how the nerds conspire to keep normal people from understanding what's going on.

Do You Have a Color Monitor?

Seems like a rather obvious question, doesn't it? If you're seeing colors on your screen, then you've definitely got a color video adapter and a monitor that can show colors. If all you see is green or amber, you may have a color screen, but just don't know it. Type this command to check:

```
MODE CO40
```

If the screen gets really weird looking (all the letters and numbers get twice as wide, but stay just as high), you've got a color adapter of some kind. Oh yes, to put it back, type this:

```
MODE CO80
```

It should pop right back into shape.

If the screen doesn't change when you type in the `MODE CO40` command, you don't have a graphics adapter on your computer.

NERDY DETAILS

> Here we go again, another exception to the rule. Although they aren't used very much anymore because color monitors cost so much, some early computers had a color video adapter with a special type of monochrome screen. If you've never seen color on your screen, but the **MODE CO40** test told you that your computer has a color video adapter in it, take a look at where your monitor plugs into the big box.
>
> If the wire connecting your monitor to the big box is a little skinny thing with a round connector plugging into the big box, you've got one of the old, obsolete *composite* monitors. These things went out with the dinosaurs. They can only display CGA graphics resolution (really chunky and awful looking) and nothing is in color. These things are so bad that a year or so ago I tried to give away a composite monitor and adapter card and no one would take it.

How Small Are Your Dots?

This is not a leading question! If you ever go shopping for a computer monitor or video adapter, whoever you talk to will want to talk about the *resolution* of the widget they're trying to sell you. Resolution means the number of dots there are on the screen. It makes sense, I hope, that the more dots you pack on the screen, the better the picture looks. It's like using sharp color pencils to draw a picture rather than dull crayons to draw the same picture.

You'll see numbers like this in the ads: "640×480 VGA Package" or "1024×768 VGA Monitor." The "640" means there are 640 dots across the screen and 480 dots up and down on the screen. (There are more dots across the screen because the screen is wider than it is tall.) The screen with 1024×768 resolution will show you a somewhat better picture.

Finally, there's a little statistic called *dot pitch*, which is the distance between dots on the screen. If your monitor has a big dot pitch (in the video world, 0.38 milimeter (mm) is a big dot pitch), you'll have a much fuzzier screen than someone with a smaller dot pitch (like 0.28 mm) because your dots will run together on the screen.

NERDY DETAILS

> Paying extra money for a high-resolution monitor doesn't guarantee that you'll be seeing things better. Your video adapter has to be able to work with the monitor at the higher resolutions, and your programs have to be able to make higher-resolution pictures.

The "640×480" means standard VGA. This is the basic resolution you get with every VGA monitor and video adapter. Every computer program that works with VGA will work with a standard VGA adapter and monitor.

Anything bigger than this (800×600, 1024×768, or even 1280×1024) is usually called *Super VGA* (or *SVGA*). The problem with SVGA is that the nerds who created these systems have never agreed how to make computer programs work with them. Just about every SVGA adapter works differently from every other one.

Give Me the Nice Bright Colors

The other figure you see in ads for a monitor tells you how many colors it can display. Good ol' standard VGA can display only 16 colors at one time with 620×480 dots on the screen. This is called *standard VGA mode*. The Super VGA adapters and monitors can usually display a lot more *modes*, such as 1024×768 in 256 or more colors.

NERDY DETAILS

Okay, I lied. There's actually a bunch of different color combinations that your VGA monitor and adapter can produce. By far the most common is good ol' 640x480 dots with 16 colors. Another commonly used mode is 320x200 dots and 256 colors. You'll see this a lot in games where lots of colors are important to show all the details of alien skin texture and exploding spacecraft.

For the most part, 16-color standard VGA is adequate for almost all kinds of work. People who make graphics, play a lot of games (many games work at very high resolutions with a lot of colors), or spend a lot of money on their computers might want to consider SVGA adapters and monitors.

NERDY DETAILS

So, we already know that nerds love to confuse you with a lot of different ways of describing the same thing, right? As it is wasn't confusing enough to talk about 16 and 256 colors, modes, resolution, and so on, a new nerdy term that is creeping into computer jargon is describing the number of colors as *bits*.

Bits doesn't mean the itty bits of color that appear on your screen. It means the way that your computer thinks of color. Simple 16-color VGA is *4-bit color*; 256-color SVGA is *8-bit color*. The real expensive *24-bit color* adapters and monitors can display as many as 16 *million* colors. This is about as many colors as your eye can see, so a picture displayed in real high SVGA resolution in 16 million colors can look *better* than a photograph.

What To Do If an Application Doesn't Work

Sometimes you'll get a game or utility program from a friend that just doesn't work on your computer. If the screen goes blank when you try to run the program, and you have to restart your computer to get it back again, it probably means you have a monochrome-only monitor and adapter. They just won't work with color games.

You might also have an old CGA monitor that just won't work with a more modern VGA-only game. Oh well!

A Video Buyer's Guide

If you plan to replace your computer's monitor or video adapter, there are some things you should keep in mind:

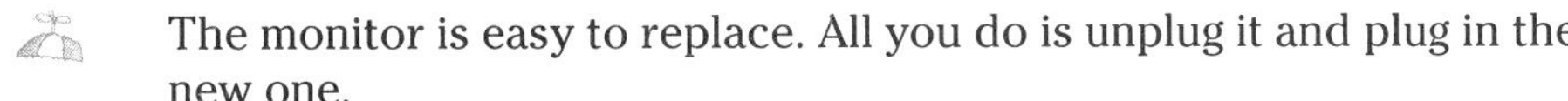

- The monitor is easy to replace. All you do is unplug it and plug in the new one.
- Video adapters are hard to replace. You have to open up your computer's big box, remove the old video adapter, and slip in the new one. Most adapters come with installation instructions. Either carefully follow the instructions or go get some help from someone who's replaced parts inside a computer's big box.
- If you don't like your computer's video arrangement, you can replace it with a better one (but it'll probably be expensive).
- You can't normally replace the screen on your laptop because it's built-in. You might be able to connect an external monitor to it with the right kind of cable, though.
- A good video system is well worth the money spent because everything will be clearer, sharper, and cause less eye strain than lower-quality stuff.
- If you're thinking about buying a Super VGA adapter and monitor, make sure it'll work with the programs you already have. Your programs have to work at SVGA resolution (800×600 and 1024×768 are the most common). Chances are, you won't have any problem at all. But it's a real disappointment to get a big, expensive SVGA monitor and adapter, and then find out that your programs won't work with it.
- When buying a monitor, the smaller the dot pitch, the better quality it is. Dot pitches that are less than 0.31 millimeters (some go as low as 0.21, most are on the order of 0.28) are pretty good.

  Really, really bad monitors are up there around 0.39 and 0.51 millimeters and will make you a contender for the Olympic Eye Strain team. The dots on a bad screen are so large you can see them from several feet away. Please, please, do not try to save money by buying a low quality monitor! You will instantly regret it.

The most expensive screens are called *multisync monitors*, and they can be used with almost any video adapter. You don't have to worry so much about matching the monitor to the video adapter, but the extra price of these things is just plain scary.

My own personal final criteria is screen size. Most computers are sold nowadays with 14-inch monitors (monitors are measured from corner-to-corner across the screen, rather than from side-to-side).

A 14-inch screen is perfectly adequate for most DOS applications such as WordPerfect and Word for DOS. If, however, you are going to be doing an appreciable amount of graphics work (AutoCAD), spreadsheets (Lotus 1-2-3 or Quattro Pro for DOS), or plan to be using Microsoft Windows much, you will probably want to spend a few extra dollars for a 16-inch monitor.

NERDY DETAILS

Something I haven't mentioned yet is that a lot of DOS applications let you change the number of lines displayed on a VGA screen from 25 (which is what you are probably looking at now) to 43 or even 50 lines. The words displayed on your screen get kind of squishy-looking when you do this, but you can see a lot more lines of your document or spreadsheet in 43- or 50-line mode.

If you're going to be doing much work in 43- or 50-line mode, consider getting a nice, big 16-inch monitor. (Look at your program's documentation to see if you can do this. Word, WordPerfect, and Lotus 1-2-3 for DOS all have this capability).

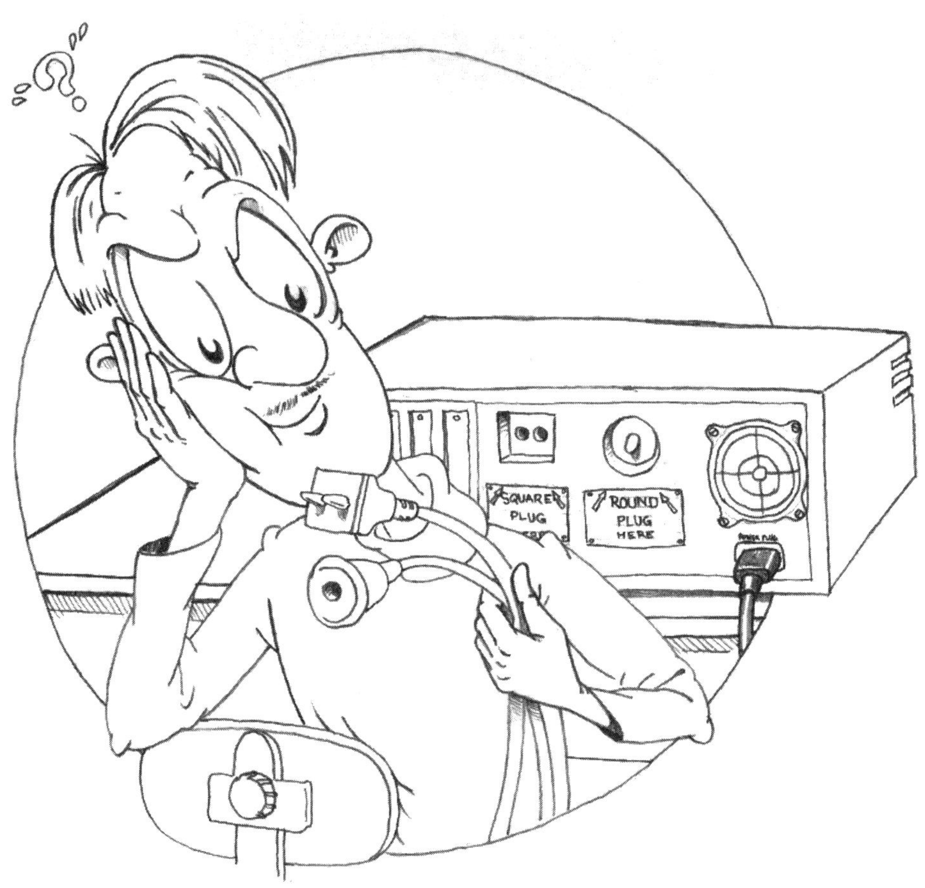
SQUARE
PLUG
ROUND
PLUG
HERE

Your Printer: A 20th-Century Gutenberg Press

Benjamin Franklin would have killed for the printer on your desktop! Back in his day, each letter on a page of paper was individually set into a printing frame, then the whole thing was inked and pressed against the paper. In contrast, your printer is truly a modern marvel. This chapter covers the whys and wherefores of turning soft copy into hard copy, including the following:

- How to print stuff
- How printers get hooked up
- Different kinds of printers
- How printers work
- Pertinent printer terminology
- Troubleshooting printers
- Printer buyer's guide

Let's Print Something!

One of the most frequent DOS tasks is to print something. Whether you've just finished a letter to your rich Aunt Mary, or are preparing the Cub Scouts' monthly newsletter, most documents and drawings created with a PC eventually end up on some kind of printer.

Although printing is usually handled by the application in which you created your masterpiece (for instance, you wrote your letter in WordPerfect and you use WordPerfect to print it), you can also print things directly from the DOS prompt.

We're going to print something just to prove that your printer works. If you have a printer connected to your computer, try these commands:

```
DIR > LPT1:
ECHO ^L > LPT1:
```

The `^L` in the second line means to hold down Ctrl (it'll be on the left side of your typewriter keys somewhere) and press the **L** key.

NERDY DETAILS

You needn't worry about the details, but the "LPT1" thing is your printer. LPT originally meant *line printer*, a special kind of printer that is never used on PCs, that prints a whole line at a whack (instead of one letter at a time). Because line printers have no relationship to PCs, the nerds decided to call the printer connections on the back of your computer **`LPT ports`**. Makes the same kind of sense as most things in DOS, doesn't it?

If, instead of a nice printout of your directory you get a nasty `Abort, Retry, Ignore, Fail?` message from DOS, it means that you don't have a printer connected to your computer, or that there's some kind of problem with the printer. Not to worry. Later in this chapter, you'll find a quick printer troubleshooting guide. (Oh yes, go ahead and type **A**, followed by Enter, to abort this command.)

If your printer doesn't immediately print the exact same thing you see when you do a plain ol' `DIR` at the DOS command line, there is something wrong. As a matter of fact, if it doesn't print, your computer might actually be hung up, and you'll have to restart it (try the Alt-Ctrl-Del three-finger salute to get it going again).

Your Printer Connections

There's not much to know about connecting your computer to the printer. There are two main kinds of connections between computers and printers: serial and parallel.

NERDY DETAILS

Nerds call the connection on the back of your printer an *interface* or a *port*. Sometimes you'll get a really obnoxious nerd insisting to know whether you've got a serial interface or a parallel interface (or serial port or a parallel port, of course). You tell him to get outtayourface and to find out for himself!

You have to know what kind of printer you've got (serial or parallel). It's a safe bet that you've got a *parallel* interface on your computer (see, even I use the nerdy expression from time to time) because most printers have this kind (a lot of printers have both kinds).

If you buy a cable, you have to get the right kind. They can't be interchanged. Here's how to tell what you've got:

1. Look at the back of your printer where the wire connecting the computer's big box plugs into the printer.
2. Unplug the wire (if it's plugged in). If it won't unplug, it may be held in with clips or little tiny screws.
3. If there are clips holding it in (one clip on either end of the connector), you've got a parallel printer and you're done. If there are little tiny screws holding the plug in, you've got a serial printer.
4. If there are no clips or screws holding the cable tightly to the printer, then check for this: parallel printers have a connector port shaped like a slot, rather than a connector with lots of tiny holes. It's as simple as that.

If it turns out that you have a *serial* printer (and some people do), be sure to read the section on serial printers near the end of this chapter.

The Different Kinds of Printers

Printers are important. Most of the work you do on your computer gets printed at some point. Printers are also fairly expensive, so you want to get one that will suit your needs fairly well.

There are lots of different kinds of printers out there, but almost all of them fall into just a very few categories:

- **Dot-matrix.** These printers use a ribbon much like an old-fashioned typewriter. A bunch of little pins inside a little thing (the *print head*) move back and forth across the paper and hit the ribbon against the paper, transferring ink from the ribbon to the paper. The pins work like very, very tiny pencils dotting the paper in the shape of letters and numbers. The constant tapping against the paper is what makes dot-matrix printers so loud. Although dot-matrix printers don't cost a whole lot, the print quality is somewhat inferior to other types of printers.

- **Inkjet.** These printers use a number of different ways to shoot ink out of a reservoir through a tiny opening onto the paper. The printer rapidly adjusts the direction of the ink so that it squirts onto the paper in the shape of letters and numbers. Inkjet printers are very, very quiet and cost more than dot-matrix printers. The print quality is similar.

- **Laser.** Laser printers work a lot like photocopiers, except that laser light is used to sensitize nerdy things inside the printer that make toner (a black powdery stuff) stick to the paper. The toner is then melted onto the paper by squeezing the paper and toner between really hot rollers. Laser printers are very quiet, produce very high-quality output, and cost quite a bit of money.

How Printers Print

All printers work like a ballpoint pen or pencil: some kind of goobery stuff is pressed or thrown or stuck onto paper as little dots that form the shape of letters and numbers. If you're printing pictures instead of plain letters and numbers, the dots of inky stuff are put on the paper closer together or farther apart to produce a "shading" effect.

The inky stuff is different for each kind of printer:

 **Dot-matrix.** It's some kind of ink soaked into the ribbon. It'll come off of the ribbon if you rub it between your fingers.

 **Laser.** It's an extremely messy, black powder called *toner*, which is stored in a cartridge or container inside the printer.

 **Inkjet.** It's ink, real ink, that is stored in some kind of container. Usually the ink is very fluid; if you shake the inkjet cartridge, you can hear it slosh around inside.

Printer Terminology You Probably Need To Know

 **On-line.** The printer may not be in the mood to listen to your computer. Before the printer can print something, it has to be listening for stuff coming down the wire. When the printer is ready, willing, and able to accept stuff from your computer it is said to be *on-line*.

There will be a little switch labeled "On-Line" somewhere on your printer (it might also be called "Select"). Make sure it's turned on. (There usually is an indicator light as well. Make sure it's on.)

 **Form feed.** When you start printing a page of text from your word processor, you probably want the printing to start at the top of the page. A form feed makes the printer move whatever page is in there all the way through it, and stop at the top of the next page. Most printers have a form-feed button that you can press to make this happen.

On dot-matrix printers and other printers that use continuous-form paper, the top of the paper may not be where the printer thinks it is. There is no way for the printer to know exactly where the top of the next page begins. If you press the form feed button, and the paper doesn't stop right at the top of the next page, you may have to roll the paper to the right spot yourself using the knob on the side of the printer.

 **Hard copy.** This is just a dumb expression for a printed copy of something.

 **Printout.** Another way to say "a printed copy of something."

 **WYSIWYG.** This really, really lame and overused word (pronounced WIZ-EE-WIG) is an overly complex acronym for "What you see is what you get." This means that whatever you see on the screen (document, picture, spreadsheet) is what prints on the printer. Yep, sure!

 **PostScript.** An early, expensive, and slow way to get WYSIWYG. PostScript is a "page-definition language" that tells the printer exactly where to put things on the page.

What To Do When the Printer Doesn't Work

Here are some very printer-specific problems:

The Printer Keeps Shooting Out Paper!

This can happen if you have the wrong kind of printer setup or printer driver installed in your application. Because every kind of printer is different from every other printer, your applications have very specific ways of communicating with the printer. These different ways of handling printers are usually called the printer setup, printer installation, or printer driver.

Most sophisticated programs such as Windows, Word, WordPerfect, Lotus, and Excel must know exactly what kind of printer is connected to your computer. If your program thinks it's printing on an Epson dot-matrix printer, but you're actually connected to an HP LaserJet, all kinds of nasty things can happen.

Here's the remedy:

1. Turn off the printer (this will empty out the storage space inside the printer where it put stuff that hasn't been printed yet).
2. Abort the printing task from inside your application unless you're connected to a network, in which case you should probably go find the system administrator (which is another way of saying "nerd") and get help.

3. Check your application's "printer setup." If it doesn't tell you that it's working with the kind of printer that's connected, you have to make some changes.

4. Consult your application's user guide to see how to set up the application to work with your particular printer and make the changes you see there.

TRICKS

Here's the good news: Generally speaking, if you have an Epson printer, almost any "Epson" printer driver will work with your printer. The same goes for HP printers, Okidata printers, and so on. Each manufacturer is pretty careful to make sure all of its printer products work together.

Here's another tip: most dot-matrix and inkjet printers will work with the Epson drivers or setup. Most laser-type printers will work with HP LaserJet setups. These printers have been the most successful within their respective markets.

Absolutely Nothing Happens When I Try To Print My Letter!

Although most applications will warn you that there's no printer connected to your computer, there are lots of things that can cause your printout to fail:

 Make sure the printer is turned on, and has paper in it.

 The printer is not "On-Line."

 The wrong type of cable is installed that connects your printer to the PC (the cable might also be missing—you should check).

 If the cable is there, and you're sure it's the right kind of cable, make sure that it's tightly plugged into the back of your computer and your printer.

 You may be trying to make your application work with the wrong printer port on back of the computer. You should check as well as you can that the application is printing on "LPT1" or "LPT2" (whichever your printer is hooked to). If you're not sure, pull the

printer cable out of the back of your computer's big box and plug it into the other printer connector (I'm assuming, of course, that you have two of the things).

The Printout Doesn't Look Anything At All Like It Does on the Screen!

It used to be acceptable if you just got the same words on your printer that you saw on the screen. No more. People now want the printout to look exactly like it does on the screen (hence, WYSIWYG). But sometimes things don't print out the way they look on the screen.

This is probably happening because your application is not sending the correct commands to your printer. Your application may think it's working with an Okidata printer when you've actually got an Epson printer attached. You should check the printer setup for your application.

The Printer Buyer's Guide

Here are some things to ask the guy at the computer store before buying a printer:

For All Printers

 Is it serial or parallel? Get parallel. There is almost no advantage to a serial printer on a PC.

 What kind of paper does it take? You don't want a printer that requires some weird, exotic, and expensive paper. I don't think there are many of this kind on the market anymore, but you might encounter something that takes "thermal" or "coated" paper. Avoid them.

 What kind of "emulations" does it do? Even if you're getting a very special deal on some Korean- or Taiwanese-built "Moon Desert Star Flower" printer, it won't do you much good if your programs won't work with it. A printer's capability to "emulate" popular printers such as the Epson or HP LaserJet means that your programs will probably work with it fine.

NERDY DETAILS

Emulation means that your programs think they're working with an HP or Epson printer and send the corresponding commands down the wire to the printer. Even though the printer may not be an Epson or HP, it'll accept the printing commands as if it were, and will print the right stuff.

For Dot-Matrix Printers

 What kind of ribbon does it take? Make sure you don't have to buy some hard-to-find, expensive ribbon that you can only get by mail order or directly from the manufacturer. It'd be a real drag to break your ribbon late at night on a three-day holiday weekend and not be able to easily replace it. Good answer: "Same as Epson," "Same as Okidata," or "Same as Panasonic."

 How many pins in the head? Remember, dot-matrix printers print by hammering little pins against the ribbon to transfer ink to the paper. The more pins your printer has, the more well-formed the characters on the paper will be. Most dot-matrix printers top out at 24 or so pins. The most common numbers of pins that dot matrix printers have are nine and 24.

For Laser Printers

 Does it come with a cartridge? Seriously, it seems silly to ask if a $900 laser printer includes a cartridge. But cartridges are expensive (some cost up to 100 clams), so buying a cartridge is an added expense you might not expect. Good answer: "Yes."

NERDY DETAILS

Cartridges for laser printers contain a drum with a light-sensitive coating and toner (the stuff that makes the printing black). The drum will eventually wear out and the toner will be used up as you print pages. The drum and toner usually need to be replaced at the same time so they are combined in one easy-to-change unit.

You can get used cartridges reconditioned or recharged. It is cheaper to recharge a cartridge than it is to buy a new one.

continues

continued

Recharging also is better for the environment because you are recycling the cartridge. Make sure that the company that recharges the cartridge guarantees its work.

 What kind of toner cartridge does it use? For the same reason dot-matrix ribbon users should be concerned about buying ribbons, you need to know whether your new printer uses a common type of toner cartridge. You don't want to have to be sending away to Taipei for replacements. Good answers are: "Same as the HP LaserJet" and "Any Canon laserjet cartridge."

For Inkjet Printers

 What kind of ink cartridge does it use? Same reason for asking about ribbons and toner cartridges. You want to be able to get them at the nearby office supply store.

 Is the ink waterproof? Time was, all the inks used in inkjet cartridges would run if you got water on them.

 How long does it take for the ink to dry? Faster-drying inks don't smear as much, and you can stack up the pages without having to worry about whether the ink is dry.

 Will it run on batteries? One of the really neat things about some inkjet printers is that you can get battery packs for them. If you have a portable computer or plan to get a laptop or notebook, you might want to consider getting a printer that travels.

Seriously Serial

Here's one of the problems with serial printers: DOS isn't too good about using them. The letters and numbers stream out of your computer down the wire to the printer at a very specific speed. Not only do you have to set the speed that the PC sends the letters and numbers to the printer, you have to set the speed at which the printer can receive the letters and numbers.

NERDY DETAILS

The speed at which stuff is sent from the computer to a serial printer is called the *baud rate.* "Baud" (pronounced BAWD) is named after J. M. Emile Baudot, a French inventor, and was originally used to measure how fast Morse code was being transmitted. Morse code was named after Samuel F. B Morse, of course, of course. Who said nerds don't have a life!

Now, suppose you want to learn how to set the baud rate on your computer. You'll have to look at the documentation that came with your printer for setting its receiving baud rate. Here's how to set your computer's baud rate:

```
MODE COM1:9600,N,8,1
```

The `COM1` in this line stands for "communications port 1." Your computer probably has one or two of these things. On the back of your computer, you'll see one or two connectors that have tiny pins (*male connectors*) in them instead of little holes (*female connectors*). One of the male connectors will be COM1.

When you discover how to set the baud rate on your printer, be sure to set it to `9600` like you did on your computer. These numbers have to match. Setting the baud rate on your printer probably involves flipping some switches inside the printer's cabinet or under a little hatch or something like that.

SAM THOUGHT HE COULD GET READY FOR VACATION...
IF HE TURNED UP THE BRIGHTNESS ON HIS MONITOR.

Interacting with the Computer: Keyboard and Mouse

Your keyboard is a pretty neat thing, in spite of its simplicity (after all, it looks a lot like a typewriter keyboard, doesn't it?). There are a lot of things you need to know about it in order to use DOS and your programs effectively. In this chapter we'll ask and answer some basic questions:

- Where's my Any key?
- What the heck is an Alt-Tab? I don't see a key for this either!
- How is Caps Lock different from Shift?
- I've got two Alt keys and two Ctrl keys. Which do I use?
- Why does the keyboard sometimes beep at me?
- What's the proper care and feeding of computer mice, joysticks, and trackballs?

The Keys to Your Keyboard

The keyboards on most computers are pretty complicated. Most current keyboards have at least 101 keys; some keyboards have a lot more. Some older PC keyboards have only 83.

Even though the positions of most of the keys are the same on all keyboards, some of the most important keys are in different places on different keyboards. Not to worry—we'll help you find them.

All About the "Any" Key

If you've ever hunted for the "Any" key (to comply with the instruction to `Press any key to continue`, you aren't alone. Here's the bad part (and you already know this): there isn't an "Any" key. Almost every key on the keyboard is the "Any" key—sometimes keys like Caps Lock, Shift, Alt and Ctrl won't do the job, but that's about it. So when something on the screen tells you to press any key, it means to press any of the keys on your keyboard. Usually it's safest to press the spacebar or Enter key.

Typing on Your Computer

Each key on your keyboard has a little tiny electrical switch inside it. When you press a key, there's a little thing inside your computer that says "I saw that!," and runs to tell the CPU. After the CPU gets the message, it puts the letter you typed on the screen and sends it to your program to work with.

NERDY DETAILS

> Actually, not surprisingly, that little thing which notices your keystroke is itself a baby computer program which busies itself waiting for your fingers to strike.

Many of the keys on your keyboard have special functions. A lot of them have special (and really stupid) names. When you press these special keys, a number of different things can happen:

- There are several keys (Ctrl, Alt, Shift) that cause all of the other keys to take on a different meaning than they usually have, but only while you're holding down the special key.
- There are a few keys (Num Lock, Caps Lock, Scroll Lock) that make some of the keys on the keyboard shift to different meanings, and stay there until you press the special key again.
- Some of the keys (such as the *function keys* described later in this chapter) have secret meanings that are known only to DOS or your programs. When you press these keys, you really don't know for sure what will happen. And sometimes you may not want to find out.
- There's a key (PAUSE) that causes everything to stop and stay stopped until you press any key. (Here's that Any key again!)

It's 11:00: Do You Know Where Your Function Keys Are?

Look at your keyboard. Somewhere on it are either 10 or 12 keys labeled "F1" through "F12" (or "F10"). If these keys (called the *function keys*) are arranged along the left side of the keyboard, you've probably got an older-style "83" key keyboard like the original IBM-PC and XT models had. If your function keys are along the top of the keyboard, you've probably got a newer "101" key keyboard (sometimes called an *enhanced keyboard*).

The basic layout of the 101-key and 83-key keyboards are similar, but the older 83-key style lacks the two little islands of cursor control keys to the right of the typewriter keys. There are many other variations on the keyboard (particularly on notebook or laptop computers), but they all have all of the keys you need—*somewhere!*

TRICKS

> Some keyboards have duplicate function keys along the top and down the left side. Take your pick—both sets work the same.

Only the enhanced 101-key keyboards have function keys F11 and F12. Not many applications even use these function keys (in fact, most applications don't use more than a few of the function keys), but they do make the row of function keys more symmetrical, don't they?

NERDY DETAILS

The keyboards used on modern PCs are different from the old "83" keyboards in more ways than one. Sure they look different, but they also act differently to the computer. You can't use one of the old "83" keyboards on a computer built for the newer "101-style" keyboard.

The reverse is not necessarily true. Most modern keyboards have a switch on them somewhere that lets you switch them from AT (newer) to XT (older) mode. Some modern keyboards can even figure out what kind of computer they're hooked up to and set themselves to talk to it. If you have to use a new-style keyboard on an old-style computer, check the position of this switch (if there is one!).

Special Keys

In addition to the function keys, there are several other keys that have very specific meanings to DOS and your programs. Of course, the key locations in the following discussion pertain only to desktop PCs with full keyboards. If you're using a notebook or laptop, you'll have to hunt around for the keys mentioned here.

Which Is It: Enter or Return?

No matter whether it's labeled Enter or Return on your keyboard (on some keyboards it's marked with a bent left-pointing arrow), the Enter key tells DOS that you're done typing on the line and it's time to go do something with whatever you typed.

The Shiftless Shift Key

Just like on a typewriter keyboard, the Shift key (actually, there are two of them, one on each side of the spacebar) "shifts" most of the keys on the keyboard to their *shifted* (or *uppercase*) meanings. (How's that for using a word in the definition of the word?) All the letters of the alphabet are shifted to capital letters, the top row keys (1 through 0, plus whatever else is on the top row) take on their punctuation meanings, and so on.

When used with Caps Lock or Num Lock, Shift reverses their effect. More on these keys in a bit.

The effects of the left and right shift keys are exactly the same. It doesn't make any difference to the computer. The shifted keys return to their original meanings when the Shift key is released.

In rare cases, a pop-up program may specify one or the other shift keys as part of the secret combination you need to access it (but you don't need a decoder ring).

Alt: The Alternative Key

You'll see the expression "Do an Alt-Tab to move to another field" or something like that. When you hold down the Alt key and press some other key, your computer sees an "alternate" meaning for the key you're holding down.

In fact, just about any time you see the name of one of these special keys (Alt, Ctrl, Shift, and so on) separated from another key by a hyphen ("Ctrl-Break"), it means to hold down the first key ("Ctrl") and press the second key ("Break"); then let 'em both go.

The Alt key is used in lots of different ways. You'll have to read the user's guide that came with your programs to see if you need to learn how to use the Alt key for them.

DOS 6 itself comes with a number of programs that use Alt to activate menus, so you can choose the option you prefer. For example, in `EDIT`, to open a new file, you begin by pressing Alt, then press Enter to choose the File menu you're already in, then press **O** to open a file.

WordPerfect, a very popular word processing program, uses the Alt key extensively. Many Windows applications such as Word and Excel also use the Alt key a lot.

Nudging the Numeric Keypad

Over on the right-hand side of the keyboard is the *numeric keypad.* Because the original IBM-PC was designed as a business computer, the designers felt that it was important to provide a calculator-like keypad for accountants and other people who need to crunch a lot of numbers.

As described earlier, the numeric keypad serves a dual function. When the Num Lock key is activated, the numbers work; when the Num Lock key is off, the arrows work (the 5 key does nothing when the Num Lock is off).

The other keys on the numeric keypad are there for accountants who might need to get at some simple math functions quickly. You'll notice (on the "101" keyboard) that there is a second Enter key. It works just like the Enter key at the right of the typewriter keys.

How Do I "Do a Ctrl-Break"?

A key that's real similar to Alt is the Ctrl key (Ctrl stands for "control"). Back in the Mesazoic era of computers, the Ctrl key allowed programmers and other nerds to send the computer secret symbols and special messages that only the nerd (and the computer) understood. You'll still see that sometimes, even on today's friendlier PCs.

If you've seen or read the message "Do a Ctrl-C to end this program" or something like that, you've discovered one of the main uses of the Ctrl key. Pressing **C** while holding the Ctrl key down (this action is called "doing a Control-C") causes many programs to stop running.

The bigger and meaner brother of Ctrl-C is Ctrl-Break. On "101" keyboards, you'll find the Break key in the very top row of keys (same row as the function keys) just above the cursor control keys. When you press the Break key while holding down the Ctrl key, almost any program will stop running. (This assumes that you've placed **BREAK=ON** in your **CONFIG.SYS** file, which most people have.) Boom! I only wish PCs had built-in sound effects.

The Break key may also be labeled "Pause."

Screeech: Pausing with Ctrl-S or Pause

Ctrl-C and Ctrl-Break end a program, but what if you just want to stop it for a moment? That's what the Ctrl-S combination is for. Try it. Enter **DIR**, press Enter, and press Ctrl-S. The display will freeze in mid-line. Press "any" key (like the spacebar) to get the display going again. You can also use Ctrl-S to get the display going again.

Pressing the Pause key, if you have one, works the same way as Ctrl-S. (A few keyboards call it Hold.)

Splish, Splash with a Backslash

Almost everyone confuses the backslash ("\") with the forward slash ("/"). DOS uses the backslash to divide up the pieces of the file paths you need to use from time to time (if this statement doesn't make sense, go back to Chapter 3 for a quick review).

For instance, on my computer I have a bunch of files in the DOCS directory on my C drive. The path to one of these files is C:\DOCS\BIRTHDAY.DOC. Notice the backslashes dividing the parts of this long thing.

In fairness to the creators of DOS, they already used the forward slash for something else: to indicate switches that adjust the way commands behave. For example, DIR /P lists a directory one page at a time.

Still, it makes typing paths a pain—most folks would find the instinctive but *wrong* `C:/DOCS/BIRTHDAY.DOC` easier to deal with than the *correct* `C:\DOCS\BIRTHDAY.`

The problem with the backslash is that it can be almost any place on your keyboard. For a key that is used so often in DOS, you'd think the keyboard-design nerds would get together and agree where to put the backslash. Sheeesh! On my big PC's keyboard it's in the lower right-hand corner. On my little PC's keyboard it's in the upper right-hand corner. I've even seen keyboards with the backslash up next to the function keys!

Look around for the backslash on your keyboard. You'll be using it from time to time.

Caps Lock

The Caps Lock key is peculiar. Although it shifts all the letter keys on your keyboard to the capital letter equivalents (like holding down the Shift key), it leaves all the number and punctuation keys alone. Also, unlike Shift, you don't have to hold Caps Lock down. Try it. Press and release the Caps Lock key (once), and then type something. You'll notice that only the letters of the alphabet are shifted to uppercase. Everything else stays the same.

TRICKS

> Most keyboards have an indicator light to tell you when the Caps Lock key is on. Because DOS is not case-sensitive (it doesn't make any difference whether you type DOS commands in capital letters or not), you can keep the Caps Lock key on all the time when using DOS commands.

Once you press the Caps Lock key, it "locks" down in the "on" position (that's why they call it Caps LOCK, silly!). You have to "unlock" it by pressing it one more time.

You can type a small (lowercase) letter while Caps Lock is on by pressing Shift at the same time. As soon as you let go of Shift, you start getting capital letters again until you press Caps Lock to turn it off.

Num Lock

Another lock key is the Num Lock. On the old keyboard, the number keys on the right side had to do double-duty. They were used both as the number keys and as arrow keys for moving the cursor in some programs. The Num Lock key was put there to change the meaning from numbers to arrows. The modern keyboard works the same way, except that you can leave Num Lock on all the time and use the separate arrow keys for the cursor.

Normally Num Lock goes on by itself when you boot. This drives some people absolutely bonkers, because it disables the numeric keypad's arrow keys. Thankfully, DOS 6 (but not previous versions) lets you turn it off by adding `NUMLOCK=OFF` to your `CONFIG.SYS` file.

Here again, you can use Shift to access the arrow keys temporarily while Num Lock is on. But realistically, if you're going to be using the arrow keys, you'll probably turn Num Lock off (or use the duplicate set of arrow keys we'll be telling you about in a little while).

A problem on most old keyboards was that the IBM nerds forgot to install an indicator light to tell you when the Num Lock key was on or off. As often as not, you'd start typing in numbers, then realize that the cursor was all over the screen because the Caps Lock key was off. Sheesh (again)!

Scroll Lock

We had to look long and hard to find a use for this key. It was intended to lock the cursor in its relative screen position, and then move the rest of the screen around if the cursor keys were hit. Practically nobody uses it anymore. (In our exhaustive research, we did notice that in Microsoft Flight Simulator, you can combine Scroll Lock with the arrow keys to change your view from the cockpit.)

Print Scrn

The Print Scrn key (or Prt Sc, either of which means "Print Screen") also isn't used much any more. Back on the original IBM-PC, you could use the Prnt Scrn key to make a hard copy (printout) of whatever was on the screen—as long as you had your computer attached to a printer that could handle a print screen.

To handle a print screen, a printer must be able to accept plain old ASCII text. Most dot-matrix printers can handle print screens. The easiest way to find out if yours can handle it is to try it. At the DOS command prompt, just press the Print Scrn (or Prt Sc) key and see if your printer prints what's on the screen. If nothing happens but your computer locks up (stops responding to your typing), wait awhile. If it remains locked up, reboot (press Ctrl-Alt-Del all at the same time) or turn the power off, wait a few seconds, and turn the computer back on.

STOP!

One of the problems with IBM-PC compatibles is that if you try to print something when there's no printer connected to your computer, the computer can lock up (or hang up) waiting for a printer to arrive. So don't use it unless you're hooked to a printer — and the printer's turned on.

If your computer is connected to a more modern laser or PostScript printer (these printers are discussed in Chapter 10), there's no way to know what'll come out of the printer. Most applications disable the Print Scrn key to keep the printer from going nuts if you accidentally touch it.

The Mystery of the Beeping Keyboard

If you're a reasonably fast typist, you know that if you continue typing while the computer is trying to do something (like read a disk or start up a program), the computer will start beeping at you. This happens because the computer can only remember 16 keystrokes at a time—that's how many fit in its *keyboard buffer*. When the buffer's full, additional keystrokes will get lost—and you'll hear a beep.

It's not easy to make your computer remember more than those 16 characters, so when the keyboard starts to beep, take a break and let your computer catch up with you.

TRICKS

Of course, if beeping continues for a long time, your computer has probably stopped running. You'll have to restart it (press Ctrl-Alt-Del all at the same time, or turn the power off, wait a few seconds, and turn the computer back on).

There's a Mouse in the House!

A real popular accessory for computers is a mouse. Your computer may or may not have a thing attached that looks something like figure 11.1.

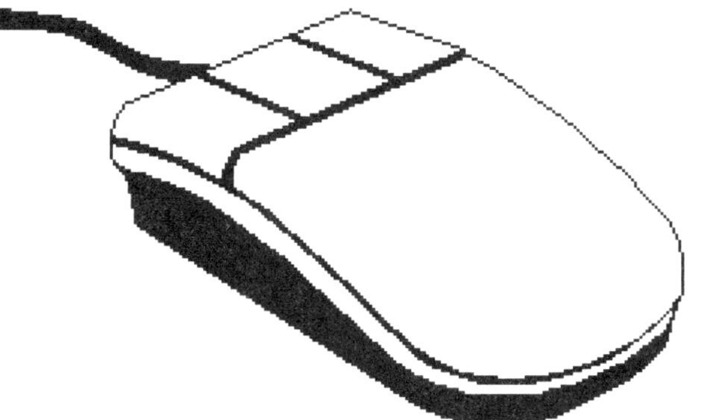

Figure 11.1

EEEK! A mouse!

The mouse is usually connected to the computer through a thin wire. As you move the mouse around on the desktop, the computer can tell which direction you move it and how far you've moved it. As you move the mouse, an indicator on the screen (called a *mouse cursor*) moves around at the same time. The mouse cursor might look like an arrow or rectangle, or it may have a special appearance.

The mouse is useful for applications such as drawing programs, in which you want to draw lines, circles, and other things on the screen. Some word processing programs let you use the mouse to tell the computer where to let you start typing or what words to delete, and so on.

Do You Really Need One?

These days, most DOS programs give you the option of using a mouse. If you have Microsoft Windows or are planning to get Windows anytime soon, or if you want to make pictures with a drawing program, you'll find a mouse indispensible. Many Windows applications require you to have a mouse. There are certain things that are nearly impossible without a mouse in hand.

Driving Miss Mouse

You don't need to know much about how the mouse works. In most cases, if you turn a mouse upside down, you'll see a little ball underneath it. That ball rolls as you move the mouse; the computer can sense the rolling ball and knows what you're doing. (Once in a while, you might get crumbs in there, and you'll have to remove the ball to clean it.)

There are other subspecies of mice, including *optical mice*, which use optical sensors and special pads to determine where you want to go.

There will be two or more buttons on the mouse. Generally, you'll use the left button. (Most *mouse drivers*, some applications programs, and Microsoft Windows will let lefties switch buttons.)

As you'll see in the next section, you *pick* things by pressing the button when the mouse cursor is on top of something on the screen.

NERDY DETAILS

Before most software can talk to your mouse, it requires some special software to be loaded into your computer as the computer starts up. Consult the instruction manual that came with your mouse to see how to get this software installed. You'll probably end up adding a line to either `AUTOEXEC.BAT` or `CONFIG.SYS`.

If you have a choice, make sure your mouse emulates (behaves like) the Microsoft mouse. The Microsoft mouse (which looks a lot like a melted bar of Ivory soap, honestly!) is by far the most popular mouse around (next to Mickey and his gang). Most software programs know how to talk to it.

Taming the Mouse

There are lots of new skills to learn when you have a mouse. Depending on the way your computer programs want you to use the mouse, you might have to move the mouse, press the button once or twice, or move the mouse while holding down the button. The trick is to learn when to do what. The following list describes common mouse features and operations:

Mouse pointer (cursor, arrow). A lot of programs change the appearance of the mouse cursor, depending on what's happening on the screen. For instance, Windows applications change the mouse cursor to an hourglass when you have to wait for something. Other programs change the mouse cursor to cross-hairs or a bull's-eye.

 **Clicking.** The most basic skill (after rolling the mouse around) is pressing the button when the mouse cursor is on top of something on the screen. Pressing the mouse button is called *clicking*, and you are clicking on the thing on the screen. This leads to...

 **Selecting (or choosing).** In most programs, when you click on a thing on the screen (let's say it's a word in a document) the thing becomes highlighted (maybe its appearance changes to *reverse video*—light letters on a black background, for instance). You have just used the mouse to select the thing.

 **Double-clicking.** A slightly more advanced action is to click the mouse button twice in rapid succession. For pretty obvious reasons, this is called *double-clicking*. Sometimes an application wants you to indicate something by double-clicking on it. Double-clicking usually both highlights something and completes an action, saving you from having to take another separate step (such as choosing an OK button) to complete an operation.

 **Dragging.** A more difficult maneuver is to *drag* something by clicking on it, move the mouse while you hold down the mouse button, then release the button. In many word processing programs, this is how you highlight a chunk of text. In many other programs, this is how you select and move something that is already highlighted. In most drawing programs, this is how you draw a line. You might first click on a little picture that represents a pencil or line drawing tool, put the mouse cursor somewhere in the drawing area, draw the line by pressing the button, move the mouse while you hold down the button, then release the button.

The Game Player's Best Friends: Joysticks and Trackballs

An indispensible accessory for incurable computer game addicts is the *joystick*. This fanciful object sits on the desktop and is essentially a little box with a handle sticking straight up out of it. As you move the handle, a cursor moves around the screen (in this way, it's a lot like a mouse, eh?).

The reason joysticks are used a lot for games is that you can rapidly move a pointer on the screen for aiming laser guns or nuclear fusion bombs. The joystick is a very intuitive thing to use for moving something around on the screen and requires very little practice to master.

NERDY DETAILS

Most joysticks require some kind of calibration exercise before you can use them. Using the utility that came with your joystick or game, you tell the computer where the "center" point is. That's the point at which the joystick is pointing straight up-and-down. The computer will do the rest as you move the joystick around.

A *trackball* is a special kind of stationary mouse. It's looks like a dead mouse turned upside-down, with the rolling ball on top. The cursor on the screen moves as you roll the ball around, just like the joystick moves the cursor, and the buttons work just like mouse buttons.

Trackball or mouse? It's a matter of personal taste. Some people claim trackballs are hard to control—since there's nothing to grab, it's hard to move them precisely. Others say just the opposite—once you get used to them, they can give you even finer control than a mouse.

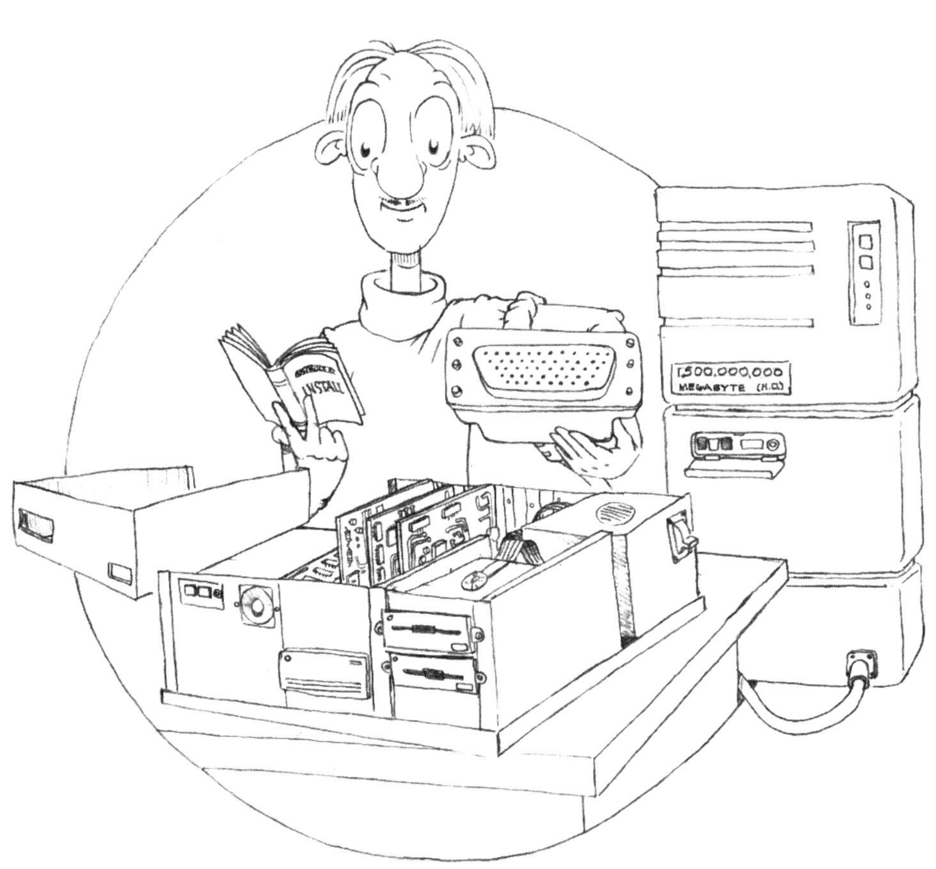
INSTALL
1,500,000,000
MEGABYTE (H.D)

Thanks for the Memories

Your computer's memory (or RAM, as the nerds call it) is where all that computing happens, data processing-wise. Without memory, your computer is nothing more than an exotic, inefficient paperweight.

This chapter is devoted to understanding your computer's memory. We'll ask the following questions and explore the following subject areas. Don't be put off by the nerdy sound of all this stuff. When it comes to your computer, understanding memory isn't just for nerds, it's for anyone who wants to get the most out of their equipment.

- What's memory good for anyway?
- Can you tell memory socks from memory underwear?
- What happens when you hit the infamous 640K barrier?
- Should you buy more memory for your computer?
- What the heck are the confusing EXs: EXpanded and EXtended?
- What's so magical about MemMaker?

In spite of the amount of really nerdy topics in this chapter, rest assured that we're only touching on part of the way your computer uses the precious stuff called memory. By the end of this chapter I'm sure you'll agree that "memory management" is a first-class oxymoron.

Why Bother with All This Memory Nonsense?

There are a couple of good reasons why it's important to understand the memory installed in your computer and how your computer uses that memory:

 Memory issues will eat up a lot of your time.

 Buying memory you don't need will eat up a lot of your money.

One of the major drawbacks to DOS (other than its daunting complexity and hostile interface with you, the user) is its inherent inability to handle really large programs. By itself, because of built-in limitations, DOS can't run really, really large spreadsheets, database applications, or graphics programs.

Over the years, however, a number of overly clever workarounds have been developed to partially overcome DOS's memory limitations. This chapter explains why memory is important to you and your computer, and describes how you can use the workarounds (a *workaround* is just a nerdism for a procedure that tricks your computer into doing something it thinks it can't) to your advantage.

Why Does the Computer Need To Remember Stuff?

After all, isn't this the purpose of "memory"? Does it make the computer smarter, or make it so it can remember things better?

Well, your computer has to think, doesn't it? When you're using your word processor to write a letter or report, you're actually using the computer's memory. *Memory* is where programs and data really live until they're given permanent quarters on your hard disk.

Other than that weird guy on Star Trek: The New Generation, data is anything like reports, letters, and databases that you might produce with your computer. I've been trying to avoid using the word data in this book, but, to tell you the truth, all your files are data. See, there's a little nerd in all of us!

When you start up a program such as WordPerfect on your computer (maybe to write that list of things you'd like to do to the neighbor's dog), DOS *loads* (another way of saying *moves*) the program from the hard disk into memory. Your CPU (see Chapter 8 to learn about CPUs and a few other TLAs) can't run WordPerfect while it's resting on the hard disk. WordPerfect has to be up there in memory, where the action is, before you can use it.

When you've run out of nasty-things-to-do-to-noisy-dogs ideas, and you save your WordPerfect document, DOS creates a nice, permanent file on your hard disk so it's there the next time you want to use it.

RAM-alama-ding-dong. What the heck does RAM mean? RAM is an acronym (another dreaded TLA) that stands for *Random Access Memory*. This means the computer can get at any little bit of memory any ol' time it wants to.

Telling Socks from Underwear, Again

Because memory and disks are both measured in the strange kilobytes and megabytes quantities, a lot of people confuse memory with disk space. Memory and disks store the same stuff: programs and data. They store these things in very different ways, however...

Memory is incredibly fast. It's a purely electronic thing, and your computer is really good at handling data electronically. A hard disk, on the other hand, has a lot of mechanical parts in it for turning the disks and moving things around in there, and all that moving takes time. The data stored in your computer's memory is available to be used at least 1,000 times faster than the same stuff stored on your hard disk.

Okay, so why don't we all have 100 megabytes of memory in our computers, and do away with disks entirely? After all, disks are slow (compared to memory), and they break more frequently.

Well, to start with, the programs and data stored in memory go away when you turn off the computer. Also, memory costs a lot more than a hard disk, on a bucks-per-megabyte basis.

Another way that memory and hard disks differ is in how much space each one's got. Your computer might have two, four, or eight megabytes of memory. A well-equipped computer might have as much as 16 or 20 megabytes of memory; its hard disk could be as large as 120 or 500 megabytes or more.

The Memory Blackboard and Hard Disk File Cabinet

Think of your hard disk as a filing cabinet of things. It's a bunch of files, some of which are instructions and some of which are collections of numbers and things you want to save. From time to time, you take the files out to use.

Your computer's memory is more like a blackboard (or white board, if you prefer), on which you write things down temporarily. If you're making the list of ways to do away with the neighbor's noisy dog, let's pretend you write the list on the blackboard first. Then, after it's done, you take a picture of the blackboard and put the picture in the filing cabinet.

Whatever is on the blackboard will get erased when you start your next project. The blackboard is a temporary place to keep things. In fact, the blackboard is only a place for works in progress. The filing cabinet is where you keep a permanent record of your work.

That's the main difference between memory and disks. Whatever is stored in your computer's memory is only there for a relatively short time. Whatever is on the hard disk will be there the next time you use your computer.

The Limitations of Blackboards

Imagine the blackboard in your third-grade classroom. It was pretty big, I bet. There was room to write a lot of things on it (if you're a fan of the Simpsons, you see Bart Simpson writing on his classroom's blackboard at the start of the show every week). But what if you had to write all the equations required to put the Space Shuttle Enterprise into orbit on a blackboard? Or you had to write the name, address, and phone number of every phone company customer in the 813 phone exchange (Florida, by the way) on a blackboard? It'd take a lot larger blackboard than you had in the third grade, wouldn't it?

Well, your computer's memory is like that. To a certain extent, the more memory you cram into your computer's big box, the more work it can do for you. Things might run faster, you'd be able to load bigger programs, and you could work with bigger damage-to-dogs lists.

Or, at least, that's what they keep telling me about adding memory to my computer. The problem is, doubling the memory in your computer does not double how fast things run, nor does it let you load two programs at once or cool stuff like that.

Hitting the Wall: The Infamous 640K Barrier

Unfortunately, like a lot of other things with computers, giving your computer lots of memory isn't as simple as that. Every PC ever built that's running MS-DOS is crippled by the infamous "640K barrier." No matter how much memory your computer has installed, the most your applications can use without intervention is 640K.

NERDY DETAILS

The "8088" CPU used in the original IBM-PC could only handle 1M of memory, and could only use the memory in pretty small pieces at a time. The clever engineers at IBM devised a workaround for these limitations that left only 640K as the upper limit of memory available for applications. At the time, I'm sure, 640K sounded immense (the typical IBM-PC sold back in '82 only had 16K of memory).

So far, Microsoft has failed to provide a workaround for the 11-year old nuisance of the 640K barrier. Even though the microprocessors in our computers are capable of using billions and billions (or "biwions and biwions") of bytes of memory, we're all stuck with this dumb limit.

The 640K of memory is usually referred to as *conventional memory*. Not only do your applications use this space, but DOS and anything DOS is doing for you (such as watching for viruses and managing your deleted files so that UNDELETE can get them back) comes out of this memory.

That's why the new MemMaker utility that comes with DOS 6 is so important. For the first time, optimizing your computer's memory is simple and easy. Before we talk about MemMaker (in a section near the end of this chapter), let's look at what you can do to add more useful memory beyond the 640K barrier.

If you'd like to see how much memory is installed on your computer, use the MEM command (if you're using DOS 4, 5, or 6) or the CHKDSK command if you're using something older than DOS 4. The display you'll get looks something like figure 12.1.

Figure 12.1

MEM at work.

```
C:\>MEM

Memory Type        Total  =  Used  +  Free
----------------   -----    -----    -----
Conventional        640K     202K     438K
Upper                 0K       0K       0K
Adapter RAM/ROM     384K     384K       0K
Extended (XMS)     3072K     832K    2240K
----------------   -----    -----    -----
Total memory       4096K    1418K    2678K

Total under 1 MB    640K     202K     438K

Largest executable program size       438K   (448368 bytes)
Largest free upper memory block         0K        (0 bytes)
MS-DOS is resident in the high memory area.

C:\>
```

The computer used for figure 12.1 has a total of 4M (MEM says it has 4096K, which is equal to 4M) installed, with 640K of "conventional" memory. The MEM display is pretty informative. The older DOS users who need to use CHKDSK will see something like figure 12.2.

You get quite a bit less information from CHKDSK. The top two sections of the display in figure 12.2 concern the disk that's installed in this computer. Only the two lines near the bottom tell you anything about the memory on this computer, and even then, CHKDSK only looks at the conventional (640K) memory that's installed.

```
C:\>CHKDSK

Volume 18_JUL_92   created 02-18-1993 10:22a
Volume Serial Number is 11DF-0840

  57556992 bytes total disk space
    278528 bytes in 7 hidden files
    212992 bytes in 26 directories
  30736384 bytes in 917 user files
  26329088 bytes available on disk

      8192 bytes in each allocation unit
      7202 total allocation units on disk
      3390 available allocation units on disk

    655360 total bytes memory
    448656 bytes free

C:\>
```

Figure 12.2

CHKDSK at work.

Should You Run Out and Buy More Memory?

You probably don't need more memory than you've already got. If your applications run well, and you're not getting any complaints when you open your documents or databases, you probably have all you need.

Even though memory costs a lot less than it did a few years ago, memory is still expensive to buy and even more expensive to get installed. You shouldn't feel compelled to pour more memory into the big box unless you're wanting to run an application (such as Windows) that requires significant amounts of the stuff.

STOP!

Sure, you can save yourself a lot of money installing your own memory upgrade. Most computers being sold have empty "slots" where you can plug in memory modules. But, do you really want to get inside the big box and mess around in there? Who knows what you'll find inside? There are a lot of different ways memory slots have been built into computers.

You should only try your own memory upgrade if you can program your VCR without VCR Plus and if you're good enough with mechanical things to replace the spark plugs in your car without help.

Expanded (an Oldie but Goodie)

One of the first and cleverest techniques was the development of *expanded memory*. Even the old 8088 and 80286 processors are able to use expanded memory, as long as it's installed and the programs you run understand expanded memory.

The limitation on expanded memory is that it can only be used to store the data your computer is working with. Spreadsheets and databases were among the first applications to use expanded memory. You can chunk in megabytes and megabytes of expanded memory, and your application can then put huge spreadsheets and databases up there.

If, for any reason, you find out you need to put expanded memory in your computer, read the following guidelines:

Older computers (8088s and 80286s) need a separate *adapter card* installed to put in the expanded memory. You also need to install a separate EMM (expanded-memory manager) program so that your application can use the memory installed on the adapter card.

NERDY DETAILS

An *adapter card* is a computer add-on that is installed more or less permanently inside your computer. They're called *cards* because that's what the nerds call 'em (really!), and they are generally card-like in appearance: flat and rectangular. (Some nerds call them *boards* instead of *cards*.)

There are thousands of different types of cards that can be installed in your computer. Two of the most popular kinds being sold nowadays are *fax/modem* cards that let you send and receive faxes from your computer and *multimedia* upgrades, such as the popular Sound Blaster sound cards that let you hear stuff as well as see it (really good for games).

If you need to buy an expanded-memory adapter card, be sure that it conforms to the *LIM 4.0* hardware standard. The details about what LIM is really aren't important, other than it's the best way to make sure your programs can work with your new adapter card.

Okay, okay. The editors have convinced me that you really want to know what LIM means. Here it is: *LIM* is an acronym for *Lotus-Intel-Microsoft*. Back in the early 80s, these three companies (Lotus Development, Intel—the people that make a lot of the electronic stuff inside your computer, and Microsoft—who makes DOS and a lot of other neat programs) got together and decided how expanded memory should work. The result of this collaboration, LIM 4.0 (there was an earlier LIM 3.2 that almost no one uses nowadays), is the most widely accepted expanded memory specification (or EMS, if you're into acronyms). LIM 4.0 requires that the adapter card be made just for it, so you need to know what LIM version your adapter card will work with. Now, are you happy you know all about LIM?

 If you buy an expanded-memory adapter card, make sure it comes with software to make it run right. You'll also need a good, easy-to-read manual with the adapter card as well. Without either of these things (software and manual) the expanded-memory adapter card is worthless.

 If you have an 80386 or 80486 computer, you don't have to buy a separate adapter card to get expanded memory to work. These computers can reserve some of the memory already installed in them to use as expanded memory.

 Another confusing TLA you might hear from time to time is *EMS*, which stands for Expanded Memory Specification. EMS and LIM, for the most part, mean just about the same thing, even though they are different three-letter acronyms. Just to be even more confusing, you might hear LIM and EMS used in the same breath, like "LIM 4.0 EMS." Kind of boggles the mind, doesn't it?

If you want to set up part of your 386 or 486 memory as expanded memory, you should look at the manual that came with DOS. The DOS 5 manual has a really nice section titled "Using EMM386 as an Expanded-Memory Emulator." EMM386 comes with DOS, so you don't have to buy anything extra.

continues

continued

Be forewarned, however, that if you want to get EMM386 running on your computer, you'll have to make changes to your `CONFIG.SYS` file. (Dum da dum dum!) See Chapter 4 for help.

The nice thing about expanded memory is that it works on virtually any type of PC ever built. Even the oldest and creakiest PC can be equipped with expanded memory. Not all applications know how to use expanded memory, however. Before you invest in the adapter card to add expanded memory to your PC, check your application's user manual to see if it can use expanded memory.

NERDY DETAILS

The nerdy detail about how your computer uses expanded memory is *really* nerdy. Suffice it to say that the LIM driver described a little bit earlier fools your computer into thinking it's getting at regular ol' conventional memory when, in fact, it's actually the expanded memory on the adapter card it's using. The expanded memory is given to your computer to use in chunks, called *pages*, of memory. As your computer needs the information on another page of expanded memory, the LIM thing *swaps* the memory pages. Hence, the clever term *page-swapping*.

That's also why you can only install expanded memory in an old PC or XT by adding an adapter card. The card contains special circuitry that lets LIM switch between the banks of memory on the card.

When you're using expanded memory with your spreadsheet or database application, you're not even aware that this page-swapping is going on. The LIM driver is quite magical.

Extended (Good Memories)

It would be better and even more useful if your computer could use memory above the 640K barrier without needing a special board or software like LIM. After all, the LIM software takes up a little bit of your conventional memory (that stuff below the 640K barrier), and (although it's not too noticeable) the memory page-swapping takes time, slowing down your computer a bit.

You can throw (which means "install") a lot of useful memory into 286, 386, and 486 computers. DOS still can't use it directly, and your applications can't simply use it without help from DOS, but with a little fiddling around, your database, spreadsheet, and other memory-hungry programs can use the extra memory you've installed.

NERDY DETAILS

> You can install an incredible amount of memory into most 386 and 486 computers. You can usually plug memory modules (called SIMMs, which stand for Single In-line Memory Modules) right into these computers without buying adapter cards—saving quite a bit of money.
>
> Memory isn't cheap, though, and a lot of 386 and 486 computers require you to install four SIMMs in the big box at a time.

This extra-special type of memory is called *extended memory* because it starts where the first megabyte leaves off. If you own a 286 or a 386SX, you can put up to 16 megabytes of memory (conventional plus extended) into your computer. 386DXs and all 486s can have as much as four *gigabytes* (billions and billions of bytes) of memory. Unfortunately, even with the billions of bytes of memory possible on your 386 or 486, good ol' DOS *still* can only use the first 640K for programs. Isn't that sad?

Only programs specifically designed to take advantage of extended memory can actually use the memory above 1M. A notable example is Microsoft Windows. If you use Windows and Windows applications such as Excel, Word, WordPerfect for Windows, or Microsoft Access, you are using your computer's extended memory.

There are only a few purely DOS programs that use extended memory. Unless you are using Windows or another application that specifically uses extended memory, you should not lay out a lot of bucks for extended memory that you won't be using.

MemMaker: The DOS 6 Memory Booster

One of the nicest things you can do for yourself and your computer is to take advantage of MemMaker, the excellent memory optimizer that comes with DOS 6. This program *very intelligently* examines the way the memory on your computer is currently being used, and builds new `CONFIG.SYS` and `AUTOEXEC.BAT` files with the correct commands to provide your computer with the absolute most usable memory possible.

NERDY DETAILS

MemMaker takes advantage of the fact that the memory in the 384K "gap" between the top of the 640K barrier and the 1024K DOS limit isn't completely used by your computer's adapters and other things that use this reserved area. There are quite large gaps in this area memory's utilization. MemMaker will search through this area, and stuff things that were formerly part of the lower 640K of memory into the 384K gap. This frees up a lot of the lower 640K for DOS and your programs to work with.

Historically, tweaking your computer's memory *configuration* has involved a lot of hocus-pocus (otherwise known as *trial-and-error*) to get the many settings in `CONFIG.SYS` and `AUTOEXEC.BAT` right. Many very good DOS experts and super nerds have never mastered the technique of memory optimization.

In the past, after many trials and a lot of errors, your system administrator would build a reasonably workable `CONFIG.SYS` for your computer and leave you with a warning to never, ever make any changes to your `CONFIG.SYS` and `AUTOEXEC.BAT` start-up files.

NERDY DETAILS

The *system administrator* is the ultimate nerd at a lot of companies. He or she is the person who's responsible for keeping all the computers and computer-related stuff running reasonably well. In most companies, the system administrator (affectionately known as the *sys admin*) also picks out the computers and software (including DOS) that you end up struggling with, so it's his fault!

Today, with DOS 6 and MemMaker, even non-nerds can expertly and accurately configure their computer's memory for optimum performance.

NERDY DETAILS

Remember the Scarecrow in the *Wizard of Oz*? I always think of him when I use MemMaker. We know the Wizard just made the Scarecrow *think* he had more brains than he did before. MemMaker does the same for your computer. MemMaker doesn't actually *make* more memory for your computer; it just makes available more of the memory it already has.

If you ever see the message **`Program too big to fit in memory`** when you try to start an application, you can easily justify the expense and trouble of upgrading to DOS 6 just to get MemMaker and put its magic to work for you.

Let's Put MemMaker to Work!

MemMaker is one of the easiest DOS 6 utilities to use. In fact, you're better off just letting MemMaker do its thing while you sit back and watch it work.

The only time you have to intervene is when MemMaker tries too hard to save your computer's memory and, for some reason or other, your computer won't restart normally after MemMaker is done. Not to worry! (Have you heard this before?) MemMaker is very good at recovering from its Type A personality and will automatically back off if you have to restart the computer yourself.

First, Make a Backup of CONFIG.SYS and AUTOEXEC.BAT

MemMaker can't make changes to your computer's memory itself. There's no way that a computer program such as MemMaker can add more memory modules to your computer or make the memory inside the memory modules bigger. MemMaker can, however, modify your `CONFIG.SYS` and `AUTOEXEC.BAT` files so that your computer will more efficiently use the memory it's got.

Just in case there's some major foul-up and MemMaker can't successfully modify your `CONFIG.SYS` and `AUTOEXEC.BAT` files, you should make backup copies of these important files, like this:

 **COPY AUTOEXEC.BAT AUTOEXEC.SAV**

 **COPY CONFIG.SYS CONFIG.SAV**

You will have reliable copies of your start-up files as they were before the process began. If there's a big failure during the MemMaker session, you can always copy the SAV files back to their respective BAT and SYS counterparts.

NERDY DETAILS

MemMaker sure is smart. It makes its own backup copies of **CONFIG.SYS** and **AUTOEXEC.BAT** before it starts, and can even restore the backup copies if necessary. But, to be on the safe side, you should not always rely on your programs to do the right thing. The DOS 6 utilities such as MemMaker, DEFRAG, and DoubleSpace are exceptionally conscientious about the possibility that something will go wrong and are well-prepared for it when it happens.

Next, Check How Much Memory You've Got

An optional first step before optimizing your computer's memory is to run MEM (if you're using DOS 4, 5, or 6) or CHKDSK (if you're using an older version). It's fun to see how much memory MemMaker gets back for you. The MEM command produced the display shown in figure 12.3 on a computer in my office before MemMaker was run.

Figure 12.3

The MEM display before running MemMaker.

```
C:\>MEM

Memory Type        Total  =  Used   +  Free
----------------   ------    ------    ------
Conventional        640K      110K      530K
Upper                 0K        0K        0K
Adapter RAM/ROM     384K      384K        0K
Extended (XMS)     3072K      832K     2240K
----------------   ------    ------    ------
Total memory       4096K     1419K     2677K

Total under 1 MB    640K      110K      530K

Largest executable program size        530K  (542848 bytes)
Largest free upper memory block          0K       (0 bytes)
MS-DOS is resident in the high memory area.

C:\>
```

As you can see, this machine has only 530K of memory free (see the line near the bottom of the display that reads `Largest executable program size` to get the amount of memory available). Although this is plenty of memory for most applications, a lot of modern programs want 512K or more before they'll run. The `530` figure also means that 110K (the difference between 640K and 530K) are being used up by different things such as DoubleSpace, `UNDELETE`, and DOS itself.

Start Up MemMaker!

When you start MemMaker by typing in **MEMMAKER** (don't forget that it has three Ms in all) at the DOS prompt (and pressing Enter, of course!), you'll see a screen something like figure 12.4.

```
Microsoft MemMaker

Welcome to MemMaker.

MemMaker optimizes your system's memory by moving memory-resident
programs and device drivers into the upper memory area. This
frees conventional memory for use by applications.

After you run MemMaker, your computer's memory will remain
optimized until you add or remove memory-resident programs or
device drivers. For an optimum memory configuration, run MemMaker
again after making any such changes.

MemMaker displays options as highlighted text. (For example, you
can change the "Continue" option below.) To cycle through the
available options, press SPACEBAR. When MemMaker displays the
option you want, press ENTER.

For help while you are running MemMaker, press F1.

            Continue or Exit? Continue

ENTER=Accept Selection  SPACEBAR=Change Selection  F1=Help  F3=Exit
```

Figure 12.4

The MemMaker welcome screen.

You can choose to leave MemMaker at this point by pressing F3, or continue by pressing Enter. Being the brave sort of people you are, go ahead and press Enter.

Shall We Take the Express or Custom Route?

The next screen (see fig. 12.5) offers you the opportunity to choose between "Express" and "Custom" setups. Unless you understand your computer's memory requirements very well and how to use all of the DOS memory-management options (not even nerds know this much!), go ahead and select Express Setup by pressing Enter.

Figure 12.5

Choosing the MemMaker Express Setup option.

```
Microsoft MemMaker

 There are two ways to run MemMaker:

 Express Setup optimizes your computer's memory automatically.

 Custom Setup gives you more control over the changes that
 MemMaker makes to your system files. Choose Custom Setup
 if you are an experienced user.

          Use Express or Custom Setup? Express Setup

ENTER=Accept Selection  SPACEBAR=Change Selection  F1=Help  F3=Exit
```

Most Microsoft programs (such as **DOSSHELL**, discussed in Chapter 5) let you choose between options by pressing Tab. MemMaker makes you use the spacebar to switch between options. Don't press Enter unless you are sure you want to accept the option that is displayed.

Some Final Checks Before Liftoff

MemMaker then asks you whether you use any programs that use expanded memory. Answer yes only if you are sure you've got a database, spreadsheet, graphics, or other program that uses expanded memory. There's no danger in making the wrong choice here; MemMaker will just make your computer so that it *can* provide expanded memory for these applications. You won't permanently lose any of your precious conventional memory by making the wrong choice. You can always rerun MemMaker later on if you discover that you have some applications that require expanded memory.

MemMaker is also interested in whether you have Microsoft Windows installed. Windows makes extensive use of extended memory, so MemMaker wants to make sure Windows is adequately supplied. If you have Windows on your computer, confirm MemMaker's question about where Windows is installed (this is almost always in the `C:\WINDOWS` directory).

Taking the Last Few Steps

You're almost done—pretty easy, huh?

MemMaker makes a few changes to your `CONFIG.SYS` and `AUTOEXEC.BAT` files (after making backups), and restarts your computer at this point. You'll see one or two screens telling you what's going on.

After your computer is going again, you'll see the screen in figure 12.6. If, for some reason, your computer doesn't restart normally, skip ahead to the section titled "The Darn Thing Didn't Restart!"

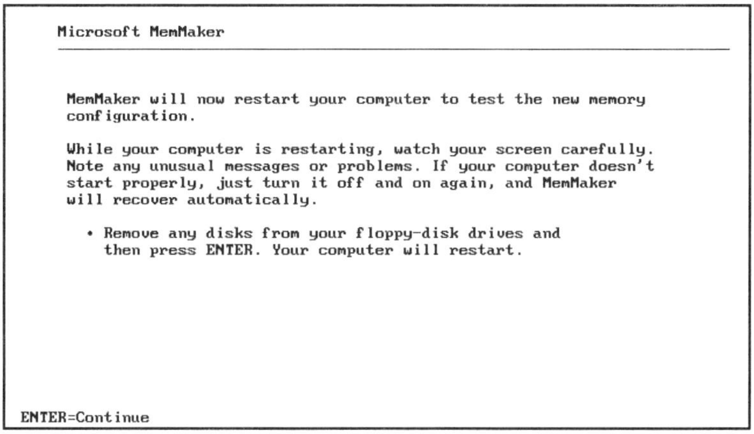

```
Microsoft MemMaker

MemMaker will now restart your computer to test the new memory
configuration.

While your computer is restarting, watch your screen carefully.
Note any unusual messages or problems. If your computer doesn't
start properly, just turn it off and on again, and MemMaker
will recover automatically.

  • Remove any disks from your floppy-disk drives and
    then press ENTER. Your computer will restart.

ENTER=Continue
```

Figure 12.6

MemMaker restarting your computer.

MemMaker is actually watching your computer as it runs, in case it has to make any last minute tweaks to the initial setup.

Success!

After making the very last adjustments, MemMaker restarts your computer one last time (after first telling you), then shows you the screen in figure 12.7.

Look closely at figure 12.7. The `Before MemMaker` column shows how poorly organized this computer's memory was. There were only 542,848 *bytes* of memory (530K, more or less) before the MemMaker session, and 631,664 (or 617K) afterwards (you can read this figure in the `After MemMaker` column).

Figure 12.7

MemMaker's success screen.

```
Microsoft MemMaker

MemMaker has finished optimizing your system's memory. The following
table summarizes the memory use (in bytes) on your system:

                                      Before        After
   Memory Type                        MemMaker      MemMaker      Change
   ----------------------------       --------      --------      --------
   Free conventional memory:          542,848       631,664        88,816

   Upper memory:
      Used by programs                      0       115,648       115,648
      Reserved for Windows                  0             0             0
      Reserved for EMS                      0             0             0
      Free                                  0        67,680

   Expanded memory:                   Disabled      Disabled

Your original CONFIG.SYS and AUTOEXEC.BAT files have been saved
as CONFIG.UMB and AUTOEXEC.UMB.  If MemMaker changed your Windows
SYSTEM.INI file, the original file was saved as SYSTEM.UMB.

ENTER=Exit  ESC=Undo changes
```

If you want further proof, after you press Enter to make the screen in figure 12.7 go away, run the `MEM` command again. Compare the `Free` column in figure 12.3 with the same column in figure 12.8. You'll see the change from 530K to 617K of free memory, which is enough to let you run a lot of programs that used to report `Program too big to fit in memory` errors.

Figure 12.8

The MEM display after running MemMaker.

```
C:\>MEM

Memory Type        Total  =  Used  +  Free
----------------  ------    ------   ------
Conventional        640K      23K     617K
Upper               179K      90K      90K
Adapter RAM/ROM     205K     205K       0K
Extended (XMS)     3072K    1164K    1908K
----------------  ------    ------   ------
Total memory       4096K    1482K    2614K

Total under 1 MB    819K     113K     706K

Largest executable program size      617K   (631560 bytes)
Largest free upper memory block       69K    (70352 bytes)
MS-DOS is resident in the high memory area.

C:\>
```

Although the 88,816-byte improvement may not seem like a lot, it's enough memory to hold a good size spreadsheet, a lot of database records, or a very large document in your word processor. (This computer will now run the Captain Keen game, which requires more than 540K!)

You have just completed a very sophisticated task that would have taken a DOS expert nerd hours and hours to complete.

The Darn Thing Didn't Restart!

Okay, so your computer didn't restart properly after MemMaker made changes to `CONFIG.SYS` and `AUTOEXEC.BAT`. Not to worry. Simply shut off your computer and turn it back on again. When it restarts this time, you'll get a screen (shown in figure 12.9) that acknowledges the problem and asks you if you want MemMaker to `Try again with conservative settings`.

```
Microsoft(R) MemMaker
________________________________________________________________

Your computer was restarted before MemMaker finished determining
the memory requirements of your device drivers and memory-resident
programs.

   If you restarted your computer because it was not working
    properly, choose "Try again with conservative settings."

   If MemMaker was interrupted for another reason (for example,
    a power failure), or if you are not sure what happened, choose
    "Try again with the same settings."

   To exit MemMaker and restore your system files, choose "Cancel
    and undo all changes."

   Try again or cancel? Try again with conservative settings


ENTER=Accept Selection  SPACE=Change Selection  F1=Help
```

Figure 12.9

MemMaker restarting after a problem.

After you tell MemMaker to go ahead with a more conservative approach, and it makes the changes once more, your computer will restart again. This time it should start up normally and proceed with the rest of the MemMaker process.

If, on the other hand, MemMaker got interrupted because of a power failure or other problem, you can retry the changes with the settings MemMaker determined in its first pass. Use the spacebar to select `Try again with the same settings`, and press Enter. It can't hurt!

If All Else Fails....

If nothing seems to work, you can make DOS bypass the `CONFIG.SYS` and `AUTOEXEC.BAT` start-up files by pressing F5 as soon as you see the `Starting MS-DOS...` message (press F5 two or three times to make sure, but only after you see the `Starting MS-DOS...` message).

Next you will see a `MS-DOS is bypassing your CONFIG.SYS and AUTOEXEC.BAT files.` message from DOS. Type:

```
COPY CONFIG.SAV CONFIG.SYS

COPY AUTOEXEC.SAV AUTOEXEC.BAT
```

Restart your computer with the Alt-Ctrl-Del restart routine, and your computer will go back to where it was before you started MemMaker.

I doubt very much that you'll need to resort to this emergency process, however. The software wizard nerds at Microsoft really put in their overtime on MemMaker, and it does a great job.

Ultimate KEYBOARD
1000

Disks, Directories, and Other Doodads

Floppy disks are the only things you actually get to take away from your computer and carry around with you. Paper printouts don't count: paper doesn't *interact* with the computer—just the printer. You can put lots and lots of stuff on disks (too much stuff, actually): love letters, dirty pictures, adventure games, your personal finances. In fact, anything you work on, use, view, or play with on the computer can be put onto floppy disks and carried around with you. This chapter tells you everything you need to know about floppy disks, including:

 How to buy floppy disks (no kidding, this is harder than it sounds!)

 How to make a new floppy disk ready to use

 How to copy everything on a floppy disk

 How to protect disks from accidental erasures

 How to double your disk space

Buying Floppy Disks

Have you ever bought floppy disks at a computer store? You'd think it'd be simple: go in, pick up a box clearly labeled "FLOPPY DISKS FOR YOUR COMPUTER," pay a few bucks for 'em, and take 'em home. Unfortunately, it isn't quite so simple. There must be a dozen different varieties in the store: "double density," "high-capacity," "double sided," "3.5"," "DS/DD," "DS/HD," and so on. Thank computer industry nerds for complicating something as simple as floppies.

Floppy disk drives are very picky. Each floppy disk drive on your computer graciously accommodates only *one* kind of floppy disk (although, like everything else about computers, there are exceptions). Even though several types of disks look alike, your drive can tell the difference. When you go to the store to buy new floppy disks, you need to get the right kind.

Each floppy disk drive takes either 5 1/4-inch (5.25") or 3 1/2-inch (3.5") floppy disks (if you're not sure, get a ruler and measure how wide the slot across the face of the disk drive is). Your computer may have both sizes of drives.

Floppy disks can be either "high-capacity" or "low-capacity." *High-capacity* floppy disks hold more information than *low-capacity* disks do. That's all there is to "capacity."

But, to complicate things, there really aren't any standard names or designations for floppy disks. The following list shows the four types of floppy disks and most of the common labels you're likely to find on their boxes:

Disk and Drive Type	Common Disk Labels
5 1/4-inch low-capacity	360K, DS/DD, 2S/2D, MD-2D, MD2-D, "Two Sided, Double Density," "Double Sided/Double Density"
5 1/4-inch high-capacity	1.2M, DS/HD, 2S/HD, MD2-HD, "Quad Density" or "Double Sided/High Density,"
3 1/2-inch low-capacity	720K, 2S/2D, MF2-DD, MFD-2DD, 2DD
3 1/2-inch high-capacity	1.44M, DS/HD, 2HD, MF2-HD, or "Quad Density"

NERDY DETAILS

For the past few years, almost every laptop and notebook computer has had a 1.44M 3.5" high-capacity floppy disk drive. Older laptops usually had 720K 3.5" low-capacity floppy drives.

Most desktop computers come with one 1.2M 5 1/4-inch high-capacity drive or one 1.44M 3 1/2-inch high-capacity drive; many include both. Low-capacity drives are generally found only on older machines.

How Much Stuff Can a Floppy Disk Hold?

Just how much stuff can a floppy disk hold? Quite a bit. As an example, the chapters in this book are between 10 and 15 pages long and contain about 5,000 words (25,000 letters, or *characters*, as literary people might call them).

Disk drives and disk capacities are measured by how many characters of information they can hold (a nerd uses the word *bytes* for "characters" and *data* for "stuff"). When you hear the term 1.44M disk, the disk holds 1.44M of information, or more than 1,450,000 characters. Wow! That means each high-capacity, 3.5" 1.44M floppy disk can hold at least two or three books the size of this one!

If you have a PC, the hard disk in it is at least 40M big. If so, your hard disk can hold about 100 books the size of this one.

TRICKS

Here's a good tip: LABEL YOUR DISKS! As soon as you start putting files on your floppy disks, mixing up valuable disks (any disk with your hard work on it is pretty valuable, don't you think?) with cheap disks (disks with nothing on them are pretty darn cheap) is pretty easy. Avoid formatting a disk with valuable stuff on it or copying over valuable stuff by labeling your disks!

If you get tired of hearing me tell you to label your disks, trust me on this one. It's an important thing to do.

That's all we're going to say about the size of things. Americans (both men and women) tend to become pretty anxious when people start talking about the size of different things and we've probably already gone farther than anyone really cares...

What Type of Disk Is This?

If you come across an unlabeled disk (usually in the middle of an emergency), you can find out how much info it can hold by its physical characteristics. Here are some clues:

Disk Size	Look For These Things
5.25"	Most of these disks have "hub rings." Look at the big hole in the center of the disk. If the hole is bordered by an extra layer of plastic (for reinforcing the hole), the disk is probably a low-capacity (360K) floppy disk. If the floppy disk does not have a hub ring, it is probably a high-capacity (1.2M) disk.
3.5"	All 3.5" floppies have a sliding metal door protecting the spinning disk. Look for the square holes you can see through near the edges of the disk. If there is only one square hole in one corner, it is a 720K (low-capacity) disk. If two square holes appear on the corners, you have a 1.44M (high-capacity) disk. (One hole may be closed with a tiny sliding door.)

NERDY DETAILS

If you want to make sure what kind of 5 1/4-inch disk you're holding, you can use the **CHKDSK** command to find out exactly how much space is on the disk (assuming that the disk has been formatted, or prepared for use). Just type **CHKDSK** at the DOS prompt, followed by the name of the disk drive:

```
CHKDSK B:
```

You'll see something like this on the screen:

```
Volume Serial Number is 1541-19BD
```

```
1213952 bytes total disk space
 235008 bytes in 10 user files
 978944 bytes available on disk
```

This is followed by a bunch of other stuff you can ignore for the time being. The `bytes total disk space` is the thing you're after. Although it's hard to instantly convert this number to megabytes or kilobytes, if you mentally put commas in the `1213952` number, you'll see that there are more than 1,200,000 bytes of total disk space on this disk, so it's a 1.2M floppy.

Generally speaking, the expressions *capacity* and *density* are interchangable. Don't let the local computer store nerd (who probably still lives with mommy) confuse you when you ask for "low-capacity" disks and he or she insists on calling them "double-density." This whole nonsense about the many names for the four varieties of floppy disks is just plain annoying, isn't it?

Also, avoid anything that says "single-sided" or "1S" (some very old, obsolete disk drives only wrote data on one side of the disk). You won't be able to use them, and nobody you know will want to take them off your hands.

NERDY DETAILS

If this little tizzy about disk formats sounds rather harsh on the computer industry, consider that the nerds who dreamed up this mess could have made it easier.

You'll notice that your 5.25" floppies have one or more notches or holes in different places around the edge of the disk. It would have been very easy to add a notch telling you (and your computer) whether a disk is high-capacity. A small thing like that would have saved millions and millions of people a lot of time over the last 10 years.

For the purposes of this book, the terms *low-capacity* and *high-capacity* are used. You will also see these kooky numbers: 360K, 1.2M, 720K, and 1.44M.

NERDY DETAILS

The hard disk in your computer and the floppy disks lying about on your desktop can hold the same kinds of files. The only difference is that a hard disk holds a lot more files (and bigger files) than a floppy (sort of like the difference betweeen a dorm- or bar-sized refrigerator and a giant commercial walk-in). And, just like a refrigerator, you've got to keep your disk clean and organized!

The Disk Fits in My Drive But Won't Work!

You put a disk in the floppy drive, lock it in, and try to read something on the disk. Suddenly, DOS flips you off with one or more of the following error messages:

 **`General failure reading drive`** ***`X`*****.** You'll see this message when you try to read data on a high-capacity disk that is placed in a low-capacity disk drive. *X* is the name of the floppy disk drive (either A or B). Use another disk.

 **`Abort, Retry, Fail?`.** This message often follows the `General failure` message. Nobody really understands this message. The best course of action may be to press **A** for Abort.

 **`Invalid media or Track 0 bad - disk unusable`.** You'll see this message if you try to *format* (described in the next section) a high-capacity disk in a low-capacity drive. Helpful message, don't you think? Why doesn't it just tell you what's going on? You might want to try the disk one more time (repeat whatever command you did when you got this message), then give up and throw the disk away.

Formatting Floppy Disks

You can't use new floppy disks right out of the box; you have to prepare them. You wouldn't bring home a bag of bagels from the grocery store and eat one without toasting it first, would you? Bagels need toasting; new floppy disks need *formatting*.

This mysterious ritual of formatting involves putting invisible grooves on the disk, which the computer fills with information whenever you use the disk.

Without the grooves, nothing can stick to the disk—everything falls off while the disk spins. (This isn't entirely true; however, the truth is really boring and a lot less picturesque.)

Formatting Is Boring

New disks right out of the box don't work until you format them. Imagine how many people have returned disks to stores because they didn't know this (probably a lot).

Every version of DOS has some form of `FORMAT` command. `FORMAT` is easy to use; just put the new floppy disk into drive A and type

```
FORMAT A:
```

Then press Enter. DOS asks you to `Insert new diskette for drive A: and press ENTER when ready....` Press the Enter key. Then wait. And wait. And (yawn) wait some more. Preparing the disk takes a minute or two, depending on the capacity (high or low, remember?) of your disk.

When DOS is finished, it asks you for a `Volume label (11 Characters, Enter for none)?`. Just press Enter. Nobody but a real nerd puts volume labels on floppy disks. If you're doing just one floppy, type **N** when you see the `Format another (Y/N)?` message.

Floppy disks last a long time. You can also *reformat* a previously used disk with the FORMAT command to wipe it clean. If you're sure you won't be need- ing anything that's on a disk and want to use it for a bunch of new files, formatting it again is the best way to ensure that the disk is ready to use. When you use the FORMAT command, it does certain tests on the disk and marks any bad spots it might find (these bad spots occur now and then just by using the disk). Later, DOS won't try to put files into the marked places on the disk.

NERDY DETAILS

If you have DOS 5 or 6 (type **VER** and press Enter to check which version you have), you can whack a few seconds off the lengthy **FORMAT** procedure if you type **/U** at the end of the FORMAT command:

```
FORMAT A: /U
```

continues

continued

This means "unconditional" format. Like a lot of things, this term is stupid because you wouldn't go to all the trouble if you didn't really want to format the disk, right?

Actually, this parameter tells DOS not to save the information required to unformat the disk. More on this later.

You can dramatically shorten the time required to reformat a disk by adding the /Q (quick) parameter:

```
FORMAT A: /Q
```

When you combine the /U and /Q parameters, the disk is formatted before you can get another sip of coffee! Now that's fast!

NERDY DETAILS

One of the reasons the **/Q** type of FORMAT is so fast is that it doesn't do all the checking on the disk that a plain FORMAT does. FORMAT won't mark any bad spots on a used disk that you format with the **/Q** parameter, so be prepared for flaky disk problems now and then.

Remember, you can only use the /Q parameter on previously formatted disks that you are reformatting.

STOP!

Never, ever, format your hard disk. This is serious business. Do not type

```
FORMAT C:
```

DOS freaks out and says (in all capital letters, no less):

```
WARNING: ALL DATA ON NON-REMOVABLE DISK
DRIVE C: WILL BE LOST!
Proceed with Format (Y/N)?
```

> DOS isn't kidding! All the files, programs, and other data on your hard disk will be irrevocably erased. Don't do this unless you have a darn good reason, such as when you're installing a new hard disk or trying to eliminate a particularly hard-to-remove virus. Remember: formatting the hard disk erases everything on it.

Formatting Foreign Disks

Some disks look a lot alike, even though they're completely different. You can format (and use) a low-capacity disk in a high-capacity floppy disk drive. All you need to know is how to tell DOS to do it. You use a different command for each type of disk:

- If you're using DOS 5 or 6, and you want to format a low-capacity (720K) 3.5" floppy disk in a 1.44M disk drive, type

  ```
  FORMAT B: /F:720
  ```

  Then press Enter (assuming that the 3.5" drive is the B drive). This tells DOS you've put a 720K disk in a 1.44M drive. Otherwise, DOS treats the disk as if it were a 1.44M drive, and says it can't format it.

- To format a 360K disk in a 1.2M drive (again in DOS 5 or 6), type

  ```
  FORMAT A: /F:360
  ```

  Then press Enter (assuming that the 5.25" drive is drive A).

Do you see the similarity between these commands? The /F: parameter tells DOS that what follows is the size you want DOS to format the floppy disk. You can put a low-capacity disk in a high-capacity disk drive and use it.

> If you're using DOS 5 or 6, you can type **FORMAT /?** and press Enter to get a help screen. In fact, all DOS 5 and 6 commands will give you help if you follow the command name with a **/?** (and press Enter, of course).

A Little Paranoia Can Be a Good Thing for Posterity

Suppose you've finished your book (or love letter, income taxes, or something really important), and it's just sitting there on a floppy disk. You know you have a copy of it somewhere on your hard disk, and you printed it out so you have a paper copy. Nevertheless, you should make another copy of the floppy disk to put in your safe deposit box, just in case.

DOS has a command that lets you make a perfect copy of a floppy disk onto another floppy disk:

```
DISKCOPY X: Y:
```

X: and *Y:* are your floppy disk drives—you're copying from disk X to disk Y.

The only rule you need to know about `DISKCOPY` is that the *from* and *to* disks must be the same type of disks. This means you can only go from a 1.44M floppy disk to another 1.44M floppy disk. You can't go from a 720K floppy to a 1.44M, even though everything will fit on the larger floppy disk. The reason is that `DISKCOPY` makes an exact copy of the disk, and the command isn't smart enough to tell the difference between disk types.

Does this mean you have to have two of the same kinds of floppy disk drives on your computer? Not really; `DISKCOPY` lets you use the same drive for both the from and to drives. The following commands work:

```
DISKCOPY A: A:
```

and

```
DISKCOPY B: B:
```

NERDY DETAILS

One last word about **DISKCOPY**: if you're copying high-capacity floppy disks, be prepared to switch floppy disks an annoying number of times. DOS is too dumb to read an entire disk in one swipe and then write the new disk in a single second swipe. Instead, it asks you over and over again to remove the **SOURCE diskette** (the *from* disk), and insert the **TARGET diskette** (the *to* disk).

Don't mix up the *from* and *to* disks during a **DISKCOPY** session. If you mix the two, you'll ruin the *from* disk (the one you want to copy) because files will be written from the *to* disk (the backup copy) and put on the *from* disk, instead of the other way around. This will happen even if the *to* disk is completely blank when you mix up the two. Write labels on them before you start, and write-protect the *from* disk (see the next section).

Protecting Floppy Disks from Stupid Mistakes

You can protect yourself from one of the most common beginner mistakes. Almost everyone has mistakenly formatted or disk-copied over a valuable disk at one time or another. Some people do it almost routinely. It's like locking yourself out of your car or apartment (unless you've got five or six sets of keys scattered around).

Write-protecting fixes your floppy disk so that it's impossible to delete files or format the disk accidentally. In fact, you can't even add new files to a disk that is write-protected. Before DOS will change the stuff that's on a floppy disk (such as when you try to `COPY` a file to it), DOS looks to see if the disk is write-protected. If it is, the message `Write-protect error` appears.

Write-protecting a floppy disk is easy. On all 3.5" floppy disks, a little square hole has a sliding plastic door on the back side of the disk. Slide the door to cover or open the hole. When the little door is opened (you can see through the hole), the disk is *write-protected*. DOS can't make any changes to the files that are on the disk. You cannot add or delete files, or format the disk.

TRICKS

If the write-protect door is missing, you can cover the hole with opaque (not clear) tape.

To protect 5.25" disks, a notch on the corner of the disk determines whether it is write-protected. When the notch is open (you can see through it), the disk is not write-protected. To write-protect it, cover the notch with tape or the special little sticky write-protect labels that come in the box of disks.

NERDY DETAILS

With some floppy disk drives, you can't use clear Scotch tape to write-protect your 5.25" disks. These disk drives use a light detector to tell whether the notch is covered. If the light gets through the tape, DOS doesn't know the notch is covered. Other floppy disk drives use a little metal finger to "feel" whether the notch is covered. You can't tell by looking at the floppy disk drive what kind of sensor it has. Don't worry about it; use opaque (not clear) tape.

Always test disks that you've write-protected. Try to copy your `AUTOEXEC.BAT` file or another small file to the disk after you've write-protected it. If DOS doesn't complain about a `Write-protect error`, your disk really isn't protected!

Stuffing Ten Pounds of Information into a Five-Pound Bag

DOS 6 includes a really nice, but very strange, utility program called DoubleSpace. This nifty program can magically convert most of your hard disk into a second, enlarged hard disk (not exactly, but you can pretend it does). As you learned earlier, hard disks are never large enough. For this reason, here's a cheap and easy way to add a second hard disk to your computer.

TRICKS

To double (almost) a hard disk, DoubleSpace squeezes a bunch of your files into one great big file. Then DoubleSpace fools DOS into thinking that the big file is actually another disk. To DOS (and to you) your hard disk suddenly becomes much, much bigger (almost twice as big!). Pretty cool, huh?

Stuffin' It: How To Use DoubleSpace

Before you start the DoubleSpace installation, make sure you've got enough time to complete the entire process. Once the DoubleSpace installation is started, don't interrupt the PC. My puny 30M hard drive took almost two hours to double; imagine a 486/50 with a 250M hard drive!

It is a good idea to clean up your hard disk a bit before using DoubleSpace. Type **DIR /S** to look for all files with last names of BAK and TMP (**DIR \ /S /P *.BAK; DIR \ /S /P *.TMP**), then use the DEL command to delete them. You should also consider moving old letters, reports, spreadsheets and other document and data files onto floppy disks before starting.

Chapter 3 tells you all about finding, deleting, and moving files.

Complete the following steps to install DoubleSpace:

1. Type **DBLSPACE**, and press Enter at the DOS prompt.
2. It'll take a second, but eventually you'll see the DoubleSpace welcome screen, as shown in figure 13.1. Press Enter.

```
Microsoft DoubleSpace Setup

       Welcome to DoubleSpace Setup.

       The Setup program for DoubleSpace frees space on your hard
       disk by compressing the existing files on the disk. Setup
       also loads DBLSPACE.BIN, the portion of MS-DOS that provides
       access to DoubleSpace compressed drives. DBLSPACE.BIN
       requires about 40K of memory.

         o To set up DoubleSpace now, press ENTER.

         o To learn more about DoubleSpace Setup, press F1.

         o To quit Setup without installing DoubleSpace, press F3.

ENTER=Continue  F1=Help  F3=Exit
```

Figure 13.1

The DoubleSpace welcome screen.

3. The next screen you see (see fig. 13.2) is the DoubleSpace Setup screen. You can choose either `Express Setup` (DoubleSpace installs itself), or `Custom Setup` (you choose the way DoubleSpace installs). Unless you are a computer nerd, you should probably choose `Express Setup` by pressing the Enter key.

Figure 13.2

The DoubleSpace Setup screen.

```
Microsoft DoubleSpace Setup

        There are two ways to run Setup:

        Use Express Setup if you want DoubleSpace Setup to compress
        drive C and determine the compression settings for you. This
        is the easiest way to install DoubleSpace.

        Use Custom Setup if you are an experienced user and want to
        specify the compression settings and drive configuration
        yourself.

          Express Setup (recommended)
          Custom Setup

        To accept the selection, press ENTER.

        To change the selection, press the UP or DOWN ARROW key
        until the item you want is selected, and then press ENTER.

ENTER=Continue  F1=Help  F3=Exit
```

4. Just before DoubleSpace goes to work, you get one last chance to change your mind (see fig. 13.3). Press **C** to kick off the DoubleSpace installation.

Figure 13.3

Your last chance to stop before DoubleSpacing the hard disk.

```
Microsoft DoubleSpace Setup

        DoubleSpace is ready to compress drive C. This will take 16
        minutes.

        During this process, DoubleSpace will restart your computer
        to load DBLSPACE.BIN, the portion of MS-DOS that provides
        access to DoubleSpace compressed drives.


        To compress this drive, press C.
        To return to the previous screen, press ESC.



C=Continue  F1=Help  F3=Exit  ESC=Previous screen
```

You can uninstall DoubleSpace later if you want to. DoubleSpace is very reliable—don't worry about it losing files or messing up your computer in any way.

5. The first thing DoubleSpace does is perform some integrity checks on your hard disk and your computer's memory. Then it automatically restarts your computer!

6. After restarting your computer, DoubleSpace displays the screen shown in figure 13.4. The wide progess bar across the lower portion of the screen shows you how far this boring process has come.

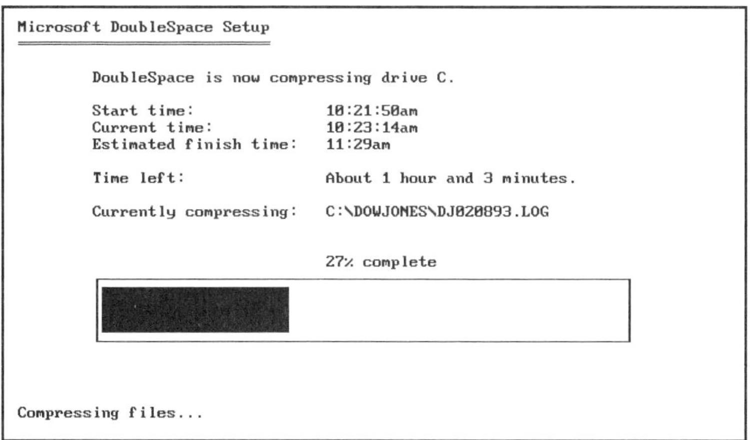
Microsoft DoubleSpace Setup
DoubleSpace is now compressing drive C.
Start time: 10:21:50am
Current time: 10:23:14am
Estimated finish time: 11:29am
Time left: About 1 hour and 3 minutes.
Currently compressing: C:\DOWJONES\DJ020893.LOG
27% complete
Compressing files...

Figure 13.4

The DoubleSpace progess display.

SAVE THE DAY!

Don't be impatient during this process. Start this boring process before you go to lunch, before you go out (wear your seatbelt!), or before going to bed. Be sure to hang a big sign on the monitor that says "DON'T YOU DARE TOUCH MY COMPUTER WHILE I'M GONE!" so that no one decides to play Wing Commander.

7. Finally, the DoubleSpace installation rewrites all the files to compress them and optimize your hard disk. This "optimizing" process (called *defragmenting*) makes the files on your hard disk easier for DOS to read. Later in this chapter, you'll learn all you need to know about the DEFRAG program.

That's it. When the DoubleSpace installation finishes, DoubleSpace displays the screen shown in figure 13.5. After you press Enter, your computer automatically restarts again. This time, DoubleSpace runs full force. When your computer is up and running, type **DIR** and admire your new, huge, hard disk.

Figure 13.5

The DoubleSpace wrap-up screen.

```
Microsoft DoubleSpace Setup

        DoubleSpace has finished compressing drive C.

            Free space before compression:    7.4 MB
            Free space after compression:    27.2 MB
            Compression ration:             1.8 to 1
            Total time to compress:         1 hour and 52 minutes

        DoubleSpace has created a new drive H that contains 2.0 MB
        of uncompressed space. This space has been set aside for
        files that must remain uncompressed.


        To exit from DoubleSpace and restart your computer, press
        ENTER.



ENTER=Continue  F1=Help
```

NERDY DETAILS

Your hard disk doesn't get bigger, of course. After your files are compressed some more room is made available on the hard disk. DoubleSpace calculates how well your files compressed, and then applies the same compression ratio to the free space left on your hard disk. When you type **DIR** to see how much disk space is available, DoubleSpace fools DOS into thinking that there's more space than there really is.

As you can see from figure 13.5, the free space on the hard disk went from a miserable 7.4M to 27.2M. The files on disk were compressed to 1/1.8 (about half) of their original size during this process, leaving quite a bit of room on the disk.

NERDY DETAILS

Later chapters discuss the need for an emergency start-up disk to get you up and running if something bad happens to your hard disk. When you put system files on the floppy disk with the **/S** option, the DOS 6 **FORMAT** command automatically puts the file that DoubleSpace needs to access your new magic disk onto the emergency start-up floppy disk. Without this file, you can't get your computer started after you've run DoubleSpace.

> If **FORMAT** can't find the DoubleSpace file (its name is **DBLSPACE.BIN**), it isn't written to the floppy disk. This means if you are using the floppy as an emergency start-up disk, you won't be able to access your DoubleSpace disk. Make sure you type **DIR** to see if **DBLSPACE.BIN** is on the disk. If it's not there, find it, and use the **COPY** command to put a copy of it on the floppy disk.

Another Word About Hard Disks

The hard disk lurking inside your computer's big box is very special. It's in there spinning about 3,600 times a minute (60 times a second!), holding zillions of little bits of love letters, dirty pictures, adventure games, and personal financial data (at least in my computer). All of this good stuff is seconds away from instant access any time you want it or need it. Try to do that with a file cabinet!

Hard disks are a lot more reliable than they used to be. They'll run zillions and zillions of hours without a problem...usually. Without much attention, hard disks deliver the goods. A little maintenance now and then, however, enhances your disk's performance and efficiency even more.

All hard disks follow a few basic rules:

 Hard disks are never big enough. No matter how big a disk you get, you will eventually outgrow it.

 All hard disks will fail someday. If you own the same PC long enough, this will happen. It will happen at the most inconvenient time, too.

 A lot of files on your hard disk are just taking up space. Everyone forgets to delete "temporary" files. For months and months after the event, for example, the party invitation you made with your drawing package will still be there, taking up space. This is the main reason hard disks are never big enough.

 You will lose things on your hard disk. Even if you are very careful, DOS or your programs will put files where you don't expect them.

There's no easy way to "look" at the files on your hard disk (remember, DIR can show you only one drawer in your DOS filing cabinet at a time unless you tell it to show you the contents of the whole disk by using the /S parameter), so it can be a tedious process to find a missing spreadsheet, letter, or drawing.

For all these reasons, please try to keep your disk clean and organized. Delete unnecessary files, or use the COPY and DEL commands (or the DOS 6 MOVE command) to move them onto floppy disks (be sure to label the floppy, remember!). You can always go to the store and buy a new box of floppy disks for a few bucks. It's not so easy, cheap, or smart to buy a bigger hard disk just to keep a bunch of useless files spinning around and around forever.

Puttin' the Pieces Together with DEFRAG

Every time you use your PC, an insiduous disease eats away at the files on your hard disk, making it work slower and slower as time goes by. DOS 6 provides a really neat program to stop this process.

STOP!

> Be forewarned; the following discussion is pretty nerdy. You might want to skip over it and go on to the next section on using **DEFRAG**!

All the files on a brand-new, freshly formatted, installed hard disk are *contiguous*; that is, each file is stored on the hard disk in one piece. As you use your hard disk—adding new files and directories, deleting files and directories, and moving stuff around—DOS tries desperately to use every bit of free space left on your hard disk.

When you delete a file, it leaves a file-sized "hole" of free space on the disk. The next time DOS needs to put a file on the disk, it uses that empty space, even if the space isn't big enough for the new file. If the new file won't fit in this "hole," DOS breaks the new file into pieces and puts the pieces wherever they will fit on the disk. If an existing file grows, such as when you add more pages to your great American novel, the file outgrows its old file space and gets broken into pieces.

Over time, lots of files on your hard disk are broken into pieces—your hard disk becomes *fragmented*. As your files become more fragmented, your hard disk goes nuts as it tries to find each little piece whenever DOS tells it to go get a file that happens to be badly fragmented. The result is that DOS takes longer and longer to find and read files. If you think your computer is getting slower, it may *not* be your imagination!

End of the nerdy stuff... Next, the solution!

Using DEFRAG To Glue Your Files Together

Humpty Dumpty would have loved DEFRAG because it puts all your files back together again! Here are the steps:

1. At the DOS prompt, type **DEFRAG**, and press Enter.
2. It'll take a while, but DEFRAG eventually displays the screen shown in figure 13.6.

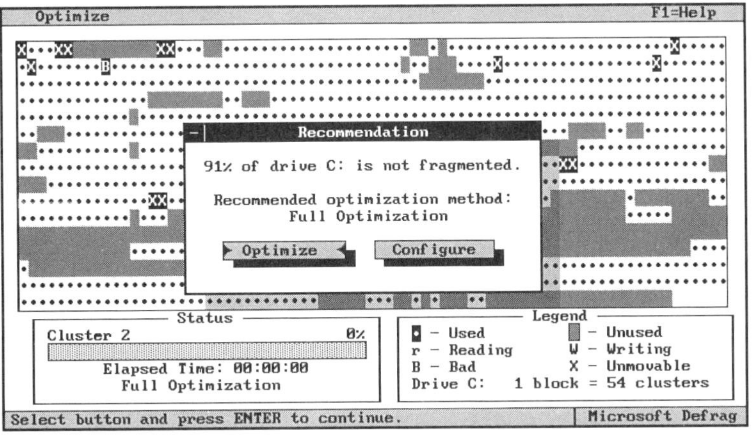

Figure 13.6

The DEFRAG start-up screen.

Look closely at the background in the figure. The white blocks with the black dots in the center indicate disk space occupied by files; darker gray areas are free space. As you can see, there are a lot more files than free space on this hard disk.

3. DEFRAG makes its recommendation to you on this screen. It's almost always best to accept DEFRAG's recommendation. Although it's not discussed in this book, you can change the optimization options (for instance, you can choose to just defragment files without moving them around to fill all the gaps between files on the disk).

4. To accept DEFRAG's recommendation, press Enter, and go away for a while. Figure 13.7 shows DEFRAG in action. The top half of the display (light gray) represents the part of the hard disk that is nicely organized. The chaotic jumble of file and free areas at the bottom of the display is the non-optimized part of the disk.

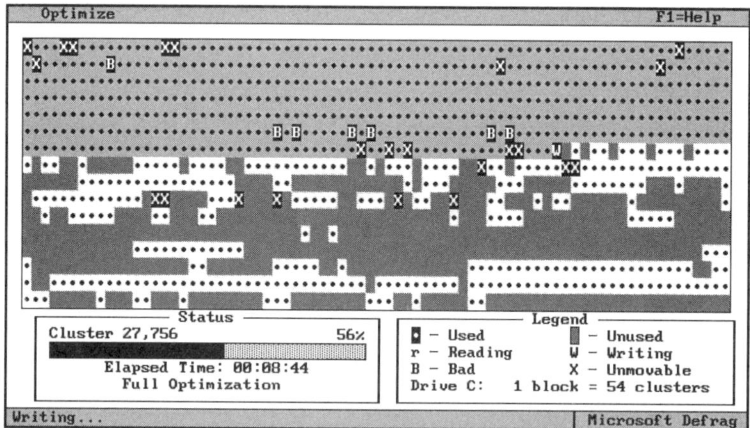

Figure 13.7

DEFRAG in action.

5. When DEFRAG is complete, the screen will look something like figure 13.8.

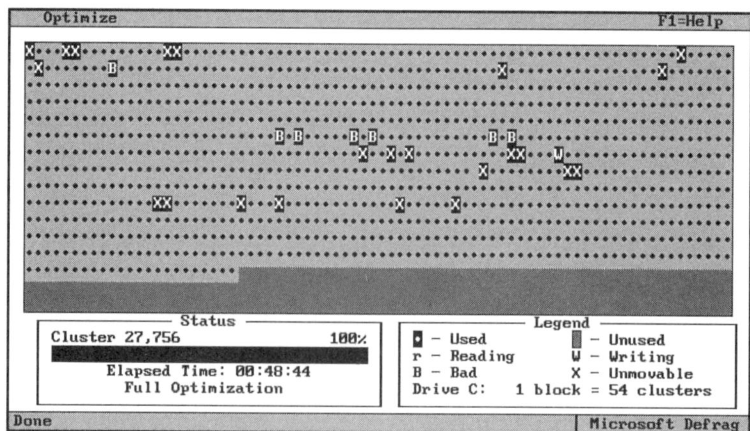

Figure 13.8

The completed DEFRAG session.

NERDY DETAILS

It's easy to overdo disk maintenance using **DEFRAG**. When you consider the amount of time required (more than an hour on a reasonably large hard disk), it's not something you want to do often. You probably only need to check the level of fragmentation on your hard disk once a month (just type **DEFRAG**, wait for the recommendation screen, then follow **DEFRAG**'s recommendation). You probably will need to defragment your hard drive only every three or four months.

That's all there is to defragmentation. When you keep your disk nicely organized and defragmented, the reward is better performance and efficiency. You won't have to wait quite as long for your big spreadsheets and document files to load from a well-maintained hard disk.

PART 4

What To Do When Something Doesn't Work Right

Things That Make You Go "Oops!"

A lot of people think of their computers as being pretty unreliable creatures. It seems as if there's always something going wrong: printer paper jams, lost or missing files, or something weird appearing on the screen.

This chapter will help you with:

- Easy-to-fix problems with printers
- Clearing up flaky file and floppy disk mysteries
- The computer not starting
- Things that go wrong with keyboards

SAVE THE DAY!

> You probably aren't reading this unless there's a problem with your computer. So I'm assuming that you are sitting in front of your computer. You're probably angry at the dumb thing (computer, printer, monitor, whatever) and are frustrated that you can't seem to make it work.
>
> Remain calm and work through the problem methodically; it broke, that's all. It's just plain unfortunate that the printer quit working just when you need it most, or the floppy disk with the only copy of the monthly report won't work. Remember, it's just Murphy's law of computing at work and, since Murphy's law has been built into every computer ever produced, there's nothing we can do about it.
>
> We can, however, fix your computer. Read on!

How To Use This and the Next Two Chapters

This chapter presents "medicine-cabinet first aid" for your computer. These are all things you don't have to go fetch the local nerd for. You won't need any tools, training, or assistance to perform the troubleshooting steps described in this chapter.

If you encounter an error message or a problem (suppose that your printer's not working, for example), start here for the most common problems and their solutions. If the things suggested in this chapter don't help, go on to Chapter 15, then to Chapter 16.

I hope you can fix things right here in good ol' Chapter 14. When you get to Chapter 15, you might actually have to open the computer's big box and check something inside. If you get to Chapter 16, you're probably in for some repair work because the problems there are mostly hard-core failures of your computer system or its components (dum da dum dum).

The Basic Rules

Boo-boos happen all the time. There's no sense in paying for help when some really trivial thing has you held up. Think of all the components of your computer as "appliances." If you think of your monitor or printer as an exotic toaster, it's a lot less intimidating, don't you think? Like appliance problems, computer problems often have simple solutions, like these:

Make sure it's plugged in. Whatever the problem is, make sure the piece of computer equipment is plugged into a "live" electrical outlet or adapter source.

Many "power strips" or "surge protectors" that allow you to plug many things into one wall receptacle have switches on them so you can turn off all of the things plugged into the power strip with one switch. If your printer is plugged into a power strip or surge protector, make sure that its switch is in the "On" position.

Make sure it's turned on. Somewhere on the printer, monitor, CD-ROM drive, or modem, will be a power switch. Make sure it's turned on. If the appliance has a pilot light, make sure the light comes on.

Make sure it's connected. A lot of computer appliances have more than one wire coming out of them. Most often, one of the wires carries information between the computer's big box and the appliance. The connections should be tight (usually the wire connections push into a socket on the back side of the appliance). Also, if there was a cable or wire there the last time you used the thing, and today the wire or cable isn't there, find out who took it.

You should always perform these basic checks before you get upset or pick up the phone and call somebody.

Each computer appliance has specific ways that it can fail. The following sections discuss the most common problems you'll encounter while working with computers.

Printer Won't Print

I'm starting with printer problems because they are very, very common. There are also a lot of different things that can go wrong with printers.

Everyone encounters really annoying problems trying to get things printed from time to time. Yesterday the darn thing worked fine. Today one of the following is happening (or rather, isn't happening):

- Nothing happens when you tell your application to print something.
- You get a strange error message on the screen; something about `Write fault error writing device LPT1`. What is that supposed to mean?
- The printer is obviously trying to print something, but the paper isn't coming out.
- The printer goes through all of its usual conniption fits, but there's nothing printed on the paper when it comes out.

What Causes Problems with Printers

After checking all of these things, proceed with the printer-specific checks described here. These are the easy-to-fix things that can go wrong with printers:

- The printer is not "On Line." Somewhere on the printer, there are one or more switches or buttons. Most often, each button or switch will have a little light next to it to tell you whether the button or switch is "active." The button or switch you're looking for is labeled "On Line" (on some printers this one may be labeled "Select"). Make sure the "On Line" (or "Select") switch or button is lit.

> If for some reason you can't make the On Line light go on, it implies there is some kind of electrical problem (like the printer isn't plugged into a working receptacle) or connection problem. Or, there may not be any paper in the printer.

- The printer is experiencing one of the following: Out of toner (laser printers), out of ink (inkjet printers), or the ribbon is jammed, missing, shredded, or otherwise damaged (dot-matrix printers):

- Make sure there's paper in the printer.

Make sure the paper isn't jammed.

Make sure the ribbon isn't jammed (dot-matrix), the toner cartridge is fresh (laser), or the inkjet cartridge has been recently replaced (inkjet printer).

If you're not sure of the definition of terms like *dot matrix* and *laser*, see Chapter 10 for explanations.

If you get an `Abort, Retry, Fail?` message when you try to print something, the printer may simply be off-line. Make sure it's on-line, then press **R** (for Retry). If you still get this message, something else is the matter.

Flaky File Foul-ups

There are a lot of bad things you can do to the files on your disk. You can delete 'em by accident, or copy over them with another file. It's also easy to just plain lose a file on the disk somewhere. Here are some solutions:

Oh, no! I just deleted a good file: Even without DOS 6's deletion protection, with DOS 5 or 6 you can use `UNDELETE` to try and recover a deleted file. The basic rule about undeleting a file is this: the sooner you try `UNDELETE`, the better your chances of recovering the lost file.

Everybody accidentally deletes a file now and then. If you've got the DOS 6 undelete protections turned on (either Delete Tracker or Delete Sentry, both described in Chapter 7), it's relatively simple to get back your deleted file. Go back to Chapter 7 for instructions on how to use the DOS 6 undelete protection.

I accidentally copied over a file: This happens when you've got a "work in progress." Here's a true-life scenario. You're working on a big report for the boss. You've been making changes all day, and you want to compare the changes you've made to the copy you put on a floppy disk yesterday. So, you do a simple copy from the floppy disk:

```
COPY A:\REPORT.DOC C:\REPORTS
```

The problem (and it's a BIG problem) is that you've just copied the *old* report over the top of the *new* report (I'm assuming the new report that you've been working on is in the C:\REPORTS directory).

Sorry, you can't get back the new report file. Once you copy over a file with another file, you can't get it back. DOS will put the copy into exactly the same disk location as the original, and you can't uncopy something.

> One of the most annoying and dangerous things about the DOS **COPY** command is that it doesn't warn you when you're about to copy a file onto a disk or directory that already contains a file of the same name. Be careful when using **COPY** to make sure you're not about to bash something valuable.

I can't find that darn file: This happens to most people from time to time. Way back in Chapter 3, we talked about how to find files with the DIR command. It's easy, and deserves repeating here:

1. Move to the root directory: **CD **
2. Do a DIR with the /S parameter:

   ```
   DIR /S REPORT.DOC
   ```

3. DOS obediently searches through all of the DOS filing drawers on your disk, and finally comes back with the name of the directory containing the missing file.

If you've forgotten the name of your file, use the * or ? wild cards in the file name with DIR /S, or move to the root directory and do the DIR command this way:

```
DIR /S /P /O-D
```

This will list *all* of the files on your disk, sorting them by date (newest at the top of the list), and pausing at every screenful of stuff. Hopefully, you'll be able to pick your file out of the mess.

If you've just lost a file because you didn't put a label on the floppy disk holding the file, shame on you! You should know better. Your only recourse is to do the `DIR` command on each and every one of your unlabeled floppy disks, like this:

```
DIR /S /P /O-D A:\
```

This assumes that you're searching disks in your A drive. Substitute `B:\` for `A:\` in the preceding statement if you're looking in your B drive.

- **Oh no! I just formatted a good disk:** This is a bit more serious than these other things. Go on to Chapter 16.

- **I just got a `Path not found` error message when I tried to open a document in my word processor:** This error will happen if you try to open a file in a directory that doesn't exist. For instance, maybe you directed Microsoft Word to open the file named `REPORT.DOC` in the directory named `REPORT`. Unless there is a directory named `REPORT`, you'll get this error message.

  The exact error you get may not be worded exactly `Path not found`. The key word of the error message is `Path`, in conjunction with a phrase implying that the path to the file is invalid or doesn't exist.

- **What's this `File creation error`?** You've just tried to create a file that has the same name as a directory. DOS won't let you do this!

- **When I tried to copy a file, DOS told me `File cannot be copied onto itself`:** This is easy. You meant to type:

  ```
  COPY MYFILE.DOC C:\REPORTS
  ```

  You left out the `C:\REPORTS` part. Unless you specify a *path* to put the results of the `COPY` command, DOS assumes that you want to make the copy in the drawer you've got open. Oddly enough, DOS won't let you copy over a file with itself, but it will let you copy over a file with another file.

- **I got an `Access denied` error message when I tried to delete a file:** This is a somewhat more complex issue and is discussed in Chapter 15.

How To Keep This File Stuff from Happening in the Future

Here's what you can do to protect yourself from problems like these in the future:

- Use the DOS 6 undelete protection. After reading Chapter 7, install either Delete Tracker or Tracker's big brother, Delete Sentry.

- Before you copy old stuff off of a floppy disk, make sure that the directory where you're putting it doesn't have something in it that will get bashed. Do a `DIR` on the floppy, then a `DIR` on the directory where it's going, and try to see where problems might arise.

  Or create a brand-new temporary directory, and put the stuff from the floppy disk there while you're working:

  ```
  MD C:\REPORTS\TEMP

  COPY A:\REPORT.DOC C:\REPORTS\TEMP
  ```

  That way, anything in the `C:\REPORTS` directory can't be overwritten by the file off of the A drive.

- It's been said before, but it bears repeating. Always label your floppy disks so you know what's on them before you reformat or copy over something that's on the disk!

Chapter 13 tells you how to *write-protect* floppies. When you've put something particularly valuable on a floppy disk, you write-protect the disk. This will prevent you from accidentally formatting the disk or deleting the files on the floppy.

The Trials and Tribulations of Floppy Disks

You'll probably use floppy disks a lot as you work with your computer. Floppies are very useful for:

1. Making backup copies of your work.
2. Sharing files with other people.
3. Making room on your hard disk by moving files onto floppies.

Floppies can also be the source of a lot of different minor problems.

Following a few simple rules will save you from most problems people encounter with their disks. Here are the basic rules for using floppy disks:

- Only one floppy disk can go into the slot at a time. Although this is obvious to most people, I've known wet-behind-the-ear users to shove two or even three disks into the slot (this can only happen on 5 1/4-inch disk drives because the 3 1/2-inch disk slot will only take one disk at a time).
- The floppy must go in the disk-drive slot, not in the crack between the floppy disk drives on your computer.
- Keep magnetic stuff away from your floppy disks! Watch out for magnetic paper clip holders and magnetized clips. Don't stick your emergency start-up disk to a filing cabinet with a magnet!
- Keep the paper jackets on your 5 1/4-inch floppy disks while you're not using them. If you've lost a jacket or two, go ahead and double up by putting two floppy disks in one jacket. It's better than no paper jacket at all.
- Don't touch the magnetic part of the disk that shows through the oval hole (5 1/4-inch), or that you can see by sliding the metal door to one side (3 1/2-inch). The disks can be damaged by even the tiniest amount of dust or goober you might have on your finger.
- Always, always label your disks so you don't mix 'em up. Do a `DIR` on a floppy before you format it to make sure there's nothing valuable on it.
- Treat your floppies as if they were a sentimentally valuable photograph: don't bend 'em, punch holes in 'em, spill stuff on 'em, or treat 'em like an inflatable party doll.

If, with a floppy disk inserted, DOS complains when you try to access a file on the disk, (or copy or save a new file to the disk). one of the following is likely to be the culprit:

- The disk may not be formatted. Do a simple `DIR` on the disk (**`DIR A:`** or **`DIR B:`**) to see what DOS reports. If you see a `General failure` error message, try formatting the disk. (See Chapter 13 to learn all about formatting floppy disks.)

- The disk may be full. Do a **`DIR A:`** or **`DIR B:`** of the floppy, and see how many *bytes free* DOS says there are on the disk. Do a `DIR` of the file(s) you want to put on the disk, and see if they'll fit on the disk.

- Make sure that the disk isn't in the drive upside down or backwards (this is only possible with 5 1/4-inch disks). Of course, the label of the disk faces up and toward you when you insert it into the disk drive.

- The floppy disk may be *write-protected*. See Chapter 13 for a description of floppy disk write-protection.

  If the floppy is write-protected, there may be a good reason why someone has gone to all this trouble. Be sure there's nothing worthwhile on the floppy disk before removing the write-protection.

- You may have exceeded the maximum number of files for the floppy disk's `root` directory (unless you use the `CD` command to change to another directory on the floppy disk, you're working in the `root` directory). You can only put 224 files into the `root` directory on 1.44M (3 1/2-inch) and 1.2M floppy disks (5 1/4-inch), no matter how small the files are. The disk might have a lot of room left over; it's just that you can't stuff any more files into the `root` directory. Older floppy disks are even worse: the old 360K disks can only hold 112 files in the `root` directory.

  The solution is simple. You can create directories on floppy disks just as you can on a hard disk. Go back to Chapter 2 to read all about the `MD` (Make Directory or Make Drawer) command. If you decide to use directories on your floppy disks, remember that you have to include the floppy directory name any time you want to use the files you put in it (Chapters 2 and 3 tell you a lot about using directories and finding the files you've put into them).

When there's some kind of screw-up when you try to use a floppy disk, the error message you get from DOS may help you understand what the problem is. For example, `Insufficient disk space` should clue you in to the possibility that the floppy disk is too full to hold your file.

Unfortunately, the `General failure reading drive A:` error message doesn't tell you much. If a `DIR` also fails on the disk, try the disk in another computer, if there's one around. If it still doesn't work, your only choice is to format the disk (either it wasn't formatted or something bad happened to the disk).

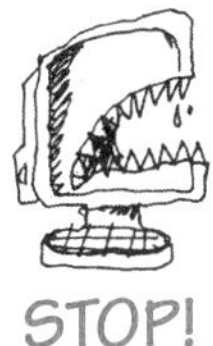

> If you ever format a disk and DOS reports a number of **bad sectors** (you DO read error messages coming from DOS, don't you?) you should check that you aren't formatting a low-density disk as high-density (see Chapter 13). If you aren't, you should probably throw the disk away. Bad sectors are often a sign of a damaged or marginally acceptable disk.
>
> Floppy disks are incredibly cheap compared to the amount of hard work that can be lost to a flaky floppy. The discussions in the next section often suggest you throw away problem-causing floppy disks. Remember, it's cheap insurance NOT to use marginal floppies.

Dumb Disk Drives

Closely related to flaky floppy foul-ups are dumb disk drive disasters. Now and then, you'll try to do something that seems perfectly natural, and DOS barks back at you with some obscure error message you've never seen before.

DOS gave me a `Not ready reading drive A – Abort, Retry, Fail?` error. I put the disk in—what's wrong now?: This is easy to fix. You forgot to pull the latch down over the disk (on 5 1/4-inch disk drives) or you haven't pushed the floppy disk in all the way (3 1/2-inch floppy drives). Fix the problem, and press **R** to retry. If that doesn't work, see the following `Abort, Retry, Fail, Ignore?` discussion.

It's also possible that you've got the floppy disk in upside down!

I get a `Write protect error` when I try to copy a file to my floppy disk: This almost always means someone has write-protected the floppy disk you're using.

What next? DOS tells me the floppy disk I'm trying to format is `Invalid media or track 0 bad`: There are a couple of reasons you might get this message. One is that you are trying to format a low-capacity floppy disk in a high-capacity disk drive. For instance, you've stuck a 720K disk (only one square hole) in a 1.44M drive (the floppy should have two square holes), and asked DOS to format it. By default, DOS will try to format the disk to the maximum capacity the drive is capable of. DOS complains when it finds out it's actually a 720K floppy.

Of course, if you really have to format a 720K floppy in a 1.44M drive (or a 360K in a 1.2M drive), go back to Chapter 13 to find out how to do it.

The second reason might be that the disk may have been formatted to use on a Macintosh computer (this applies only to 3 1/2-inch floppy disks). Most of the time there's no problem formatting a Mac disk in your PC's 3 1/2-inch floppy drive. From time to time, however, even when you do everything right, you can't change a floppy disk from being a Macintosh to DOS disk just by formatting it.

Shoot! What the heck does `General failure reading (or writing) drive A: (or B:)` mean? Usually this just means that the floppy in drive B isn't formatted yet (see Chapter 13 for formatting instructions).

This is a bad, bad message if you're sure the disk is formatted and has some valuable files on it. You may have exposed the disk to a magnetic field, a virus has attacked it, or some other bad thing has happened to damage the delicate magnetic surface on the disk. You might try the disk in another computer; if you get the same result, the disk is almost certainly ruined. Go ahead and see if you can format it. If you can't even format it (you'll see the Invalid media message), throw it away, or use it for a hot drink coaster or something.

What is `Abort, Retry, Fail, Ignore?`: This annoying message means that DOS has encountered some kind of problem reading or writing stuff to your floppy disk, and DOS wants you to tell it what to do about the problem.

You may have put a 1.2M disk into a 360K disk drive or a 1.44M disk into a 720K drive. These low-capacity drives just can't read high-capacity floppy disks.

The file you're trying to copy may be damaged somehow. Tell DOS to Retry by pressing **R**. The drive might go "waaagh waagh waaggghh" a couple of times and you'll get this message back again. If the file is important to you, press **I** to tell DOS to Ignore the problem, and it'll jump over the bad spot on the disk.

If you end up having to do the Ignore bit, you may not be able to use the file you're copying because DOS didn't copy the bad spot in the file.

Okay, so neither Retry nor Ignore worked, so do an Abort by pressing **A**. DOS will just pretend you never tried to access the floppy disk. You can either try your copy, write again, or throw the disk away.

SAVE THE DAY!

Okay, so I lied again, sort of. If you get a lot of `Abort, Retry, Fail, Ignore?` *messages (or messages like this one), you may be heading for trouble with your disk drive. Write down the message so you won't forget it when you call the repair shop. The exact wording of the error message might be helpful to the repair nerds when you take your computer in for fixing.*

You can try the Fail option any time you want. What this means is that you're telling DOS to forget the whole thing. It's as if you never typed in the command in the first place (sort of like "Never mind!"). You might get a weird message from DOS like `Fail on INT 24`, but you can ignore it.

TRICKS

If you are sure the disk is the right size for the disk drive, the disk is inserted fully into the drive, the latch is pulled down (5 1/4-inch drives), and you get an `Abort, Retry, Fail, Ignore?` *message, it's a good sign that the disk can't be trusted. You're better off throwing the floppy disk away as soon as possible, rather than risk losing a valuable file.*

`Bad sector reading drive A:` This is a good one. It means that the floppy disk can't be trusted. Try `DIR`, `COPY`, or whatever it is that you were doing, then throw the disk away.

You may also get an `Abort, Retry, Fail?` message when you try to print something. See the section on printing problems earlier in this chapter.

What To Do When Your Monitor or Computer Won't Come On

There's not much to keeping a monitor or big box running. Because there are so few moving parts, they're normally about as reliable as a TV set or table radio. If the darn thing just won't come on, it's almost surely a problem with electrical power from the wall outlet. Check the connections between the box and the wall just to be sure.

Almost all problems with monitors and the big box (outside of really big failures that require professional help) can be fixed by the simple instructions given earlier in this chapter. If these things don't fix the problem, you've got more trouble than can be handled at home.

Crummy Keyboard Capers

Keyboards are a *lot* more reliable than they used to be. But, from time to time, like everything else plugged into your computer, bad things will happen:

Nothing happens when you type on the keyboard: Make sure that the keyboard cable is plugged into the computer. Most keyboard cables plug pretty tightly into the back of the computer. But some keyboard plugs don't stick quite so well and can wiggle out.

If your computer has a keylock mechanism on the front, make sure that the key switch is turned on. All the lock does is disable the keyboard; it's not really locking up the computer.

NERDY DETAILS

A funny story was told to me by the New Rider's Publishing staff while I was writing this book: "When my son was 5, I gave him a dead keyboard to play with. He used the cable as a leash and took it for a walk like a dog. There were keycaps all over the driveway!"

One or more keys don't work at all, or work only sometimes: Your keyboard is probably on the way out. Most keyboards, after all, contain more than 100 mechanical switches. Any one of those switches can fail at almost any time at all. It's probably time to replace the keyboard.

TRICKS

You might want to clean out the most obvious dirt and crumbs that have fallen into the keyboard. Turn it upside down and shake it. If you've got a "real" vaccuum cleaner, put the nozzle right down on the keys and try to vaccuum out the stuff that's between the keys.

My keyboard has gone wacko! Everytime I type "M," I get a carriage return instead (or anything else unexpected): This pertains only to "programmable" keyboards such as those that come on Gateway computers (you can tell if there's a key labeled "program" or "macro" or something like that). You may have accidentally hit the macro key and reprogrammed the M key (or any other key) to substitute for the Enter key (or any other key or combination of keys).

You'll have to dig out your owner's manual to find out how to return your keyboard to its "default" state. On some keyboards, it's not enough to just turn the computer off and on again, or to unplug the keyboard. These "special" keyboards remember how they were last programmed, and you can't unprogram them by unplugging them.

Another strange thing that can cause a problem like this is if the Ctrl key is stuck down. Your computer reads all kinds of different things when the Ctrl key is held down and other keys are pressed. Any time your keyboard goes a little nuts, be sure the Ctrl (and Alt, Caps Lock, and so on) aren't stuck down. There might be a piece of an old M&M down in there!

I get a `KB/Interface` error when I start my computer and the keyboard doesn't seem to work: You may have recently replaced your keyboard with the keyboard off of an old IBM-PC, IBM-XT, or clone. The old PC/XT type of keyboards just doesn't work on newer computers. This is especially likely if you've only got 10 function keys, and they are arranged down the left side of the keyboard (see Chapter 11 to learn more about keyboards).

If your keyboard is a "modern" 101-key type (it has 12 function keys arrayed across the top, and you get some kind of "keyboard" error when your computer starts up (that's what the `KB` in `KB/Interface` error stands for), someone may have switched the functioning of your keyboard from "AT" to "XT". Turn the keyboard over and look for some kind of switch (it may be hidden under a cover or hiding in a recess in the bottom of the keyboard). Not all keyboards have this switch, so if you don't find one, there probably isn't one! Some label or other indicator should tell you that when the switch is in one position, the keyboard is an "XT" keyboard; while in the other, the keyboard is an "AT" keyboard. Make sure it's in the AT position.

Kinda Serious Things That Can Happen

You know how problems are. They just get worse—after the easy kind come those that require a little more work to fix and cause a little more anxiety when they occur. You might have to find and edit a file, for example, or open your computer's cabinet to fix something. This chapter covers some of these common problems:

- Bad things that happen to good computers
- What to do when your video goes wacko
- Petulant printers
- Computers that can't wake up
- Flaky files
- Jump-starting your computer's battery

All of these dilemmas can be solved by non-nerds. For the most part, these are just common-sense fiddles and twiddles to get your computer working again, or at least help you figure out what to tell the computer doctor when you take your sick machine to the hospital.

So, when one of the things discussed in this chapter happens to your computer or its equipment, go ahead and get the "oh-ohs" out of the way, 'cause you've got work to do!

What Could Go Wrong

As Murphy's Law suggests, your computer will always work perfectly until the time that you need it the most. For example:

-  Yesterday you printed a 150-page summary report without a squawk. Today the printer won't even spit out a simple two-page memo.
-  Your monitor won't come on at all after lunch, but you used it all morning without a flicker.
-  You can't load the spreadsheet that contains your household budget, but the darn thing worked fine last week when you made changes to it.

These are the kinds of things that can drive people absolutely nuts.

As always, when you've got a problem with your computer, you should always check the simpler stuff described in Chapter 14 before beginning something that requires a lot more work. 'Nuff said.

Your Monitor Goes Wacko

Video problems don't happen all that often. In general, the monitor and its adapter card are very reliable components of your computer system and rarely cause problems. But, let's say the screen has suddenly gone blank, changed color, or the picture is wiggling. Before you totally freak out, try the following:

-  **Stupid Rule #1 as always.** Make sure it's turned on and plugged in. Better you discover this and save yourself the embarrassment when you call a nerd for help.
-  **The screen appears overly dark or blank.** Make sure the brightness and contrast controls aren't turned all the way down. Brightness is often marked with a little sun, contrasted with a half dark/half light circle.

The screen suddenly goes blank, fades out, or begins to display fireworks or other strange things. Make sure it's not just a screen saver in operation. Press any key (such as the Shift key or spacebar) to see if the picture pops back on the screen.

NERDY DETAILS

Screen savers make the screen blank or display some sort of constantly changing image if you haven't pressed any keys for a while. So, if you go away for a few minutes to get coffee, you may come back to a blank screen. If your screen saver becomes an annoyance, find out from someone how to adjust the length of time before it kicks in.

The screen is displaying only red or blue or green. Check both ends of the cable connecting the monitor to the computer—it might be loose or only partially plugged in. Most cable connectors have little screws—be sure they're nice and snug.

There's an annoying "flicker" or "waver" to the screen. If possible, try turning off the fluorescent lights in your office. A lot of computer screens operate at nearly the same *frequency* (now there's a nerdy word!) as fluorescent lights. All computer monitors waver a little bit. (The better the monitor, the less waver.) When the wiggles on your screen coincide with the wabbles from fluorescent lights (all fluorescent lights waver, too!), the result can be nearly stroboscopic. You might think you've slipped into a time warp and landed in a 1970s disco bar.

Screen quivers can also happen if you're too close to another screen (the wiggles and wabbles apparently can float through the air from monitor to monitor!) or by being too close to a power supply. Maybe you're screen is too close to another PC or awkwardly placed so that a wiggle—prone part of the monitor is too close to the power supply (it's a part down inside the PC's big box) in your PC.

NERDY DETAILS

Good, high-quality (and high-priced) computer monitors are *non-interlaced*. They paint the whole screen in one pass. Lesser-quality (*interlaced*) monitors paint half of the screen in each of two passes, causing a noticeable flicker to the screen picture.

continues

continued

If you determine that you are sensitive to the flicker of an *interlaced* screen, you should get a good quality *non-interlaced* monitor. Also, a high *refresh rate* (72Hz is better than 60Hz) reduces flicker.

The picture on the screen is too small! Most monitors have knobs to adjust the horizontal and vertical size of the picture, much like adjustments on your TV set. Look for these knobs and experiment with them.

Printer Doesn't Print Anymore

After you've read about checking the wires, paper, ribbon/ink/toner, and so on (see Chapter 14), and the thing still won't print, try some of these remedies:

Make sure the ribbon, toner cartridge, or inkjet cartridge is full. This is Chapter 14 stuff, but you should check it to be sure!

Make sure the paper isn't jammed. If this is a laser printer, you may have to open the printer up and look inside. The difficult thing here is usually *finding* the button or latch or lever that opens the printer. Most of the time it doesn't even look like a button, latch, or lever. Experiment a little bit and see if you can open the printer.

A lot of laser printers open up like giant clam shells. Open up that clam and look inside. Do you see a piece of paper obviously stuck in the printer's innards? If you do, just grab hold of the paper and gently pull it out of the printer.

One of the dangers involved with laser printers is that they use heat (a *lot* of heat) to fuse the toner to the paper. Somewhere inside the laser printer is a very, very hot *fusing roller*—don't touch it! (The hot fusing roller is why the paper just coming out of a laser printer or photocopier sometimes feels warm!)

Normally, the hot roller will be shielded one way or another to keep you from accidentally touching it. But, since the interiors of laser printers are normally the domain of nerds, the danger from the hot roller may not be obvious to the unwary normal person.

If you replaced the inkjet or toner cartridge, did you put it in correctly? (Just to be safe, you *might* consider reading the instructions.)

NERDY DETAILS

Most laser printer toner cartridges and inkjet cartridges have a strip of tape or a plastic shield over the place where the toner or ink comes out of the cartridge. If you have just installed a new toner cartridge or inkjet cartridge, and nothing prints on the paper even though the printer seems to be working, make sure you've removed the plastic tape or shield. Read the instructions that came with the new cartridge!

Your laser printer is printing unevenly across the page. Take out the cartridge and shake, rock, and roll it from side to side. What you're trying to do is get the fine toner powder evenly redistributed around the cartridge.

Computer Won't Come On

Before we talk about what can go wrong with starting your computer, let's review the steps that your computer goes through as it starts:

1. The power comes on when you throw the switch.
2. The pilot lights come on, you hear the fan start, and possibly hear the disk drive start up.
3. DOS starts up.
4. DOS reads the `CONFIG.SYS` and `AUTOEXEC.BAT` files and then presents you with the `C:\>` prompt (or something similar).

During this start-up sequence, the only time you see anything on the screen is when DOS is reading the `CONFIG.SYS` and `AUTOEXEC.BAT` files. All of the other steps are done invisibly. Each of these four steps is a potential source of failure. As you learned in Chapter 14, the most common failures are, fortunately, the easiest to rectify, as well.

Okay, so you turn the big box on and nothing happens—no lights, no hum, no nuttin'. Your computer is obviously not following the four steps to computing nirvana outlined a few paragraphs ago. Or maybe the lights work, but it never really starts up. Look through the following descriptions to see which comes closest to your particular situation:

Absolutely nothing happens. It's gonzo. Assuming you checked everything included in Chapter 14, this is not good news. If you're sure there's power from the wall receptacle, the power strip (if there is one) is turned on, the switch is on, but you just don't hear or see anything, skip on through to Chapter 16. You've got more than just a simple problem.

You get lights, you hear a hum or fan noise from inside, but the screen's still blank. The reset button on the front of your computer might be stuck. Try snapping it a couple of times to make sure it bounces in and out like it's supposed to. Check the monitor, too.

You get a `Bad or missing Command Interpreter` error message: Oops. Something happened to the very important file named COMMAND.COM. It might have been just a software error, so first try restarting the computer (hold down the Alt, Ctrl, and Del keys all at the same time for a second, or turn the power off, wait ten seconds, and turn it on).

If that doesn't work, take out your emergency start-up disk (see Chapter 4 and the later section in this chapter "Using the Emergency Start-Up Disk"), put it in drive A, and restart the computer.

When the computer starts, it should use the files you put on the emergency start-up disk to get going again. When the computer is going well, use the COPY command to put a fresh copy of COMMAND.COM onto your C drive. Type:

```
COPY A:COMMAND.COM C:\
```

Press Enter. This only works if something happened that bashed the COMMAND.COM file on your C drive. If something else bad happened, you still might see the `Bad or missing Command Interpreter` message. You also might have to copy the COMMAND.COM file to another location, such as your DOS directory, or edit your start-up files, as shown in the Nerdy Detail that follows.

NERDY DETAILS

There's probably a line in your **AUTOEXEC.BAT** file that looks a bit like this:

```
SET COMSPEC=C:\COMMAND.COM
```

There should also be a line in your **CONFIG.SYS** file that looks something like this:

```
SHELL=C:\DOS\COMMAND.COM C:\DOS\ /e:384 /p
```

These lines tell DOS where to find the all-important **COMMAND.COM** file. If **COMMAND.COM** is not *exactly* where these lines say it should be, you may see that pesky **Bad or missing Command Interpreter** error.

To fix the problem, you'll have to put on your horn-rimmed glasses and pocket protector here because this is a fairly nerdy operation. Got 'em?

Check the contents of your AUTOEXEC.BAT or CONFIG.SYS start-up files by typing **TYPE AUTOEXEC.BAT** (press Enter) and **TYPE CONFIG.SYS** (and press Enter again) to see if they contain those lines. Then use the **DIR** command to make sure the **COMMAND.COM** file is where these lines say it is.

The directories in each of these lines should agree, of course. If one says **C:\DOS**, the other should as well. You can use the **EDIT** command to change these lines so that they agree. You might as well have these lines just say **C:\DOS**:

```
SET COMSPEC=C:\DOS\COMMAND.COM
```

and

```
SHELL=C:\DOS\COMMAND.COM C:\ /e:384 /p
```

COMMAND.COM must be in the **DOS (C:\DOS)** directory anyway or your computer might not start up properly. The DOS installation program automatically puts a copy of **COMMAND.COM** in the **C:\DOS** directory, so these lines will almost always work.

Your computer won't start right after you made a change to CONFIG.SYS or AUTOEXEC.BAT: OK, you've just installed a scanner on your computer and (carefully following the instructions that came with the scanner) you've made a couple of changes to CONFIG.SYS. Now the doggone thing won't start! Jeez! To get started again, see Chapter 4 and the next section in this chapter called "Using the Emergency Start-Up Disk."

How To Do an Emergency Start-Up

You need an emergency start-up disk to attempt many of the remedies described in this chapter. Some of these fixes require you to make changes to your AUTOEXEC.BAT and CONFIG.SYS files, and it can make your computer pretty hard to restart if you do something wrong. Chapter 4 describes the process of creating this disk.

If you are a DOS 6 user, you can bypass both CONFIG.SYS and AUTOEXEC.BAT if you make a mistake editing either of these files (see the next few sections in this chapter). If you're a DOS 5 or earlier user, go on ahead to "Using the Emergency Start-Up Disk."

Instantly Bypassing Sick CONFIG.SYS and AUTOEXEC.BAT Files

DOS 6 gives you a really cool way to get past errors in both CONFIG.SYS and AUTOEXEC.BAT. As soon as you see the `Starting MS-DOS...` message on the screen, press the F5 key. Press it twice to be sure DOS saw it, then sit and wait. It should only take a few seconds until you see a second message that reads `MS-DOS is bypassing your CONFIG.SYS and AUTOEXEC.BAT files.` and you'll get a very simple `C:\>` prompt.

Before you get all carried away, remember that your computer is not ready for use. Even though it looks like a duck and quacks like a duck, you don't have a duck yet. You've bypassed all of the normal start-up stuff, so DOS won't even be able to find most of your programs.

What you have to do now is repair the damaged CONFIG.SYS and AUTOEXEC.BAT files. Use the EDIT command to look at these files and make changes (type in **EDIT CONFIG.SYS** or **EDIT AUTOEXEC.BAT**, and press Enter). Once EDIT has your file on the screen (you can only work with one at a time, of course), recheck the changes you made to them.

If something has happened to really bong up your start-up files, you might have to replace the bonged-up ones with good copies from somewhere else. You should have made backups of these files before you made changes to them; use the COPY command to restore the backup copies (from floppies, or from the hard disk) with **COPY CONFIG.SAV CONFIG.SYS** and **COPY AUTOEXEC.SAV AUTOEXEC.BAT**—assuming you named each of your backups with a SAV last name.

As a last resort, copy the CONFIG.SYS and AUTOEXEC.BAT files from your emergency start-up disk:

```
COPY A:CONFIG.SYS C:\
COPY A:AUTOEXEC.BAT C:\
```

Unless you are very good about keeping these important files updated on your emergency start-up disk, though, it's possible that the ones on the start-up disk are outdated. But try anyway.

NERDY DETAILS

> If you've run MemMaker (described in Chapter 12) or made other changes since the last time you updated the CONFIG.SYS and AUTOEXEC.BAT files on your emergency start-up disk, you'll have to redo these steps after you copy the files from the start-up disk. Go back to Chapter 12 to learn about MemMaker. It's easy! It's fun! It's good for your computer to run MemMaker!

Bypassing Parts of CONFIG.SYS and AUTOEXEC.BAT

Well, maybe you made one little change to CONFIG.SYS, and now your computer won't start or it's acting kind of weird. With DOS 6, you can selectively bypass lines in your CONFIG.SYS file so that you can find the line that's causing a problem.

As soon as you see the `Starting MS-DOS...` message on the screen, press the F8 key. After a few seconds, you'll see the message `MS-DOS will prompt you to confirm each CONFIG.SYS command.`, immediately followed by the first line of your `CONFIG.SYS` file. Figure 15.1 shows you what this screen might look like.

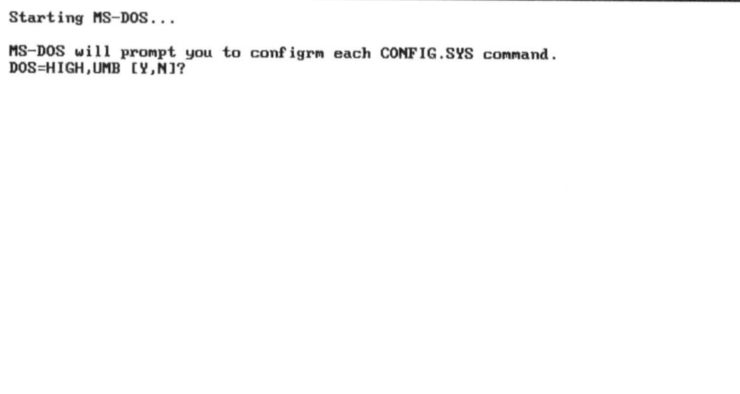
Starting MS-DOS...
MS-DOS will prompt you to configrm each CONFIG.SYS command.
DOS=HIGH,UMB [Y,N]?

Figure 15.1
Selectively bypassing `CONFIG.SYS` commands.

Answer **Y** to each of the `CONFIG.SYS` commands you want DOS to complete. Usually, this means you can answer **Y** to all of the lines that *weren't* changed recently. When you get to the offending line in `CONFIG.SYS` (at least, the line you *think* is causing you trouble), bypass it by answering **N**.

TRICKS

> Another way to figure out which line in **CONFIG.SYS** is giving you trouble is by answering **Y** to each and every line. When DOS reads the bad line, it will probably be obvious, since your computer will start acting weird as soon as the line is read.

Your display will look different than figure 15.2. I just put this picture here so you can see how it might look as you bypass `CONFIG.SYS`. You'll notice I answered **N** to the line that starts `DEVICE=C:\SCANNER\HHSCAN`. In this case, I entered one of the dumb things at the end of this line wrong when I installed my nifty new scanner. I fixed the bad line by using the `EDIT` command to change it the way it was supposed to be.

The stuff on the screen in figure 15.2 looks pretty weird, doesn't it? Most of the lines in **CONFIG.SYS** (like **DEVICEHIGH=/L:1,12048 =C:\DOS\SETVER.EXE**) have to do with your computer's *memory management*. On my computer, this line (and a lot of others in **CONFIG.SYS**) were added by MemMaker when I ran it. Don't lose any sleep over the exact meanings of the lines in your **CONFIG.SYS** file. Only a true nerd wants to know these things. DOS and your computer know for sure—that's what's important.

When you get to the end of CONFIG.SYS, DOS will ask you Process AUTOEXEC.BAT [Y,N]?. If your computer didn't start because of some change you made to CONFIG.SYS, of course you can go ahead (see fig. 15.2).

```
Starting MS-DOS...

MS-DOS will prompt you to configrm each CONFIG.SYS command.
DOS=HIGH,UMB [Y,N]?Y
DEVICE=C:\DOS\HIMEM.SYS [Y,N]?Y
DEVICE=C:\DOS\EMM386.EXE NOEMS [Y,N]?Y
BUFFERS=30 [Y,N]?Y
FILES=30 [Y,N]?Y
LASTDRIVE=E [Y,N]?Y
FCBS=4,0 [Y,N]?Y
DEVICEHIGH=/L:1,12048 =C:\DOS\SETVER.EXE [Y,N]?Y
DEVICE=C:\SCANNER\HHSCAN /V:129 /Q:876 /F [Y,N]?N
Process AUTOEXEC.BAT [Y,N]?
```

Figure 15.2

So many questions!

After you've gotten your computer started again by bypassing the bad lines, either repair the bad line(s) in CONFIG.SYS or AUTOEXEC.BAT, or copy the safe files from your emergency start-up disk or from the SAV backup copies you made before you made changes to it.

If it's something in **AUTOEXEC.BAT** that's giving you trouble, you can revert to the time-honored technique of typing in **REM** in front of the lines in **AUTOEXEC.BAT** that you suspect are the cause of the problem. **REM** tells DOS to jump over the line, instead of executing the command contained on the line.

continues

continued

For instance, on my computer I've got the following line in my `AUTOEXEC.BAT` file:

```
REM C:\MSMOUSE\MOUSE.EXE
```

The REM on this line tells DOS to just jump over this line and not to start the MOUSE.EXE program on my computer. If you "REM out" (a nerdy phrase, to be sure) the offending line, your computer should start normally, which tells you that you've narrowed the problem down to a single line in `AUTOEXEC.BAT`.

Using the Emergency Start-Up Disk

If you've got DOS 5 or an earlier version installed on your computer, you can't use the F5 or F8 tricks to get around `CONFIG.SYS` and `AUTOEXEC.BAT`. Let's try another approach.

Suppose that every time you try to start your computer, it stops right in the middle of one or the other of these files and refuses to go any farther.

No matter which DOS version you use, here's how you get around this hangup:

1. Put your emergency start-up disk in drive A.
2. Restart your computer by doing the Alt-Ctrl-Del thing.
3. When your computer starts again, it'll use the start-up files on your emergency start-up disk rather than the broken start-up files on your hard disk.

Once your computer is going again, you can fix or replace your `CONFIG.SYS` or `AUTOEXEC.BAT` file (whichever one is broken), as described in the previous section.

More Flaky File Things

If you thought we'd covered all possible file problems in Chapter 14, guess again! Here are some of the more complicated problems:

`Access denied` error message: You might see this love letter when you try to delete, copy over, or otherwise alter a file that has been marked read-only. Some applications make themselves or their support files read-only when they are installed.

Let's say the file that you're trying to remove is named REPORT.DOC. Enter the following at the keyboard:

```
ATTRIB -R REPORT.DOC
```

Then try the delete again:

```
DEL REPORT.DOC
```

That should take care of the problem.

NERDY DETAILS

So, you wanna know about the **ATTRIB** command, eh? Files and directories on your computer have a number of characteristics (or *attributes*) associated with them. For instance, if you have activated Delete Sentry, it builds a *hidden* directory called **SENTRY** in the **root** directory of your computer (this is where it keeps the files that have been deleted but not removed from your computer yet). The hidden attribute means that it doesn't show up when you do a **DIR** command on the root directory.

If you type **DIR **, you won't see a directory named SENTRY. (I'm assuming you have Delete Sentry activated. See Chapter 7 for an explanation of Delete Sentry and Delete Tracker.) You can alter the DIR somewhat:

```
DIR \ /AH
```

You'll see all the files that have the *hidden attribute* (that's the /AH) turned on. There are four attributes in all, but only two of them are important now: Hidden and Read-only. You can make a file (such as REPORT.DOC) read-only with the following command:

```
ATTRIB +R REPORT.DOC
```

Later, if you try to delete or write over the REPORT.DOC file with another file, DOS will complain with this message:

```
File creation error
```

If you type **ATTRIB**, followed by the name of a file (and press Enter), you'll see something like this:

```
C:\> ATTRIB REPORT.DOC

  A    R      REPORT.DOC
```

The A means this is an archive file (we don't have to pay attention to this attribute); the R means this file is a read-only file and can't be erased or changed.

You also use the ATTRIB command for removing file attributes:

```
ATTRIB -R REPORT.DOC
```

Notice how DOS cleverly uses the plus (+) and minus (-) signs to indicate adding and removing attributes.

Recovering an Accidentally Formatted Disk

If you've accidentally formatted a valuable floppy disk, DOS 5 or 6 can "unformat" the disk and recover the files that were on the disk. The UNFORMAT command is pretty easy to use. For this example, let's assume you're unformatting a 5 1/4-inch disk in drive A. Simply put the accidentally formatted disk in drive A, and enter the following command:

```
UNFORMAT A:
```

Then follow the directions. As long as you don't format the floppy disk with the /U parameter (which means *unconditional*, but you might remember it as "un-unformattable"), you should be able to unformat the disk.

"DANGER, WILL ROBINSON!" said The Robot. If DOS unformats a disk, any new files on it will be lost. Let's say you've got a disk with some old files on it. You format the disk to use it over again and copy a few new files to the disk. Then you realize the files you really need are the old ones that were on the disk in the first place.

> Sometimes you can unformat a disk even if you've added new files to it. The new files you've added, however will be lost unless you first copy the new files to another disk or a temporary directory first, then do the **UNFORMAT**.

Even though you can sometimes unformat a disk that has a few new files on it, the new files will often overwrite critical data that UNFORMAT needs to do its job. If you've put very many files on a newly formatted disk, it is very unlikely you will be able to UNFORMAT it.

NERDY DETAILS

> When you use the **FORMAT** command on a floppy disk, it reports **Saving UNFORMAT information**. What **FORMAT** is actually doing is looking at the floppy and saving all the directory information that will be needed to successfully use the **UNFORMAT** command later on, if necessary. This information is saved in two hidden files named **MIRROR.FIL** and **MIRRORSAV.FIL**.
>
> If these two files get overwritten when you add files to the disk, or the old file space gets written over with new files, you can't unformat the disk at all.

Twilight Zone: It's Always January 1, 1980

Have you ever thought about how your computer knows what time it is every time you start the thing up? Easy! It just looks over your shoulder at the clock on the wall...

Actually, there is a clock inside of your computer (surprise, surprise), which runs off of a battery like any digital watch or cordless wall clock. Once in a great while, the battery will go dead, causing all kinds of problems.

You have two choices:

 Take your computer to a repair shop and wait two weeks to pay the guy a few big bucks to replace your battery.

 Buy the battery (should cost about $10) and replace it yourself.

If you can't figure out how to set the timer on your VCR, you shouldn't try to replace your computer's battery. It's well worth whatever the nerd in the computer shop charges you to replace it rather than replacing a much more expensive component on your system.

If you're very lucky, you may find a shop that'll replace the battery while you wait. It really doesn't take long, and it'd be a shame for you to be without your computer for a week or two for it to be done.

Computer repairs are expensive, and you should try to protect yourself from sham artists. When you take your computer in for repairs or parts replacements, you should ask that the shop give all "replaced" components back to you (especially if the shop "finds" a problem that you didn't know you had). Most reputable auto service shops are happy to return replaced parts to you and will even show you why the parts needed replacement in the first place—why shouldn't a computer repair shop?

But, if you're brave and somewhat mechanically inclined, you might want to try this job yourself:

1. Buy the new battery. All computer stores have them. Batteries are essentially the same for all computers, and look like a little box with a wire hanging out of it. On the end of the wire is a teensy, weensy little plug that attaches to your computer somewhere.
2. Turn off your computer and unplug it.
3. Look at the back of your computer for some screws, tabs, or other turning things that are obviously holding the cover onto the big box. You might have to gently pull out some of the cables to get at them.

> If you can't figure out which screws are the right screws, take it to the shop. Don't just start taking out screws back there without knowing what they're holding in.

4. When you get the cover loose, gently pull it forward (that's towards the front of the computer) until it's clear of the inner part of the computer. You also might have to tilt it a little.

5. Look around inside (don't touch anything!) for something that looks like the battery you just bought. If you don't see one, carefully put the cover back on, return the battery to the store, and take your computer to a competent repair shop.

6. If you find the battery, look to see where it's plugged into your computer's innards. That's exactly where the new battery will plug in. Look to see if the old battery has both red and black wires (or white and some other color) coming out of it, and notice the orientation. You want the red (or white) and black (or "other" color) wires on the new battery to plug into the same orientation as the old ones.

7. Before removing the old battery, touch some piece of metal on the back of the computer (like the grid covering the ventilating fan) or the big squarish power supply inside the cabinet to let off any static electricity that may have built up. This may seem weird, but you can do serious damage to the delicate electronics inside if you happen to touch something and zap it with the static electricity that is on you and your clothes.

8. Gently pull out the old battery. Most computer batteries are held in with Velcro (honest!) or double-sided sticky tape. Some might even have a special ledge or other holder that they rest on. As you pull the old battery out, be careful not to bend the prongs that its wires are plugged into.

9. Once the old battery is out of the way, install the new battery exactly as the old one was. The red-wire side of the plug goes where the old red wire went, and the black-wire side goes where the old black wire was. (Elementary, my dear Watson!)

10. Carefully re-install the cover on the computer, making sure that you don't snag any of the wires and other stuff inside the box. Put all the screws back in, replug all the cables and the power cord, and you're done! (Now that wasn't so bad, was it?)

After you get the new battery in, you'll have to run your computer's setup program to enter all the information your computer needs to know (you see, it forgot what kind of hard disk, floppy disks, and what day it was when its battery went dead).

The batteries inside computers last quite a long time. Long enough, certainly, that the warranty has long expired by the time it goes dead.

Zzzt!
Zzzt!
Zzzt!
Zzzt!

The Simplest Mistakes Everyone Makes

Because DOS involves a lot of typing, and because there are so darn many different DOS commands, everyone makes certain mistakes from time to time. The mistakes discussed in this chapter are all just dumb mistakes. Always remember that you're not a dummy if you do any of the following:

- Make stupid spelling mistakes
- Forget to press the Enter key
- Put extra spaces in a command
- Leave out a directory name or backslash
- Delete or copy over a valuable file
- Format a valuable disk

Misspelling a Command

Without a doubt, misspelling a DOS command is the most common mistake. It's also one of the most frustrating for new users. "Learning a command is hard enough (you ask); you mean it's gotta be spelled a certain way, too?"

Some very common misspellings include typing the following:

"**DRI**" when you mean DIR

"**TPYE**" when you mean TYPE

"**CPY**" when you mean COPY

Any time you see a Bad command or file name error message, check your typing. Odds are you misspelled the command.

Forgetting To Press the Enter Key

DOS can't know that you're done typing your command until you press Enter. DOS just sits there and waits until you figure out that it's waiting for you to press the Enter key.

NERDY DETAILS

You often see "Enter" applied to DOS commands and other things that you're supposed to type in. For instance, you might see something like this:

```
Enter your first name
```

This tells you to type in your name and then press Enter. It's much easier to say "Enter your first name" than it is to say "Type your first name and press the Enter key." DOS nerds use a lot of shortcut ways of saying things.

Putting Spaces Where They Don't Belong

DOS is real fussy about where you should put spaces. A lot of people want to put spaces in the middle of DOS commands where they don't belong. Here's a good example: DISKCOPY is the command you use for duplicating a floppy disk (DISKCOPY A: A:). The command is *not* DISK COPY. If you try typing **DISK COPY A: A:**, DOS complains: Bad command or file name.

Always make sure you know where spaces go and where you *can't* use spaces.

Leaving Out the Colon When Referring to a Drive

You must always use a colon (:) after the letter name of your floppy disk drives when copying a file to or from the floppy. If you enter the following, the file named REPORT93.DOC is copied to a file named A:

```
COPY REPORT93.DOC A
```

Without the colon behind the A, DOS thinks you want to copy the file to *another* file named A. What you *should* type is:

```
COPY REPORT93.DOC A:
```

The second COPY command makes an exact copy of REPORT93.DOC on the floppy disk in drive A.

The only time you can omit the colon is when you're copying to the current drive. In this case, you should also omit the drive letter. For instance, **COPY REPORT93.DOC REPORT93.SAV** copies the REPORT93.DOC document to another file called REPORT93.SAV on the disk you're currently using (which will usually be C).

Leaving Out the Directory Name or Backslash

People are always forgetting where they are in the file system. Remember that you might have layers upon layers of files and stuff on your computer (like drawers in a filing cabinet). And each directory can have files and directories in it—it sure gets confusing!

If you're trying to get to a file (such as REPORT93.DOC) that's in a subdirectory (\DOCS), be sure to include the subdirectory as part of the file's name:

```
COPY \DOCS\REPORT93.DOC A:
```

You'll see the word *subdirectory* used a lot when you read about DOS. *Subdirectory* is another way of saying *directory*. Just another example of the way nerds give two similar-sounding names to the same thing.

Accidentally Deleting a File

It's easy to accidentally delete an important file, especially when using wildcards. Any time you use **DEL *.*** to delete all of the files in a directory, DOS warns you with the following message:

```
All files in directory will be deleted!
Are you sure (Y/N)?
```

DOS is not kidding (DOS never kids)! You're about to delete every file in the directory you're in, so be sure that's what you mean to do.

The same thing will happen if you enter the name of a directory instead of a file. Let's say you have a file named REPORTS.DOC and a directory named REPORTS. Suppose you type this (leaving off the file's last name, DOC):

```
DEL REPORTS
```

DOS thinks you want to delete all of the files in the REPORTS directory and will give you the `All files in directory will be deleted!` message. Pay attention when DOS talks to you!

What if you went ahead and accidentally deleted a file? Have no fear! Your best defense against accidental deletions are the new UNDELETE options with DOS 5 and 6. In DOS 6, Delete Sentry (the biggest and meanest of the undelete options) *guarantees* that you will be able to get back any accidentally-deleted files. Go back to Chapter 7 to learn all about UNDELETE.

Copying Over a Valuable File

Let's say your annual report is in a file cleverly named REPORT93.DOC. If, for some bizarre reason, you copy over this file with another file, like so:

```
COPY REPORT92.DOC REPORT93.DOC
```

The original file (REPORT93.DOC) is *absolutely, totally* gone. Nothing in DOS protects you from this error.

The COPY command is completely uncontrollable. You can't make it warn you before it copies over another file; it just goes ahead and copies without caring about what it's copying or where it's copying it to. This often happens if you copy a bunch of files into a directory without checking to see what's in there first.

A Real-Life Scenario

Suppose that the working version of a report (REPORT93.DOC) is on your hard disk. Last week, you made a backup of your file by copying REPORT93.DOC to a floppy disk (COPY REPORT93.DOC A:\). You probably felt pretty safe because you did the right thing, and the backup protects you in case something bad happens on your hard drive, right?

In the meantime, you spend 40 or 50 solid hours on your report. You even stay up all Saturday night (forsaking that great party you were invited to) so you could get those last few figures inserted into the report just right,and spell-check the darn thing for the umpteenth time.

Come Monday morning, bleary-eyed and strung out by too much black coffee and Crispy Creme donuts, you decide that you really should back up your masterpiece before something bad happens to it. Putting the back-up disk in drive A, you enter (you think) the magic back-up command:

```
COPY A:\
```

or

```
COPY A:\REPORT93.DOC
```

If you type the first version of the COPY command (you forget to put the name of the file between COPY and A:\), you soon find out that it copies everything from drive A onto your hard disk.

If you type the second command (when you mean to *restore* your back up after something bad has happened), you copy the week-old file named REPORT93.DOC over that beautifully crafted document on your hard disk that you worked on so diligently over the weekend. It's gone for good.

Be careful copying files around your disks. It's easy to lose something valuable.

Accidentally Reformatting a Valuable Disk

Nearly everyone who has used a computer for more than a few weeks has accidentally reformatted a disk. It usually happens like this: because you need a fresh disk for some files, you pick up a disk from your work table, insert it in the drive, issue the FORMAT command, and then press Enter:

```
FORMAT A:
```

Uh oh. What you mean to do, of course, is to make sure that you're working with a perfectly clean disk. Well, the disk is now clean all right. Anything that was on there (REPORT93.DOC) is now gone!

If your system has DOS 5 or 6, you can use the UNFORMAT command to try to retrieve that file. UNFORMAT, however, doesn't always work (particularly if you don't discover the error until after you've added some files to the floppy), and it won't work if you include the /U (unconditional) parameter on the FORMAT command line (the /U parameter is discussed in Chapter 13).

Your best bet is to always carefully label your disks! As soon as you put anything on a disk, you should use one of those labels that come with new floppy disks and stick it on the disk. Write a description of the disk's contents on the label (if you use a pencil or hard-tipped pen, don't press hard!).

Always remember that the files contained on a floppy are more valuable than the disk itself. Before formatting a floppy or deleting all of the files on it (DEL A:*.*), do a DIR on it first to see what's there.

PART 5

The Biggest and Best Things To Remember

YUM
YUM
NOTEPAD
CROZZI

The Very Best Things You Can Do

Although your computer will run a very, very long time without major problems, no computer runs perfectly forever. Fortunately, there are a few simple things you can do to minimize the inconvenience caused when something does go wrong. This chapter will show you the best things you can do to increase your computer's efficiency, help you avoid boo-boos, and help you recover from things that can go wrong (both self-inflicted and externally-caused). You learn:

 Why it's good to make copies of the stuff on your computer.

 When the normally useless computer manuals can actually help!

 How to keep your silverware in the silverware drawer and underwear in the underwear drawer: the importance of file management.

 How to keep viruses from eating your hard disk.

 When it's bad (and possibly a felony!) to make copies of the stuff on your computer.

 How to feed and water your computer.

 How to remember important things that your computer will eventually forget.

Back Up Your Work!

When you become a serious computer user, it's too bad you have to keep thinking about disasters. In spite of all the care and attention you might lavish on your little silicon buddy, he can turn funky real fast when his time is up.

Computer systems are prone to failure from a lot of sources: electrical surges and brownouts, component burn-out, bad disks, dirt, viruses, even stupid users. Your only true protection is a little up-front investment in frequent, good, reliable backups of your system (see Chapter 7 for ways to make backups with MSBACKUP).

Whatever bad thing befalls your system, you can always go out and get another hard disk, motherboard, monitor, or complete computer (assuming, of course, that your budget will allow it). What you may not be able to replace (without backups) are the software and data that live on your hard disk. There's no way you can reconstruct from memory every letter, report, spreadsheet, database, or drawing you've every produced. After all, that's what you were expecting the *computer* to do.

Always remember that all of that stuff is whirling around inside your computer, stuck to the hard disk through the magnetic magic that keeps it in place and lets your computer read it off of the disk for you to use. If the magic goes away, so do all of your files and all the hard work they contain.

Do a complete backup of your system pretty soon, and perform incremental backups every month or so, or more often if you are a heavy computer user. The alternatives are just too scary!

Get Help When You Need It

Don't be afraid to ask for help. There is no reason why you should expect to perfectly understand (or care about) every DOS command, or to diagnose and fix everything that might go wrong with your computer.

A lot of things that you try for the first time will seem pretty strange. Because DOS is so hostile and unhelpful, you can't always rely on prompts or error messages to help you understand what DOS wants you to do. Sometimes, you're just better off finding someone (even a geek) who's familiar with the task you're trying to complete and getting him to help you.

But, please respect the fact that people that are good with computers tend to be pretty busy. From time to time in this book I've made fun of the nerds and geeks of this world, but—for the most part—they're pretty hard-working people.

TRICKS

> The best thing you can do is to read up on what you're planning to do (let's say it's creating a directory to store your report documents in), then to try it yourself. If it doesn't work the first time, sit back a moment, breathe deeply (say "oooommm"), and check to make sure that you put spaces where spaces should go and pressed the Enter key when you were supposed to. Then try it again.

Only after you've given it a really good try should you go get help. Don't beat yourself up because you can't understand what DOS wants from you. Even the most advanced nerd needs a hand now and then.

Save the Manuals

Computers are a lot like cars. All computers share certain things in common (such as keyboards and monitors), and each computer has a lot of things that are unique to the particular model you've bought (where the reset switch is or what kind of hard disk is installed inside). If you ever have a problem with your computer (or want to add new equipment to it), the manuals that came with it can sometimes save your cake.

SAVE THE DAY!

> For the same reason, you should also save the sales receipt and other papers that came with your computer and its peripherals. These documents often specify the "base configuration" of your computer and the optional equipment that may have been installed when you bought it.

Keep Your Disk Organized and Tidy

Over and over again I've found the same situation on users' hard disks: all kinds of unrelated files are stuffed into one or two directories on the hard disk. Sometimes there are several programs installed in the same directory, or data files (such as spreadsheets are living in the same directory as the spreadsheet program files).

A much better approach is to learn how to make and use DOS directories. Make a directory for each kind of file you have on your disk: one directory for monthly reports you wrote with WordPerfect, another for spreadsheet data files you made with Lotus 1-2-3, and so on. It's like installing a separate file drawer for each kind of document you want to store in your big DOS filing cabinet.

Later, when you're trying to find something (like the monthly report you wrote in November) there are only a few places it's likely to be. It's also much easier to make backups of a few selected directories than to haphazardly back up files from one great big directory.

Protect Yourself from Accidental File Deletions

If you have DOS 6, use Delete Tracker or Delete Sentry! Chapter 7 tells you all about the DOS 6 deletion-protection brothers: Tracker and Sentry. Of the two, Delete Sentry provides a higher level of protection, but it costs you some disk space. Delete Tracker is better to use when your hard disk space is somewhat limited, but at the expense of somewhat less reliable deletion protection.

Your best bet is to add one of the following lines to your AUTOEXEC.BAT file. To automatically install Delete Sentry when your computer starts, add:

```
UNDELETE /SC
```

To invoke Delete Tracker when your computer starts up, add:

```
UNDELETE /TC
```

Use the DOS 6 Anti-Virus Protection

Chapter 7 talked about viruses that can eat your hard disk. Unless you never share files with other users, and have never put a "foreign" program on your hard disk, you should use the DOS 6 anti-virus protection.

If you have DOS 6 on your computer, you've got VSAFE (it was free). VSAFE requires very little of your computer's resources—only 23K of memory.

If you don't have DOS 6, you really ought to plan to put it on pretty soon. The virus protection options, disk defragger, DoubleSpace, and other features of DOS 6 are awfully nice to have.

NERDY DETAILS

Although it's pretty good, the DOS 6 anti-virus protection isn't the last word in virus fighting. A lot of viruses are able to get around the protection provided by DOS 6. Your best bet is to practice safe computing by not using pirated or unknown software, back up your system from time to time, and pay attention to what's going on with your computer.

If you are really interested in a rigorous description of viruses, how they infect computers, how to keep from getting 'em, and how to eliminate them once you get 'em, read *Inside MS-DOS 6*, which is available from New Riders Publishing.

Although *Inside MS-DOS 6* is a much more complex book than this one, it's got a real good discussion of the anti-virus and disk-optimization features of DOS 6.

Respect Software Copyrights

At the risk of sounding corny, software providers invest a great deal of time, effort, and money creating and preparing the software products you use. A well-designed program such as Microsoft Excel or WordPerfect can take months and months of hard work and effort by the programmers, project managers, and support staff at the software companies.

Using *pirated* software (for instance, a copy of a popular word processor or spreadsheet that your buddy made for you at work) not only deprives the software company of its hard-earned income, it leaves you with only half of the product. You won't be entitled to support or updates to the software (which may fix some software problems that you have to deal with), and you won't have access to the product's packaged documentation. Furthermore, using pirated software is illegal and puts you and your employer at risk (copying over $2500 worth of software is a Federal felony!).

NERDY DETAILS

Making backup copies of your software as part of normal computer backups as described in Chapter 7 is legal. Making copies and giving them to friends, or accepting copies of software is illegal.

Assuming that you use only licensed, legally-owned software, be sure to register each program you own. Almost all computer programs come with some kind of mail-back card that registers you as the bona fide user of the software. The software company uses this information to learn a little bit about its users and to contact you in the event of a bug fix or other upgrade to your program. They may even offer you special discounts on other programs (really!).

Finally, if you use commercially-purchased software, you should give the manufacturers feedback about their product. It is very expensive for software companies to survey the general public for ideas for new programs or for tips on how to improve their existing products. The best information is obtained from users of their programs. When we think of "feedback" we usually consider only complaints or problem feedback. Even positive information (like which features you use the most) is important data for software developers.

Defrag Your Hard Disk Now and Then

Chapter 13 tells you all about DEFRAG, which is the DOS 6 hard disk defragmenter. As this chapter explains, the files stored on your hard disk get broken up into more and more pieces as you add new files to the disk and take old ones away. Over time, there will be a noticeable degradation of efficiency and performance as you use your computer.

DOS 6 comes with a built-in disk defragmenter. DEFRAG will return your hard disk to a nice, neat, orderly condition that enables DOS to access your files as fast as possible.

DEFRAG runs quite slowly; defragmenting a large disk may take several hours. There is no reason to run DEFRAG more often than necessary. Refer to Chapter 13 to learn how DEFRAG recommends what level of optimization to apply to your system, and then follow the suggestions.

SAVE THE DAY!

Because DEFRAG may take hours to clean up your hard drive, you may want to let it run when you don't need to use your computer. Just start DEFRAG before you leave the office for the evening and your hard drive will be clean and ready to go when you get back!

Protect Your Hardware with a Good Surge Protector

Deep down inside your computer are a lot of pretty fragile electronic components. These things can be damaged or destroyed if your computer receives even a very short burst of extra electricity from the wall socket (this happens more often than we think). These surges come from a wide variety of sources: problems with the transformer in your neighborhood, lightning strikes or other random sources of extra electricity, and so on. I've heard that car accidents and wind storms that cause damage to the power company's transmission equipment (poles, wires, and so on) can cause some pretty severe surges.

Just about your only defense against power surges is to equip your computer with a good surge protector. Most surge protectors plug into the wall outlet near your computer; you plug your computer, monitor, printer, and other equipment into the outlets on the surge protector.

After they have trapped a really big surge, protectors are no good any more. A good surge protector will alert you if there's been a big surge. Some are equipped with lights that light up after a surge has occured (don't confuse them with a light that just tells when it's on). Others may warn you audibly; some will even quit passing electricity to your computer when their protection is gone. A poorly designed surge protector will continue passing electricity to your computer even though it is no longer protecting your valuable equipment.

When you buy a surge protector, be sure to get one with visible and audible alerts. If one of the new fail-safe models is available, you should get it. Good surge protectors are not expensive (even good ones are scarcely more expensive than an extension power strip), yet they protect your equipment from expensive damage.

Provide Enough Ventilation Around Your Computer

Wherever you install your computer, be sure to provide enough space around it so that air can get to all sides of the computer's big box and monitor. For instance, you shouldn't cover the monitor with a cloth or plastic covering while you're using it.

Your computer needs air flowing through it to keep it from overheating. Temperatures inside your computer's big box can reach over 150 degrees (even higher on a hot day). Because some electrical components and connections start to fail at temperatures that are not much higher than this, your system can be in danger of failure without adequate ventilation.

Computer fans usually start squeaking or squealing just before they get ready to break. If your fan starts making funny noises, get it replaced. If your fan stops completely, shut your computer down *immediately* (so it doesn't overheat) and get a new fan installed.

Should I Leave My Computer On All the Time?

Some people suggest that you leave your computer on all the time. I think this is a bad idea for a number of reasons. First, you will wear out certain parts of your computer (like the fan and hard disk) sooner than you will by turning it off when you're not using it.

Second, all the time the computer is running, the fan is drawing air out of the room and blowing it through your computer system to keep it cool. Even under the best circumstances, this air contains a certain amount of dust and other crud that builds up inside your computer. You should see some of the dust build-up that occurs after a few months with the fan on continuously! Under very humid conditions, this dust can actually become electrically conductive, causing all sorts of intermittent crashes and problems.

Third, even with adequate surge protection, your computer can be subjected to brownouts, surges, spikes, and other electrical junk coming through the power cord.

NERDY DETAILS

Another true story: the air conditioning failed over a weekend in the building where I used to work. When we came in to work on Monday morning, one of the computers that had been left on all weekend was completely fried: the hard disk light was on all the time (even though the hard disk wasn't running anymore), both floppy disks were turning, turning endlessly, and the monitor was blank, blank, blank. The computer had been reduced to a heap of junk from overheating.

Fourth, running your computer all the time costs money! Your PC can use over $200 worth of electricity during the course of a year. If you are using your computer intermittently during the day, you should probably leave it on between sessions. It'll be more gentle to the components in your machine if it's left on for an hour or so at a stretch than turning it off and on multiple times during the day. I suggest you don't leave it on overnight or over weekends, however. Too many bad things can happen to it while you're not there.

If you need to leave your computer on all the time, you should equip it with an after-market air filter and a good power-line conditioner that will really protect your machine from these hazards. Auxiliary filters are relatively cheap (a kit should cost you less than $20). Power-line conditioners are quite a bit more expensive ($100 or more). It's your choice.

Make a Printout Copy of Your AUTOEXEC.BAT and CONFIG.SYS Files

If you've read Chapter 10, you know something about getting your printer connected and working. Use this knowledge to print out your AUTOEXEC.BAT and CONFIG.SYS files, and keep the printout with your other valuable computer papers. You might need this information some day.

How To Remember Stuff That Your PC Will Eventually Forget

Perhaps you've made the conversion from paper-based record keeping to a completely computerized filing system. You've got all of your important documents on-line, your household budget and income tax data is safely stored in a bunch of different spreadsheet files, and you've even converted all of Aunt Bessie's recipe cards to an electronic format. With all of this computer power at your disposal, why would you want or need to write anything down? Because, friends, even the best-laid plans of computer mice and men may go awry. Read on.

SEE-MOSS, Shmee-Moss. Why Can't My Computer Tell Time?

Your computer stores a certain amount of vital information only in a very fragile portion of memory called the CMOS (pronounced SEE-MOSS). If the battery goes dead, the information stored in the CMOS area will disappear and your computer (and DOS) won't even know what time it is, much less what kind of hard disk or floppies are installed. Without this information, you (and DOS) *can't run your computer.*

SAVE THE DAY!

> You should write this CMOS information down—it gives you a paper backup of information that isn't recorded anywhere else. If you've written down the CMOS information and the CMOS is wiped out by a dead battery, you can reconstruct the CMOS information after you've replaced the battery.

Most computers have some kind of "Setup" program that allows you to alter the data stored in your computer's CMOS memory. On most modern computer systems, the Setup program is built into the computer's hardware. On these computers, it is generally quite easy to invoke the Setup program to change or view the information stored in the CMOS.

You had to have a Setup floppy disk with the setup program on it to change the CMOS in the old IBM AT and many other older computer systems. This was an incredible pain since you only have to change the CMOS once or twice a year (for instance, to change the clock for daylight savings time or when the battery would go dead). Fortunately, most modern computers have done away with separate setup disks.

How To Record What the SEE-MOSS Has To Say

You're going to look at the CMOS information, write down what you see there, and save your written notes someplace safe so you can get at them when you need to later, right?

The first step is to find out how to invoke the Setup program so you can see the CMOS data. Watch your computer when it starts up. If you see a message that says something like `Hit <Del>`, if you want to run SETUP you're in luck. This means you've got a very easy-to-use Setup program that can be used any time you start your computer.

I'm going to describe how to start up two of the most common Setup programs. These Setup programs are found in many different types of computers from many different manufacturers. If your computer doesn't have either of these Setup programs built into it, look in your computer's manuals; the principles will almost certainly be the same as described here:

 If your computer says something like `ROM BIOS (C)1990 American Megatrends Inc` at the top of the screen when you turn on the power, you've got the very popular AMI-type of Setup program.

 If, on the other hand, you see something that says `Phoenix Technologies Ltd`, you've got the Phoenix Setup Utility built into your computer.

The American Megatrends Inc, Setup Program

Computers that are equipped with the AMI BIOS display the message `ROM BIOS (C)1990 American Megatrends Inc` at the top of the computer screen when they start up. Press Del to stop the start-up procedure and go to the setup program. You'll see a screen that looks something like figure 17.1.

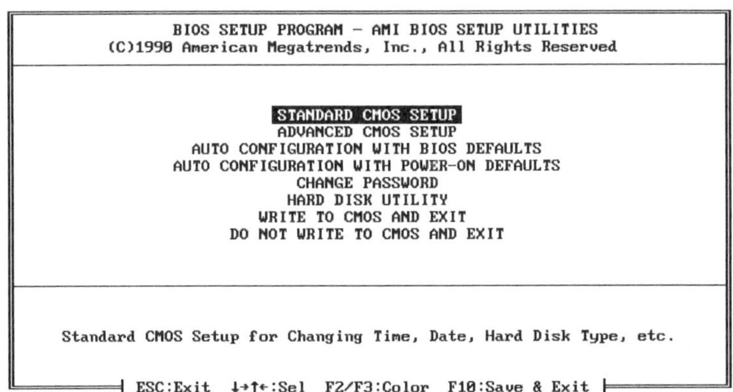

Figure 17.1
The AMI Setup program opening screen.

Just press Enter to go to the main Setup screen (see fig. 17.2). This screen has the information you're looking for.

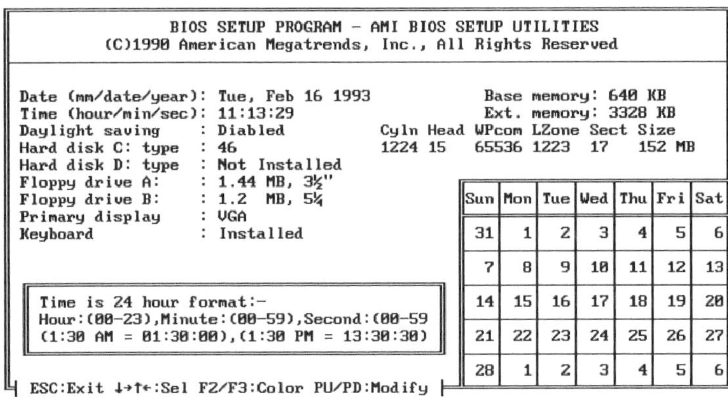

Figure 17.2
The AMI main Setup screen.

You're not going to change anything here. Just take a piece of paper (you might use the inside front cover of your computer user's guide) and write down the following information:

Hard disk C: type ____________________

Floppy drive A: ____________________

Floppy drive B: ____________________

In figure 17.2, the computer has hard disk type 46, floppy drive A is a 1.44 M, 3 1/2-inch drive; floppy drive B is a 1.2 M, 5 1/4-inch drive. This is all information your computer will forget if the battery dies.

You can only start up the AMI Setup program while your computer is starting up. Once your machine is running, you can't simply switch to the Setup program.

The Phoenix Technologies Ltd, Setup Program

If your computer displays a message indicating it has the Phoenix BIOS as it starts up, try this:

Again, while your computer is booting, press and hold down these keys simultaneously: Alt, Ctrl, and Esc. You should see a screen something like figure 17.3 pop up.

```
                Phoenix SETUP Utility (Version 1.00)
          Copyright 1985-1990  Phoenix Technologies Ltd.

                                                      Page 1 of 2

                  ** Standard System Parameters **

System Time:          10:37:30       NumLock on at boot:   No
System Date:          Feb 16, 1993

Diskette A:           5.25", 1.2 MB
Diskette B:           3.5", 1.44 MB      Cyl  Hd   Pre   LZ   Sec  Size
Hard Disk 1:          Type 30            1024  10    0     0   17    85
Hard Disk 2:          Not Installed
Base Memory:          640 KB
Extended Memory:      7552 KB
Video Card:           VGA/EGA
Keyboard:             Installed

 ESC       F1        F2                    ↑↓       +/-       PgUp/Dn
 Menu      Help      Sys Info            Field     Value       Page
```

Figure 17.3

The Phoenix Setup screen.

This screen is somewhat simpler than the comparable AMI-type screen. Write down the following information:

Diskette A: ____________________

Diskette B: ____________________

Hard Disk 1 ____________________

Diskette A in the computer in figure 17.3 is a 5 1/4-inch, 1.2M; diskette B is a 3 1/2-inch, 1.44M. The hard disk in this machine is a Type 30.

If you would rather not fiddle with your computer's CMOS setup program, you can use the DOS 6 program MSD to show you what is stored in your CMOS. Just type **MSD** at the DOS prompt (exit Windows first, if you have it), and you'll pop right into the diagnostic program. Press **D**, and MSD will show you the disk drive types used in your computer.

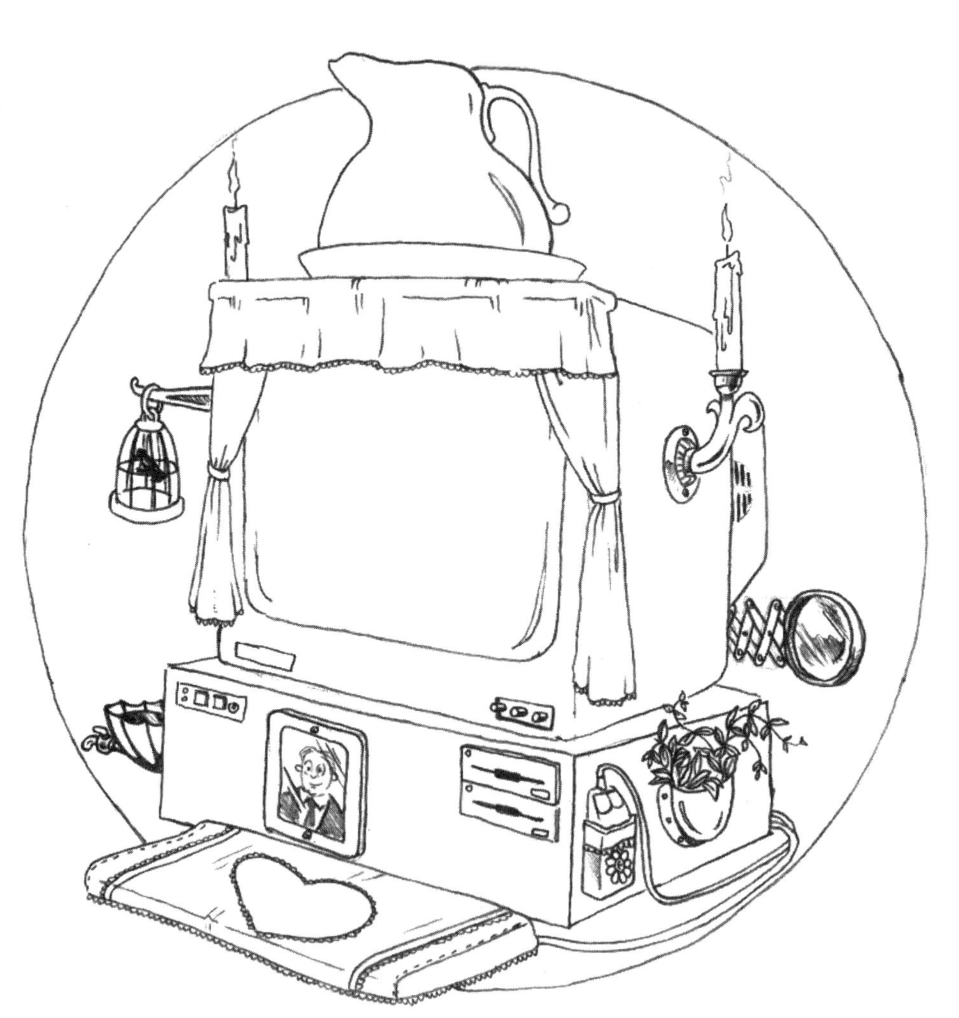

The Best Things To Never, Ever Do

Remember when your mom would yell at you when you opened the oven to see what was baking? Or when your dad yelled at you because you put the car into Park when it was still rolling a little bit? Just like these things, there are a few things you should *Never, Ever Do* with your computer. This chapter covers:

- Things to Never, Ever Do to your computer.
- Some things you shouldn't do to your disk drives.
- Why you should pay attention to the weather while using your computer.
- Why you should pay attention when DOS is trying to tell you something!
- How to practice safe computing!
- What's a DOS command that can really, really mess things up?

Never, Ever Pull the Plug While the Machine Is Running

Okay??? This shouldn't take a rocket scientist to figure out. There are a zillion things going on inside your computer while it's running. It might be in the middle of saving a file to the hard disk, or it might be reading something from the disk. Some hard disks need a more-or-less orderly shutdown to keep them happy and healthy.

Pulling the plug (or pressing the Reset button, or suddenly shutting off the power switch) is NOT a good thing to do. Exit your application gracefully and get back to your friendly DOS prompt before shutting the machine off.

A lot of software (Windows is an example) relies on an orderly shutdown so that they can write certain information to the hard disk before they go away. If the machine is suddenly jerked out from under them, they don't get the chance to perform their housekeeping tasks before leaving.

NERDY DETAILS

Restarting your computer with the Alt-Ctrl-Del three-finger salute (a process called *softboot* or *rebooting* by nerds) is NOT quite as bad as pulling the plug, by the way. At least with Alt-Ctrl-Del the machine has a chance to briefly think about what's happening before restarting. But, you should try to avoid using Alt-Ctrl-Del unless you are at the `C:\>` DOS command prompt and all drive lights are off.

There are occasions (particularly after an application has crashed) when your only option is restarting it with Alt-Ctrl-Del, or even to turn off the machine. In some situations, DOS is so far gone that it can't respond to the Alt-Ctrl-Del request anyway, so you have to shut the machine off with the power switch. If so, you should wait ten seconds for the electronics to clear before turning it back on.

STOP!

Shutting your computer off, or rebooting it while a program is still on your screen confuses DOS and causes it to leave file fragments on your hard drive. These fragments build up over time, wasting disk space and further confusing your computer.

To clean up these fragments, type **CHKDSK /F** at the DOS prompt, and press **N** when you are asked if you want to save the fragments to disk.

Don't Open a Drive Door While the Light Is On

If the light on your floppy disk drive is on, it means that an application or DOS is reading or writing something on the disk. If you open the door, not only won't DOS like it (you might get an error message on the screen), but the file that is being read or written gets scrambled. This is good for eggs, not for files.

Never Use Your Computer During a Thunderstorm

Even if you've installed a surge protector (as described in Chapter 17), you risk computing on a smoking cinder if you insist on using your computer during a thunderstorm.

Surge protectors and power-line conditioners, even very good ones, are only able to trap transient voltage spikes. High-voltage events that last more than a few milliseconds (if lightning strikes a power transformer near your house, for example) will blow away even a very good, very expensive surge protector or power line conditioner.

TRICKS

Rule of thumb: if you unplug your TV during a storm, treat your computer the same way.

Story time: I used to live in Boston near the subway tracks. One day a squirrel decided to commit suicide by bounding across the bare wire that supplies the 600 volts of electricity needed to run the train. After the squirrel made contact between the 600 volts and a ground, the 600 volt wire snapped and fell across the power line supplying my apartment building, filling the electrical system in the building (temporarily) with a healthy 600 volts of pure, clean power. I happened to be watching TV at the time.

After the smoke cleared, I was able to put my TV back in working order by replacing the TV's fuse (it was completely blown up inside). I can't imagine what would have happened if I'd been using my computer at the time.

Don't Use Your Computer During Brownout Conditions

The electrical power in Boston tends to be somewhat unreliable during the summer. On some days, when all the air conditioners in town are running full force, the picture on the TV shrinks, lights dim, and the refrigerator makes weird sounds. This is not the time to be using your computer.

The power supply in your computer needs around 110 volts of electricity in order to supply adequate power to your hard disk, memory, and other components. If the electricity coming out of the wall falls very far, your computer may crash (if you're lucky), or it may begin to suffer from a number of other problems.

For instance, the fan may slow down, causing overheating. The motor in the hard disk may slow down, causing mistakes when reading or writing data. The hard disk motor can even slow down so much that the fragile heads in your hard disk touch the surface of the spinning platters. This is a bad, bad thing and can ruin your disk.

If you know you're experiencing a brownout, go outside and play, take a nap, bake some bread, write to the president; just don't use your computer.

Don't Ignore Error Messages!

If you start seeing a lot of spontaneous `Parity error` or `Sector not found` error messages when you try to read or write a file on your hard disk, you may be in for some trouble.

Eventually, dirt and dust can build up around the delicate electrical connections inside your computer. This dirt and dust can become partly electrically conductive, particularly under conditions of high humidity during the summer, causing all kinds of problems. It's time to take this machine to a shop for a good cleaning and checkup. Don't put it off. A good servicing by a reliable shop (ask around for recommendations) can save you a lot of trouble later on.

Error messages arising as a result of disk activity (such as `Sector not found` or `Error reading/writing drive`) may indicate that it's time to service your hard disk. What may have happened is that the accuracy of your hard disk is fading away and needs to be renewed.

This is not a common ailment and servicing hard disks is well beyond the scope of this book. You really are better off trusting some well-meaning nerd to help you out. Or you can take your beloved machine to a reliable PC repair shop for maintenance.

Servicing a hard disk is a big job. Everything on the disk has to be reliably backed up to disk or cartridge tape, a low-level format is performed, then a high-level (DOS-style) format is done on top of the low-level format. This renews the disk's accuracy and will also reveal any deterioration of the magnetic media on the spinning platters inside the disk.

Low-level formatting is a chore best left to experienced PC nerds, especially because not all drives can be successfully low-level formatted. For example, the most common type of hard drives, known as IDE drives, should NEVER be low-level formatted!

Never, Ever Use Unknown Software

This scenario has been repeated thousands of times: The local nerd bounds into the office on Monday morning with a really awesome game he downloaded from a bulletin board system (BBS) over the weekend (probably on Saturday night when everybody else was out on a date). He insists on showing you how he achieved his incredibly awesome score blasting away at the invading Thermigids and saved the universe from eternal subjugation and earned the rank of All-Conquering Galactic Hero.

After this jerk finally leaves, you get back to work and soon discover you've got problems. First, you wonder where your document directory went. All of your reports and correspondance have been mysteriously erased. Then you realize your WordPerfect directory is gone, too, and you can't start Windows anymore. Finally, your computer restarts itself, and you get a `No boot device` error message as your machine tries to get itself started again.

Welcome to the wonderful world of viruses! I'm not kidding—this kind of damage has happened to a lot of people. There is a particular type of high-tech, low-ethic vandal who derives a perverted pleasure from writing software to destroy the files and directories on your hard disk. The agent of this destruction is commonly called a computer virus, and the person who writes viruses is called a lot of really, really bad names. (Chapter 7 tells you about viruses and what DOS 6 can do to help you avoid them.)

The message is this: Let the jerk run unknown software on his own computer. Practice safe computing! Use the DOS 6 anti-virus (MSAV is described in Chapter 7), back your system up once in a while, and don't use contraband software on your system.

Never, Ever Use the RECOVER Command

And I'm not kidding! The `RECOVER` command (which comes with DOS), in spite of its helpful-sounding name, can really, really mess up your hard disk. Its job is to try to repair files that contain corrupted data. It splits a damaged file into two pieces—one piece contains all of the file contents that came before the damaged part; the second part contains all of the file contents that come after the damaged part. The original file is gone, and the pieces are given the very, very unhelpful names of `FILE0001.REC` and `FILE0002.REC`. `RECOVER` makes no attempt to name the pieces anything useful.

The problem with `RECOVER` and your hard disk is the following: if you omit the name of the file you want recovered, that is, you just type **`RECOVER`** at the DOS prompt instead of `RECOVER MYFILE.DOC` (if that was the name of the damaged file), `RECOVER` will split all of the files in your directory into pieces, even the good ones! It's up to you to try to reassemble your files and reassign them their original names. The truth is, not even most nerds know how to use RECOVER.

> Because the **RECOVER** command is basically a nightmare waiting to happen, I recommend that you just delete the **RECOVER.EXE** command from your hard drive. You'll always have the command on your original DOS floppies—where it won't do any harm.

RECOVER is so dangerous to files and so difficult to use that I have deleted it from my hard disks. On the rare occassion that I get a corrupted file, I use a well-written set of third-party utility programs (called the Norton Utilities) to repair my file.

Don't Panic!

Last, but not least, is: don't panic. If something goes wrong, you can fix it. Or someone else can fix it for you. The worst thing you can do is flip out and start erasing files, re-installing software, and making a nuisance of yourself.

Whenever you're faced with what appears to be a serious problem, sit back for a moment to assess what's going on. What are the symptoms? Is it just a misplaced or accidentally erased file or is it something more serious like a disk-sector error? If you're sure you've got a virus, run the MSAV program and have it scan for bugs before you throw in the towel.

Don't always assume the worst. Unless there is smoke pouring out the back of your computer, you can probably recover from even the most serious disaster. Although a lot of really serious problems are beyond the scope of this book, there are lots of books and magazine articles that can help you out and many, many things you can do on your own.

Then again, you can always go ask that nerd for help, can't you?

PART 6

Graduate-Level Topics

"WELL, IF YOU DON'T LIKE THIS ONE...
I GOT A '89 YUGO OUT BACK THAT I CAN SELL YOU...
FOR THE SAME PRICE."

DOS 6: A New and Improved DOS

If you're using a version of DOS that's older than version 5, you ought to schlep yourself to the software store and plunk down some dough for DOS 6. Even if you use DOS 5 (which is pretty good, for DOS), you'll probably like DOS 6 more.

The "new and improved" DOS has loads of features that no other version has ever had. DOS 6 even has some fun stuff built in. It lets you manage memory without even thinking about it (sounds just like your brain, doesn't it?), store more files on your hard disk, and protect your PC from viruses and other menacing critters.

You'll see what makes DOS 6 so much better later in this chapter. You'll also learn how to load DOS 6 on your PC without causing a meltdown. This chapter shows you how to:

 Understand what's new in DOS 6

 Get ready to upgrade to DOS 6

 Understand the installation process

 Master installation options (become a Master of the DOS Universe)

What's New in DOS 6?

If you've read many of the earlier chapters in this book, you have an idea of what's new in DOS 6. Just in case you haven't, or if you've turned to this chapter first, here is the condensed list:

- DoubleSpace: Doubles the usuable space on your hard disk. It makes 20M into 40M, 80M into 160M, and so on.
- Virus fighters: MSAV scans and eliminates computer viruses. You can also install VSAFE, which will constantly monitor your computer for new infections. Virus fighting is discussed in Chapter 7.
- Memory management: MEMMAKER automatically configures your computer for optimum memory use. Very, very cool thing to do. Read all about MEMMAKER in Chapter 12.
- Delete protection: Really, really good UNDELETE features. You can decide what level of protection you need. Delete Tracker and Delete Sentry are explained in Chapter 7.
- Disk optimizer: DEFRAG, discussed in Chapter 13, optimizes your hard disk for better performance.
- Backup utility: The new DOS 6 MSBACKUP is a lot more intelligent and friendly than earlier versions of BACKUP were. MSBACKUP is discussed in Chapter 7.

DOS 6 does not automatically provide these new features—you have to go through a "mini-installation" for each of them. Once you have DOS 6 installed, you can read the chapters that discuss these features, and get instructions for ways to make them work on your computer.

A Message About Upgrading for the Faint of Heart

Once upon a time, only the most die-hard computer nerd had the guts to load DOS onto a computer. It was touch-and-go all the way, and if you (or DOS) made the teensiest mistake, the whole thing went into the toilet. To get ready to load DOS, you had to take steps that were like performing brain surgery.

Things have gotten easier over the years, and now you just have to be able to read in order to load DOS like a pro. And you won't have to read very much!

Before you load DOS 6, you only have to do two things:

1. Make sure that you really want to do it.
2. Make sure that your hard disk has enough space to hold the new DOS programs.

For help with the first step, read the section about the new features of DOS 6. Then make sure you've got enough cash to actually buy it. You'll learn how to take the second step in a few pages.

When you install DOS 6, it makes a copy of your existing DOS directory and saves all the old DOS files that already are on your hard disk. DOS 6 saves those files in case something goes wrong during the installation process. You shouldn't expect anything to go wrong, because DOS 6 is pretty smart. But if your computer won't work with DOS 6, you can easily "uninstall" DOS 6 and go back to using your old version of DOS. (You'll learn what nerds mean by "uninstall" later in this chapter.)

Here's How It Works

Before you actually load DOS 6, it's a good idea to understand what's going to happen when you start flinging those floppy disks around. This section gives you a quick overview of what happens when you upgrade.

DOS 6 comes on three or four floppy disks; you can get either 5 1/4-inch or 3 1/2-inch disks. The disks contain a lot of DOS 6 program files and other stuff that the installation program uses to install DOS 6 on your computer.

When you install DOS 6, a program called Setup takes control of your computer. Don't worry: Setup is one of the smartest and easiest-to-use programs around. It knows exactly what it's doing, and it can help you through lots of problems. Setup performs the following tasks:

1. Checks your hardware to see if you're using a network, mouse, or other special hardware that DOS 6 needs to know about.

2. Copies files from the floppy disks to your hard disk.
3. Lets you decide whether you want to install some optional programs.
4. Modifies your DOS start-up files (AUTOEXEC.BAT and CONFIG.SYS).

When Setup is done, all you have to do is restart your PC. And Setup even tells you how to do that!

You met the **AUTOEXEC.BAT** and **CONFIG.SYS** files in Chapter 4. DOS gets initial directions from these files after you turn on your computer. Once in a while, you have to change some of the stuff in these files—for example, when you want **VSAFE** (the anti-virus guard) to start up every time you use your computer.

Only Computer Nerds Could Invent a Word Like "Uninstall"

OK, OK. You're right. There's got to be a catch. If you're doing something as difficult as installing DOS, there's got to be a catch, right? Right. You've got to learn a new nerd word—uninstall—and be prepared in case you have to uninstall DOS 6.

In computer geek-speak, *uninstall* means "bail out," "clean up this mess," and "put it back the way it was before you started." If we're lucky, it'll be a long time before uninstall appears in dictionaries used by normal people.

When it installs DOS 6, Setup creates an emergency start-up floppy disk. This disk is called the UNINSTALL disk. With this disk, you can restart your computer and get to the files on your hard disk. You may have to do this if a disaster strikes, and DOS 6 decides that it won't run on your computer.

Just so you're forewarned, you should prepare your UNINSTALL disk before you start the installation process. Take a nice, new floppy disk and format it. Although Setup can format the disk for you, the setup process will take longer because you have to wait (or take a potty break) until the disk is formatted in the middle of Setup.

If you can't restart your computer after you install DOS 6, you can put the UNINSTALL disk in drive A, and restart your computer by giving it the computer nerd's "three-finger salute." That is, you press the Ctrl, Alt, and Del keys all at the same time. (This action is called the "three-finger salute" because it takes three fingers for most people. This means that the typical computer nerd has to take at least one finger out of his nose first.) The computer then uses the good start-up files on the UNINSTALL disk, and should start running normally.

Setup copies some of your original DOS files on the UNINSTALL disk. It then saves these files—and others—on your hard disk in a directory named `OLD_DOS.x`. With these files, you can get DOS 6 off your computer and restore your original version of DOS, if necessary.

A Special Warning for the Meek and Overly Cautious

So now you may be ready to load DOS 6. But then again, maybe not. Check the following note with the mean-looking picture to find out why not.

Don't do anything unless you read your DOS 6 manual first! Sad but true, it may actually be necessary for you to read a manual in some cases, and this is one of them.

The following steps are pretty general and should guide you through your DOS installation, but you may have a customized version of DOS that was made especially for your computer. This is particularly true if you're using a laptop or other specialized computer system. In that case, you may need to do something special to make sure that DOS 6 will run on your PC.

Now That You Understand It, Go Ahead and Do It

All right, already. You know so much about installing DOS by now that you could fly a rocket. Go ahead, then! Load it up!

1. Put the first DOS floppy disk in drive A. Then type this at the DOS prompt:

   A:SETUP

   If you use drive B rather than drive A, type **B:SETUP**. It's all the same to DOS.

2. You should see a simple "checking-configuration" screen, which quickly disappears.

3. The next thing you'll see is the welcome screen, which is shown in figure 19.1. If you're getting butterflies about the whole thing, this screen's message gives you the chance to bail out before it's too late. If you feel brave, you can also choose to charge ahead.

   If you want to go ahead and install DOS, press Enter.

   Press F3 twice to leave the Setup program and return to the DOS prompt. Watch the screen—it'll tell you when to press the F3 key.

```
Microsoft MS-DOS 6 Setup

        Welcome to Setup.

        The Setup program prepares MS-DOS 6 to run on your
        computer.

        • To set up MS-DOS now, press ENTER.

        • To learn more about Setup before continuing, press F1.

        • To quit Setup without installing MS-DOS, press F3.

ENTER=Continue  F1=Help  F3=Exit
```

Figure 19.1

The MS-DOS 6 Setup welcome screen.

If you don't think you understand what's happening on your computer's screen while you're loading DOS, just press F1. DOS shows you a quick help screen, which explains that the Setup program will scan your system to look for optional hardware you may have installed.

Get the UNINSTALL Disk Ready

4. Next, DOS asks you to prepare your UNINSTALL disk, as shown in figure 19.2. If you read the earlier section that described uninstallation, then you understand the need for this important disk. This disk is easy to prepare—you just need a blank, formatted disk that will work in drive A. The disk should be high-density (if your drive A is high-density); if your computer only uses double-density disks, you'll need two disks, labelled UNINSTALL #1 and UNINSTALL #2. When you have the disks ready, press Enter.

The UNINSTALL disk(s) doesn't have to be formatted (see Chapter 13 to learn all about "formatting"). Setup is smart enough to do that for you if it's not already done. You're better off using an already-formatted disk, though, because it'll save you time during the install process.

Setup will put the files onto the UNINSTALL disk later. This screen is here to remind you that you need to prepare the UNINSTALL disk.

```
Microsoft MS-DOS 6 Setup

        During Setup, you will need to provide and label one
        or two floppy disks. Each disk can be unformatted
        or newly formatted and must work in drive A. (If you
        use 360K disks, you may need two disks; otherwise,
        you need only one disk.)

        Label the disk(s) as follows:

           UNINSTALL #1
           UNINSTALL #2 (if needed)

        Setup saves some of your original DOS files on the
        UNINSTALL disk(s), and others on your hard disk in a
        directory named OLD_DOS.x. With these files, you can
        restore your original DOS if necessary.

          • When you finish labeling your UNINSTALL disk(s),
            press ENTER to continue Setup.

ENTER=Continue  F1=Help  F3=Exit
```

Figure 19.2

The UNINSTALL disk screen.

Make Sure Things Are Right

5. Like I said before, Setup is pretty smart. The next screen you see displays what Setup knows about your computer. DOS calls this information the *system settings*. In the case of the computer shown in figure 19.3, DOS reports that we are installing generic MS-DOS 6 (not a version that was customized to work on a laptop or other specialized computer), the DOS home directory is C:\DOS, and the display type is VGA.

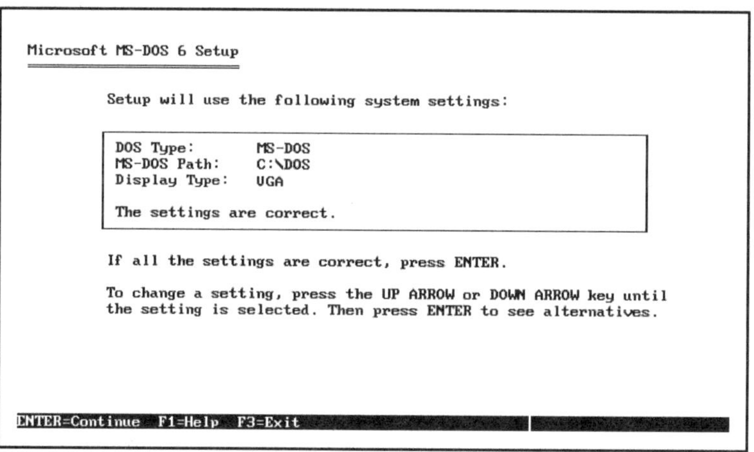

Figure 19.3

The system settings confirmation screen.

The system settings list is almost always correct and you probably won't need to change it. If you need to make any changes in these settings, however, use the up- and down-arrow keys to move the highlight bar to the item you want to change, and press Enter. Figure 19.4 is typical of the screens you use to make changes to the system settings.

This screen is easy to use. Simply move the highlight bar up or down the screen until the option you want is highlighted. Then press Enter. Setup returns to the screen shown in figure 19.3, and your change is made to the list of system settings.

6. The next screen lets you install optional software (see fig. 19.5). These optional programs (Backup, Undelete, and Anti-Virus) are all new DOS 6 features. As long as you have enough disk space, you should install all of them.

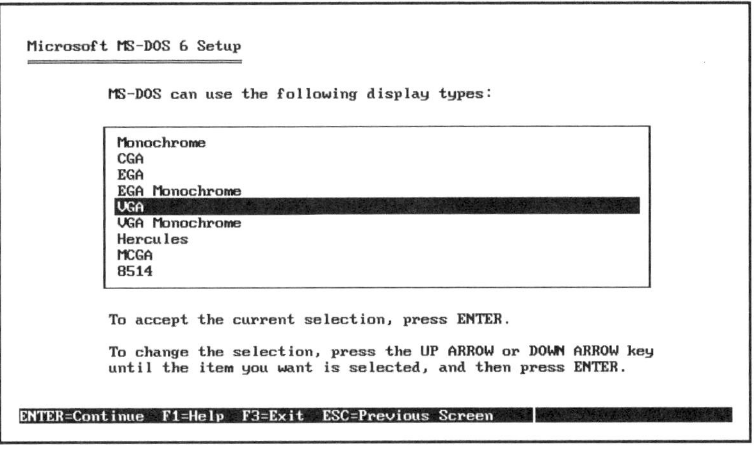

```
Microsoft MS-DOS 6 Setup

        MS-DOS can use the following display types:

          Monochrome
          CGA
          EGA
          EGA Monochrome
          VGA
          VGA Monochrome
          Hercules
          MCGA
          8514

        To accept the current selection, press ENTER.

        To change the selection, press the UP ARROW or DOWN ARROW key
        until the item you want is selected, and then press ENTER.

ENTER=Continue  F1=Help  F3=Exit  ESC=Previous Screen
```

Figure 19.4

A change system settings screen.

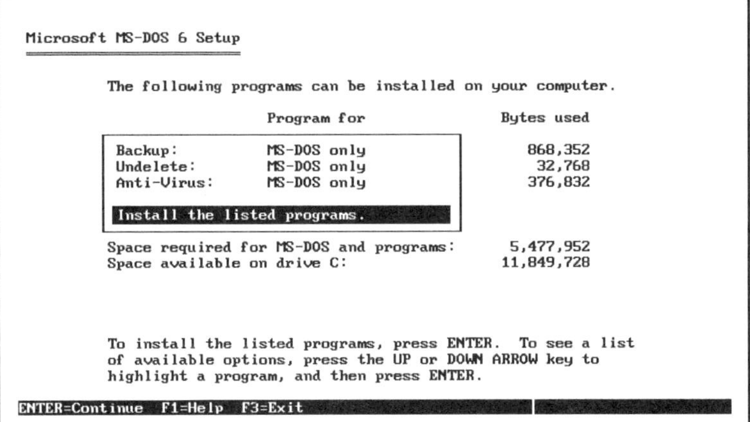

```
Microsoft MS-DOS 6 Setup

        The following programs can be installed on your computer.

                            Program for              Bytes used

          Backup:           MS-DOS only                 868,352
          Undelete:         MS-DOS only                  32,768
          Anti-Virus:       MS-DOS only                 376,832

          Install the listed programs.

        Space required for MS-DOS and programs:       5,477,952
        Space available on drive C:                  11,849,728


        To install the listed programs, press ENTER.  To see a list
        of available options, press the UP or DOWN ARROW key to
        highlight a program, and then press ENTER.
ENTER=Continue  F1=Help  F3=Exit
```

Figure 19.5

The optional programs selection screen.

NERDY DETAILS

If you plan to use Windows, you should install the Windows versions of these programs. To do so, follow the change procedure described in step 5.

The DOS 6 install is clever enough to find your Windows directory, and will ask you to confirm its location.

Let 'er Rip!

7. After you make your selection from the optional software screen and press Enter, you will have one last chance to verify that you intend to install DOS 6. If you're squeamish, now's your last chance to back out! If you decide to go on, Setup will begin copying the DOS 6 files from the floppy disk to your hard disk.

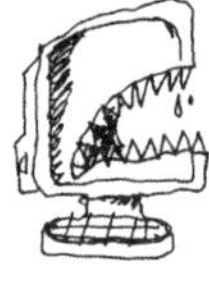

Do not disturb your computer while Setup is copying the DOS files. Just leave the computer alone while it copies the files. It knows what it's doing. All you have to do is sit back, take a potty break, get some java, and wait for DOS to ask you to put in a new floppy disk.

The Setup program does a lot of different things:

 It creates a new directory called `OLD_DOS.1`, in which DOS 6 saves some of your old DOS files in case you need to uninstall DOS 6 later.

 It asks you to insert your UNINSTALL disk (see fig. 19.6). Setup makes the UNINSTALL disk for you. Remember that if this disk has any files on in, they'll be erased.

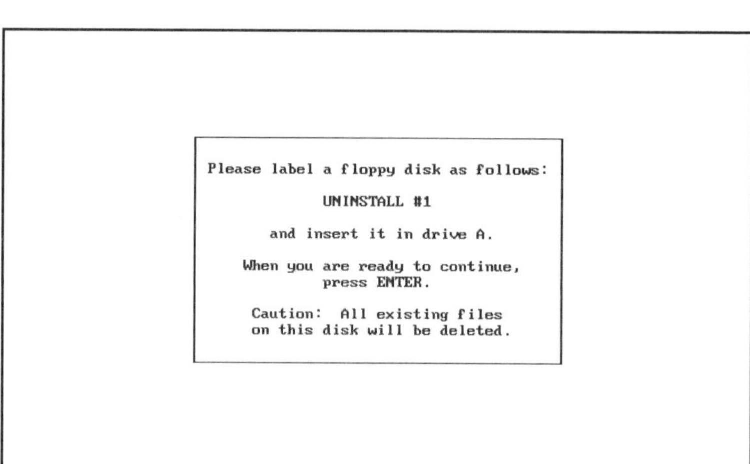

Please label a floppy disk as follows:
UNINSTALL #1
and insert it in drive A.
When you are ready to continue, press ENTER.
Caution: All existing files on this disk will be deleted.

Figure 19.6

The UNINSTALL disk prompt screen.

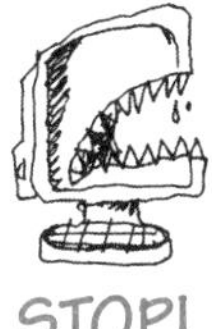

Do NOT forget to remove your DOS installation disk from the floppy drive and replace it with your carefully labeled UNINSTALL disk. Everything on the disk that is in the drive when you press Enter will be erased and replaced with uninstall files! This means you could easily erase your DOS installation disk if you do not take it out of the drive and replace it with the UNINSTALL disk. Take heed!

8. Setup asks you to flip-flop between your DOS setup disks and the UNINSTALL disk once or twice. Each time you put your UNINSTALL disk in the drive, Setup writes new files to it that are necessary for a successful uninstall.

9. While Setup is copying files from the floppies to your hard disk, from time to time it'll ask you to take the disk that's in the drive out and replace it with one of the other installation disks. Don't mix up your disks! Always make sure that you're putting in the right disk.

10. Finally, after the last disk is copied, Setup asks you to remove the last floppy disk from the disk drive, and press Enter. Setup reports that DOS 6 was successfully installed on your system. Press Enter and your computer automatically restarts. (Make sure that there are no disks in any of your floppy disk drives.) When your computer restarts, DOS 6 wakes up and goes to work.

Remember that your computer simply may not be able to run DOS 6. If your system fails to restart properly, jump down to the "Using the UNINSTALL Disk" section in this chapter. If things get really bad, you may have to call Microsoft for special help.

Otherwise, you have just successfully installed DOS 6 on your computer!

In Case Disaster Strikes

What do they say about the best-laid plans of mice and men? Or maybe Murphy said it best: if anything can go wrong, it will. If anything went wrong with DOS 6 and your computer, now is when you will probably find out. But don't worry. You're prepared!

If your computer refuses to work after you've installed DOS 6, you may need to use the UNINSTALL disk that you prepared earlier. Using this disk is simple:

1. Insert the UNINSTALL disk in drive A.
2. Restart the computer by pressing Ctrl-Alt-Del.
3. Your machine starts up by reading files from the UNINSTALL disk in drive A.
4. A message appears, as shown in figure 19.7. Notice that you must press **R** to continue with the uninstall process. If you press **E**, this "uninstallation" ends and your computer gets restarted yet again. (You have to remove the UNINSTALL disk from the drive if you decide to exit at this point.)

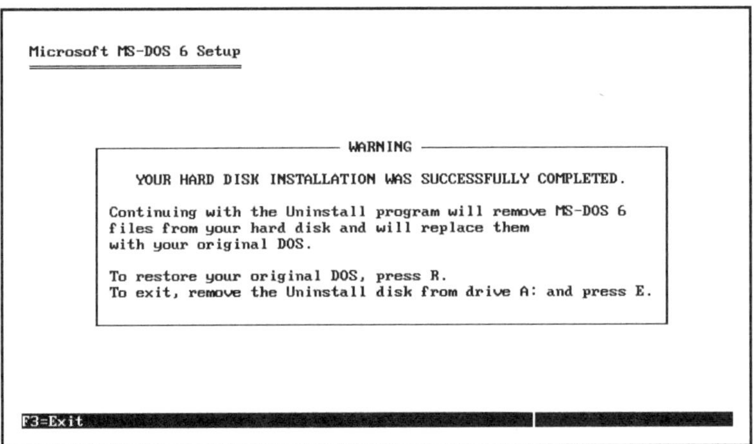

Figure 19.7
The UNINSTALL start-up screen.

He Who Uninstalls and Runs Away, Lives To Uninstall Another Day

Even a nerdy invention like UNINSTALL has its drawbacks. Sometimes it won't help you out of this jam. So don't try to use UNINSTALL:

-  If you've used the DOS 6 DoubleSpace disk-compression program.

 If you've deleted the OLD_DOS.1 directory from drive C. You may have deleted the directory so that you could use the disk space it was taking up. Ooops! If you can live with the disk space OLD_DOS.1 takes up, you should leave it just like it is for several weeks until you're sure that DOS 6 works.

 If some crazy nerd has repartitioned or reformatted your hard disk. (This is a very unlikely event. Chapter 14 briefly explains hard-disk partitioning. It is a quite advanced topic and is not required reading for non-nerds). If you think some nerd may have done this to you, however, find him and grill him. If he confesses to it, make him fix it, and then take away his propeller hat.

 If another dork has moved or renamed two secret DOS files (IO.SYS and MSDOS.SYS) in your hard disk's root directory. This is also a very unlikely event, but punishment is required if you find out that some nerd did it to you.

You cannot use an UNINSTALL disk that was created on another computer. Each UNINSTALL disk is a little different. Each one sets itself up to match the way your computer is set. An UNINSTALL disk will only work correctly on the PC in which it was created.

Killing Off Your Old Copy of DOS

Once you're sure that DOS 6 is working, go ahead and remove your old copy of DOS from your hard disk. Remember that DOS 6 put the old DOS into a directory called OLD_DOS.1. You may even have an OLD_DOS.2, OLD_DOS.3, ad nauseum, if you installed DOS 6 more than once. The OLD_DOS.x directory contains more than a megabyte of files. On a small hard disk, this can be a lot of room.

DOS 6 has a handy command called DELOLDOS that lets you kill off your old version of DOS in a snap. Just look at this as one chance to get even with DOS! Figure 19.8 shows DELOLDOS in action. The screen asks you to confirm that you want to delete the OLD_DOS.x directory.

Figure 19.8

DELOLDOS in action.

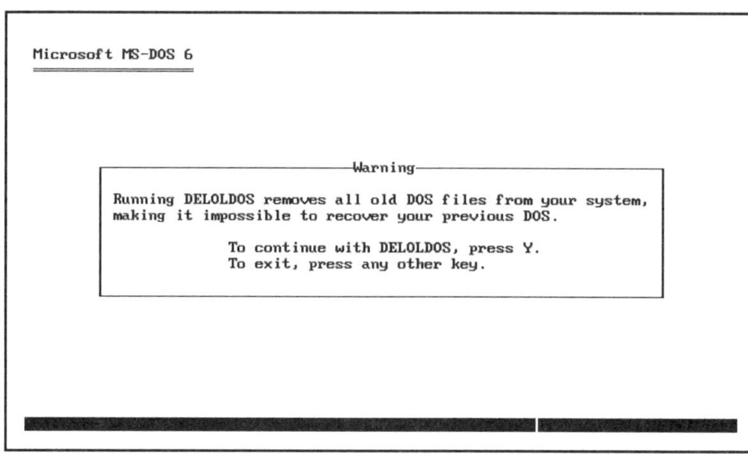

Microsoft MS-DOS 6
Warning
Running DELOLDOS removes all old DOS files from your system, making it impossible to recover your previous DOS.
To continue with DELOLDOS, press Y.
To exit, press any other key.

Press **Y**; DELOLDOS not only removes the `OLD_DOS.x` directory, it removes itself from your hard disk! Self-destructing DOS! What a concept!

Jump-Starting Your PC

I don't care how long you've been using computers. When the thing won't start, your first thought is to panic. Having your computer fail just before a big meeting is like having your car stall out in a bad neighborhood. Even the tough get squeamish.

Your computer can poop out and decide not to work for the following reasons, just to name a few:

 The start-up files on the hard disk have been damaged.

 A power failure or sudden jolt has damaged your hard disk.

 God is getting even with you for being mean to your younger brother when you were a kid. (God's funny that way, sometimes.)

In any case, you may turn on your PC and see this message:

```
Bad or missing Command Interpreter
```

Or this one:

```
Boot device not found
```

You can laugh at such messages if you're prepared. (Hey, even very experienced PC users fail to prepare for this one, so if you're smart about this, you'll be one up on the office nerd.) This section tells you how to create an *emergency start-up disk*. With such a disk, you can start your sick computer and figure out what the heck's wrong with it.

If your computer refuses to start, your first step should be to use the emergency start-up disk. Then you can turn to Part Four to find out how to get under way again.

For now, then, you need to make an emergency start-up disk and hide it away in a safe place. (Just don't forget where you put it. I've done that before.)

Making an Emergency Start-Up Disk

Follow these steps to create an emergency start-up disk:

1. Take a nice new floppy disk and stick it in drive A. (The disk does not have to be brand-new. It should, however, be in good shape and not beat up very much.)
2. Type in the following command:

   ```
   FORMAT A: /S /U /V:DOS6_BOOT
   ```

   If you don't know what formatting is, don't worry. For now, you just need to know that you are preparing the disk for use. If you want to save yourself some typing, you can leave out the `/U` and `/V:START_UP` portions of this command, but do not leave out the `/S` parameter.
3. When the `FORMAT` process has ended, DOS asks if you want to format another disk. Press **N**, and then press Enter.
4. Issue the following commands:

   ```
   COPY AUTOEXEC.BAT A:
   COPY CONFIG.SYS A:
   ```

   These commands will put the essential DOS start-up programs on your emergency disk.

Sometimes you may need to update some of the files on your emergency start-up disk. You may add commands to the AUTOEXEC.BAT or CONFIG.SYS files on your hard disk, particularly if you decide to use DoubleSpace or MSAV. (Both are described briefly in the next section and more completely in Chapter 14.)

The general rule is this: Whenever you change AUTOEXEC.BAT or CONFIG.SYS on your hard disk, you should take out your emergency start-up disk and update it.

Using the Emergency Start-Up Disk

Using your emergency start-up disk is easy:

1. Stick the emergency start-up disk in drive A.
2. Restart the computer by pressing Ctrl-Alt-Del.
3. Pray.

After a little while (maybe 30 seconds or so), your computer will start up by using the files on the floppy disk.

OK, What's So Great About DOS 6?

You probably think that anything as nerdy as DOS is not going to get your attention for very long. And it shouldn't. But you should know that your life at the computer can be made easier if you use DOS 6. Here's why.

Improve Your Memory!

One of the best-kept secrets of DOS 6 is MemMaker. Until DOS 6, PC memory management has always been a hit-or-miss, trial-and-error process. Even among the nerdiest of nerds, very few people really understand how to set up their computer's memory under older versions of DOS.

Make Your Hard Disk Bigger!

The second-best new feature of DOS (you may think it's the best one, but I don't, so there; NYYAAHHH!!!) is DoubleSpace. This truly magical DOS 6 feature transforms your wimpy little disk into a big, hefty whopper with twice the space you once had.

DoubleSpace makes your hard disk appear bigger than it really is by making your files smaller. DoubleSpace creates a new hard drive for you so that you end up with two hard disks when you only had one before. Sounds like something you've gotta have, doesn't it?

Organize Your Life (and Your Disk)!

As you use your disk over weeks and months, the files on your disk become *fragmented*. As you'll read in Chapter 14, this really can't be avoided, so don't worry about it. In short, it means that your files get scattered all over your hard disk. It's very disorganized, and it can really slow down your PC. The new DOS 6 DEFRAG program reorganizes your disk, restoring its former snappy performance.

NERDY DETAILS

> By the way: if you use DoubleSpace (and you really should), you should use only **DEFRAG** to optimize your disk. If someone has installed another disk optimizer on your computer, get rid of it, and use **DEFRAG** instead. It's good, reasonably fast, and it knows how to handle a DoubleSpace drive.

Protect Yourself from Antisocial Nerds!

Some socially unbalanced nerds like to write computer programs that destroy the files on the hard disk of an innocent bystander (that's you). These evil programs are called *viruses*, and they make trouble in many ways. See the following note if you want to know more about viruses.

NERDY DETAILS

Viruses work by attacking the master index that DOS uses to look up the files stored in your DOS filing cabinet. A virus might also reformat certain sensitive parts of your hard disk.

Chapter 7 is devoted to a discussion of viruses and other bombs that can explode inside your computer. Chapter 7 also discusses Microsoft Anti-Virus (MSAV), a life-saving program that comes with DOS 6.

C:>

The Most Common DOS Commands

Until now, you haven't had to deal much with the blank stare of the MS-DOS command line. Now you're headed into the belly of the beast.

As of DOS 6, there are more than 70 MS-DOS commands. You're still exonerated from knowing roughly 70% of them. The rest? Frankly, you can even avoid using some of these, if you're really determined to. Some of these tasks can be done through the DOS Shell, and certainly through Windows if you have it.

But the fact is, the fastest way to do many tasks is still the command line. It's like driving; now that you know the terrain a little, you can start taking the shortcut—which takes you squarely into `C:>` territory. And, even here in the mid-90s, a few things can *only* be done from the command line. So without any further ado...

This chapter discusses the most common commands, including:

 `DIR`

 `PATH`

 `COPY`

 `DISKCOPY`

- CD
- MD
- TYPE, MORE, EDIT
- DEL
- UNDELETE
- DELTREE
- FORMAT

Looking at Directory Contents with DIR

Let's start with an easy question: What files are in your computer?

You're at your C:> prompt, right? If it says A:> or some other letter, type **C:** and press Enter. Now, type:

DIR

Then press Enter. DOS responds with something like:

```
Volume in drive C has no label
Volume Serial Number is 1A56-422A
Directory of C:\
AUTOEXEC BAT       183 02-05-93  10:23a
DOS          <DIR>     02-15-93   6:15p
WINDOWS      <DIR>     02-15-93   6:54p
OLD_DOS  1   <DIR>     02-22-93   8:02a
COMMAND  COM     52925 02-12-93   6:00a
CONFIG   SYS       375 02-15-93   6:22p
MOVEDIR      <DIR>     02-28-93   7:47p
PSFONTS      <DIR>     02-15-93   7:38p
WINA20   386      9349 02-12-93   6:00a
        9 file(s)      62832 bytes
                    52912128 bytes free
```

This listing shows you file names and extensions (last names), whether an item is a file or directory, its size in bytes (roughly equal to characters), when files were last changed or directories created, the number of files listed and space (in bytes) that they take up, and the space in bytes left free on the disk.

NERDY DETAILS

Note that only files have file sizes listed. Although the file size is not listed for directories, they take up space—from 512 to 8192 bytes per directory. That can be a little misleading if you want to know how much space you have left (bytes free).

If you've been using your computer awhile, and especially if you've been careless about organizing your files, you might have a *very* long list of files in the `root` directory—too many to see at once. To see them a screen at a time, type:

```
DIR /P
```

Press Enter. DOS will pause after each screenful with a `Strike a key when ready...` or `Press any key to continue...` message.

You might want to see just the file names. The `/W` option displays the file names five across, with subdirectories shown in brackets.Type this:

```
DIR /W
```

You then see this:

```
Volume in drive C has no label
Volume Serial Number is 1A56-422A
Directory of C:\
AUTOEXEC.BAT [DOS]   [WINDOWS]       [OLD_DOS.1]     COMMAND.COM
CONFIG.SYS   [MOVEDIR]      [PSFONTS]        WINA20.386
        9 file(s)      62832 bytes
                    52912128 bytes free
```

The `/P` and `/W` options are all you have in earlier versions of DOS, but DOS 5 and 6 have a whole lot more tricks you can use, as follows.

Seeing Files with DOS 5 or 6 in Any Order You Want

Now let's work on the order in which the listings appear. DOS 6 (and 5) gives you all sorts of control with the `/O` (Order) option:

`DIR /O:N` lists files alphabetically, A to Z.

`DIR /O:E` lists files alphabetically by extension.

`DIR /O:D` lists files by time (date), oldest to newest.

`DIR /O:S` lists files by size, smallest to largest.

`DIR /O:G` lists directories first, then files.

With a simple minus sign, you can make DOS do somersaults for you. This example lists files alphabetically, Z to A:

```
DIR /O:-N
```

The colon (:) after the `/O` isn't required, but it makes it a little easier to read. `DIR /O:S` is the same as `DIR /OS`.

You can even combine sorting methods. For example, `DIR /O:NE` or `DIR /ONE` sorts by name, then by extension.

Getting Even More File Information with DOS 5 or 6

Like Chuck Connors in the old TV western *Branded*, every file you possess contains a secret byte that brands it in the eyes of DOS. It's called the *attribute byte*, and it tells DOS your file has one or more of these attributes:

Archivable	This file's changed since you last backed it up.
System	DOS needs this file or it won't work.
Hidden	This file is hidden from normal listings.

Read-Only	You can read or copy this file, but not delete or change it.
Directory	This is a directory, not a regular file.

You can sort directory listings by attribute, using the `/A` option:

`DIR /A` lists all files, including system and hidden files.

`DIR /A:A` lists only files that have changed since the last backup.

`DIR /A:S` lists only system files.

`DIR /A:H` lists only hidden files.

`DIR /A:R` lists only read-only files.

`DIR /A:D` lists only directories.

And the minus signs work here, too. This example lists files that haven't changed:

```
DIR /A:-A
```

The colon (:) after the `/A` isn't required, but it makes it easier to read. You can also combine atributes; for example, `DIR /A:SH` or `DIR /ASH` lists only files that are both system and hidden.

NERDY DETAILS

Although the **DIR** command lists the files with the attributes you specify, it doesn't show the specific attributes with the files. You can use the **ATTRIB** command to list the files and show the attributes, or to change most of these attributes. Type **HELP ATTRIB**, and press Enter to learn how. Note that when you specify multiple attributes, DIR lists only files with *all* of them, but **ATTRIB** lists files with *any* of them.

Looking in Subdirectories for Files with DOS 5 or 6

Ever leave a file somewhere, and forget where you put it? DIR's nifty /S option can help with that, too. Type this to see all occurrences of FILENAME.TXT on drive C:

```
DIR C:\FILENAME.TXT /S
```

Combining the /S option with wild cards is a great way to search for lost files.

Tailoring Searches with Multiple Options

You can mix and match these different DIR options. For example, you can list your files from newest to oldest, and from largest to smallest. You can also include all system and hidden files, and list the files five-across ("wide"). To do this, type:

```
DIR /W /O:-D-S /A
```

Heck of a thing to try to remember. Fortunately, DOS lets you create a default DIR listing. Just include the parameters in your AUTOEXEC.BAT file, like this:

```
SET DIRCMD=/W /O:-D-S /A
```

Don't include DIR here, just the parameters. These new parameters will go into effect as soon as you restart your computer. Then, when you use DIR without any options, it will use the options you put in your AUTOEXEC.BAT file. When you use DIR with other options, it ignores the options you put in your AUTOEXEC.BAT file.

Telling DOS Where To Find Things with PATH

You learned about root directories and subdirectories in Chapter 13. Think of PATH as clearing the snow out of all your friends' driveways, so you can get directly to any house you expect to visit.

What's your PATH statement right now? Type:

```
PATH
```

Press Enter and DOS will tell you.

Duplicating a File with COPY

You learned how to use this whizzy command in earlier chapters.

Here's a simple COPY file :

```
COPY FILE1.DOC FILE2.DOC.
```

This takes the file FILE1.DOC, makes a new, identical copy named FILE2.DOC, and places it in the same directory.

COPY also works with the nifty * and ? wild cards you learned about in Chapter 13. To copy all files in a subdirectory onto a floppy, type:

```
COPY C:\DIRECTRY\*.* B:
```

Assuming that they fit, that is. If you run out of space, COPY will quit dead in its tracks—leaving you to figure out what still needs to be copied.

COPY can also *concatenate* files, which means that it can combine multiple files into one. Once every century or two, you might actually want to concatenate files. But for every person who does this intentionally, 100 people do it by accident—and destroy their data as a result.

Most data files simply don't cotton to concatenation. They include formatting commands that belong in specific locations and can't be scrunched together with formatting commands from other files.

Here is how you can screw things up royally. We'll show you this in slow motion. Let's say you want to use a wild card to copy multiple DOC files to a single subdirectory, C:\FILES. You type:

```
COPY *.DOC C:\FILES
```

But you forgot: you don't have a C:\FILES directory. *Or* your FILES directory is on drive D. *Or* you spelled FILES wrong. In any case, DOS will copy all the DOC files in your current directory into one big, useless concatenated file. Good luck sorting through the wreckage!

Duplicating a Disk with DISKCOPY

So you want to be a good computing citizen, and back up your new program the way you're supposed to. DOS comes with a utility called DISKCOPY that copies everything on a diskette onto another identical diskette. Hidden files, system files, subdirectories, even empty ones—everything. See Chapter 13 for the real skinny on DISKCOPY.

Changing to Someplace Else on the Disk with CD

We've talked a lot about using full path names to help DOS get to a specific file. But what if you simply want to change current directories yourself? That's what CD (change directories, or the identical CHDIR command) is for.

In the simplest case, suppose that you're in the root directory of drive C, and you want to go to a subdirectory called JONES. Type this:

```
CD JONES
```

This tells DOS to look in its current directory, and change to the directory C:\JONES. (It also works if you are in C:\OUTLAWS and want to go to the subdirectory C:\OUTLAWS\JONES. It works as long as the subdirectory you want to use is in the current directory.)

But what if you're in C:\SMITH, and C:\JONES isn't in your current path? Your disk structure ("tree") looks like this:

```
C:
¦
________________________________
¦                ¦                ¦
SMITH          WESSON          JONES
```

You have to tell DOS to start at the `root` directory, and then "root around" from there. So the following command does the job:

```
CD \JONES
```

Suppose you're buried deep in some subdirectory structure. You've been messing around in `C:\PROGRAM\DATA\SUBDATA`, and you want to change your current directory to the `root` directory. Again, you can use the backslash:

```
CD \
```

Here's a shortcut. Pretend you're back in the depths of **C:\PROGRAM\DATA\SUBDATA**, and you want to move horizontally, within the same structure, to **C:\PROGRAM\DATA\OTHRSTUF**. DOS recognizes two dots (..) to mean that you want to go one step up, and work from the parent directory. You can just type:

```
CD ..\OTHRSTUF
```

You can use .. with any DOS command that accepts a path, by the way. (Impress your friends!)

`CD` always changes the directory on the current drive unless you tell it otherwise. However, you can actually change current directories on *another* drive without going to that drive by using the drive name in your `CD` command:

```
CD D:\JONES
```

When you later change drives, you'll find yourself in the D:\JONES subdirectory.

Making a New Directory with MD

What if you need to create a new directory? Let's say you're in the root directory of drive C, and you want to create C:\NEWSTUFF. Child's play—you use MD (make directory, or the identical MKDIR command) like this:

```
MD NEWSTUFF
```

All the variations on this theme are identical to those of CD. If you're buried deep in some subdirectory, and you want to create a new directory one level under the root directory, use the backslash:

```
MD \NEWSTUFF
```

If you want to create the subdirectory on another drive, specify the drive:

```
MD D:\NEWSTUFF
```

And if you're deep in a subdirectory structure and want to create another subdirectory "next to" the one you're in, type:

```
MD ..\NEWSTUFF
```

Viewing the Contents of a File with TYPE, MORE, and EDIT

Since its first version, DOS has offered a clumsy way for you to see what's in a file: TYPE. You just type the command plus the file name, and press Enter. (You also have to include the full path if it's not in your current directory, but that's true for all DOS commands, so I'll stop telling you that.)

For example:

```
TYPE README.TXT
```

The information scrolls by on the screen. If it's a long file, it scrolls off the top of the screen. But you can use `MORE` instead of `TYPE` to pause it so that you can read it:

```
MORE < README.TXT
```

Now the information appears a screen at a time, and pauses with a `—More—` prompt; just press any key to see the next screen. Notice the < character (if you forget it, you see a `Too many arguments in command line` error).

A file with a `TXT` extension is the best kind of file to view using `TYPE` or `MORE` because it's usually all ASCII characters (mostly normal letters and numbers). Software vendors use files with names like these to include information that wasn't ready in time for the manual (such as new bugs).

You shouldn't use `TYPE` or `MORE` with formatted files, such as those files that most programs create. The formatting or data generally shows up as gibberish, may beep at you, and often won't display the whole file.

Another way to view (and edit) files is `EDIT`, which loads the file into the Editor program. Now you can at least scroll around and try to find the evidence you're looking for. To do this, type:

```
EDIT README.TXT
```

Press Enter. (See Chapter 5 for information on using `EDIT`.) If you really want to rummage around, View File Contents in the DOS Shell will show you the file in ASCII and hexadecimal at the same time!

Removing a File from the Disk with DEL

`DEL` and its identical twin `ERASE` do a masterful job of eliminating files you don't want. (The trick, as always, is to keep them from trashing anything you do want.)

To delete a file in your current directory, type **DEL** followed by the file name:

```
DEL USELESS.TXT
```

To delete a file elsewhere on disk or on another disk, include the full path name:

```
DEL D:\WORTHLES\USELESS.TXT
```

To delete everything in a subdirectory, use something like:

```
DEL D:\WORTHLES\*.*
```

To which DOS will respond:

```
All files in directory will be deleted!
Are you sure (Y/N)?
```

Y kills them, **N** spares them.

If you're preparing to do some serious damage, you might want to know about these two precautions:

First, before deleting files with a wild card, try the same file specifications with DIR—so you know exactly what you're terminating. For example, try this first command before you try the second:

```
DIR D:\FILES\*.*

DEL D:\FILES\*.*
```

You can also ask DOS to prompt you for each file deletion using the /P option:

```
DEL D:\FILES\*.* /P
```

Just don't get that itchy trigger finger—by the time you realize you've deleted a file, it's long gone.

Fixing the Damage with UNDELETE

By the way, what if you've just deleted a file you need? DOS now offers a fairly sophisticated UNDELETE capability (covered extensively in other chapters). But you've got to use it right away. Think of UNDELETE as you think of antidotes for poison: stop what you're doing, and deal with the problem *right now*.

Deleting Whole Trees, Files, and Directories with DELTREE

Before DOS 6, you had to delete one subdirectory at a time. If a subdirectory had subdirectories, all of the contents had to go, too. First, you had to delete everything in each subdirectory, including any hidden or read-only files. Finally, once you had stripped each subdirectory clean, you had to use the RD command to delete it.

Now, with DOS 6 and DELTREE, it's easy. DELTREE is like some deadly ancient curse: it kills your directory, and all its contents, and all its "child" subdirectories, and all their contents... wiping out the entire line of directories and files in the path you choose.

To use DELTREE, type **DELTREE** followed by the name of the directory you plan to zap, and press Enter:

```
DELTREE DEADFILS
```

You'll be prompted for each directory or subdirectory you wish to delete:

```
Delete directory DEADFILS and all its subdirectories? [Y/N]
```

Press **Y**, and they're gone.

Preparing a New Disk for Use with FORMAT

You're an expert at this now (to brush up, refer to Chapter 13).

In Chapter 21, we'll extend your knowledge of DOS commands—giving you more control over your computer. By the end of Chapter 21, your computer will know who's boss...even if *you're* still not quite convinced.

A Bunch of Other Useful DOS Commands

This chapter gives you a quick intro to a few commands that tell you what's going on inside your computer... and what you can do about it if you don't like what you see:

- `VER` tells you what version of DOS you're running.
- `CHKDSK` reports on the status of your disk and fixes some logical errors.
- `MEM` gives you a detailed report on your memory usage.
- `MSD` gives you an incredibly detailed report on everything that's going on inside your computer.
- `TIME` and `DATE` let you set the time and date.
- `PROMPT` lets you change the looks of your command prompt.
- `LABEL` lets you name a disk.
- `VOL` lets you check your disk's name and serial number.
- `REN` lets you rename a file.
- `MOVE` lets you move files and rename directories.

What DOS Are You Using? Ask VER

That's easy enough. Maybe you just upgraded to DOS 6... so that's what version of DOS you're running.

If you're using an earlier version of DOS, you're missing out on some useful capabilities and some other features may work a little differently—especially if you're using a version of DOS earlier than DOS 5.

 **If you're using DOS 5...** you're missing disk compression, MemMaker, defragmentation, anti-virus protection, easy backup...

 **If you're using DOS 4...**you're also missing the improved DOS Shell, partitions larger than 32M, UNFORMAT and UNDELETE, the capability to load DOS outside conventional memory, on-line help for commands...

 **If you're using DOS 3...**you're also missing any shell at all, extended partitions...

 **If you're using DOS 2...**you're also missing all network support, support for high-density diskettes, Windows compatibility...

Now that we've finished shilling for Microsoft's upgrade business, go ahead and type:

```
VER
```

Then press Enter. DOS will report the version it's running, like:

```
MS-DOS Version 6
```

VER checks the version of two hidden DOS files. You can also use COMMAND.COM to check the version (and copyright) of DOS. Just type **COMMAND**, and press Enter at the DOS prompt. Check to be sure that it reports the same version as VER. Sometimes weird problems are caused by different VER and COMMAND versions, which can happen if a different COMMAND.COM accidently gets copied to the root directory. After using COMMAND to check the version, type **EXIT** and press Enter (for reasons too nerdy to go into).

How's Your Hard Disk Today? Ask CHKDSK!

You may not be able to determine whether life makes sense, but you *can* make sure that your *disk* makes sense (to make sure its logical structure is intact). And you can even fix things if it isn't. Sort of. That's what CHKDSK is for.

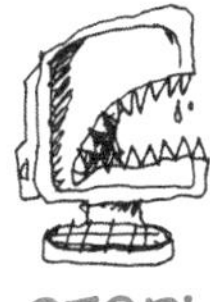

STOP!

> Before you run **CHKDSK**, always exit any running program, Windows, or the DOS Shell. (Don't use a command prompt from within Windows or the Shell. *Exit!*)
>
> If you don't, **CHKDSK** may find problems where there aren't any. Quite naturally, you might ask it to fix them—and that will *cause* problems!

CHKDSK always gives you this basic information about your disk:

-  Disk name and serial number.
-  Total disk space.
-  Space available.
-  Cluster or allocation-unit size.

Especially if you've been using your disk a while, you're likely to see a message like this, too:

```
Errors found, F parameter not specified
Corrections will not be written to disk
   12 lost allocation units found in 7 chains.
   24576 bytes disk space would be freed
```

Say *what???*

Don't sweat it, this happens all the time. CHKDSK simply checked your disk's *FAT* (*File Allocation Table*, a table that tells DOS where all parts of all files are), and found some fragments—chunks of files that no longer have a matching directory entry. These fragments are *lost allocation units*. Orphaned.

What's in them? Probably garbage. Maybe you turned off a computer before it had a chance to save temporary files. (Don't do it again!) Don't worry too much; if it was something really important, you'd probably have noticed.

Still, you might as well fix them—you can't use that disk space until you do. So type:

```
CHKDSK /F
```

Press Enter, and DOS responds:

```
Volume Serial Number is 1A56-422A
  12 lost allocation units found in 7 chains.
Convert lost chains to files (Y/N)?
```

You should press **N**, which simply deletes the lost chains without further rigamarole.

You might run into things that CHKDSK can't fix: for example, a *cross-linked cluster*, which is a cluster that DOS thinks belongs to more than one file (which, of course, isn't possible). The best you can do is to copy each of those files to other locations, erase the originals, and hope for the best.

CHKDSK is good for one other thing—it gives you a complete list of every file on your disk. Type the following, and press Enter:

```
CHKDSK /V
```

V stands for *verbose*, and is aptly named. You may want to slow down the flood of output to one page at a time:

```
CHKDSK /V | MORE
```

By the way, some people think CHKDSK does all kinds of things it really doesn't do. It doesn't fix physical disk damage. It doesn't prevent you from using damaged disk sectors. It doesn't even fix lost allocation units and chains unless you tell it to with the /F option.

I Can't Remember! Where Your Memory's Gone with CHKDSK and MEM

I skipped over the last two lines of your CHKDSK listing. They tell you how much conventional memory you have. For example:

```
655360 total bytes memory
578380 bytes free
```

You may be thinking: he's got 578K out of 640K available—not too shabby! But it's not quite as good as it looks. Remember, these are *special* Ks: they have 1,024 bytes, not 1,000. So 578380 bytes is really less than 565K.

As your available Ks plummet down through the 500s and into the 400s, some programs will slow down—or refuse to load. So available memory is pretty important.

You may very well want more information about your memory than CHKDSK can give you. For example, CHKDSK doesn't tell you about extended memory, which Windows eats as if it were Audrey, the bloodthirsty plant in *Little Shop of Horrors. ("Feed me... now!")*

See Chapter 12 for all the memory particulars.

Hercule Poirot Reports on Your PC with MSD

It's shocking. One day you'll have a problem you can't solve. And when you call the technical support line, you may be asked some very bizarre questions. What interrupts are you using? What's in your WIN.INI file? What TSRs are you running?

This is *not* the stuff of everyday conversation.

But if you have DOS 6 you'll be ready, thanks to MSD, which is your computer's very own system detective. It looks under every rock and takes notes, preparing an incredibly detailed report about your computer's guts. Print yourself an MSD report, file it away, and when the worst happens, you'll be ready to answer any question they throw at you. Here's how:

1. Load your printer full of paper. You'll need at least 30 sheets. If you're running Windows, load 50 sheets to be on the safe side.
2. At the command prompt (*not* from within Windows or the DOS Shell), type **MSD**.
3. Press Alt-F to activate the File menu.
4. Press **P** for Print Report.
5. Press Enter twice. Now go have coffee.

By the way, in extremely rare instances, Poirot behaves more like Clousseau, and crashes the system. Don't sweat it, just reboot and go about your business like nothing happened. No harm, no foul.

It's About Time To Use TIME and DATE

What's today's date? Chances are, your PC knows. Type:

```
DATE
```

Press Enter, and DOS responds with something like:

```
Current date is 06-14-93
Enter new date (mm-dd-yy):
```

If your computer says 01-01-1980, you *definitely* need to wind its clock. Well, not quite wind it. You just type the new date, following the correct month/day/year format:

```
06-17-93
```

Press Enter. If your computer has a working clock and battery, you're in business. If not, it'll keep track until you turn your computer off, and then softly return to the days of Jimmy Carter and Ayatollah Khomeini.

By the way, DOS won't accept 2-29-93... it *knows* 1993 isn't a leap year.

Unless you live in Indiana (where this book was published), you'll need to change the TIME at least twice a year to deal with Daylight Savings Time. Also, you should check it periodically because most computer clocks aren't real accurate.

TIME works the same way. Type **TIME**, and press Enter for the current time. DOS responds to within one-hundredth of a second:

```
Current time is  5:35:58.03p
Enter new time:
```

You can enter the new time like **6:35** (which DOS assumes to be a.m.), tell it a.m. or p.m.: **6:35A** or **6:35:59P** (the seconds are optional), or use military time: **18:35** (6:35 p.m.).

All of this "timefoolery" is actually useful, of course, if you want to *time-stamp* a document so you know when you created it and when you revised it. It won't hold up in a court of law, but it can keep you from copying an older version over a newer one.

Customizing the DOS Command Prompt with PROMPT

Chances are, when you type **C:**, the prompt C:> appears, indicating that you're now working on drive C.

Or, perhaps, the prompt shows your current subdirectory, too:

```
C:\WINDOWS>
```

This type of prompt is set by the standard prompt command that DOS 6 installs in your AUTOEXEC.BAT file:

```
PROMPT $P$G
```

$P gives you the path; $G gives you the more-than symbol ">".

Most people are so used to this prompt, they can't envision anything else. And it is fairly useful. If your system doesn't display it, you should add it to your AUTOEXEC.BAT file. But you might also check out some options. For example, you can add the time, using $T for the time:

```
PROMPT $P$G$T
```

This gives you a prompt something like this:

```
C:\WINDOWS14:04:03.52>
```

We can clean that up a bit.

```
PROMPT $P$G $T
```

This gives you:

```
C:\WINDOWS 14:04:03.52>
```

Adding a space in the command adds a space in the prompt. You can add any text you like to the prompt:

```
PROMPT IT'S $T! GET BACK TO WORK!$G
```

This gives you (or your favorite colleague):

```
IT'S 14:04:03.52! GET BACK TO WORK!>
```

Note that the text itself doesn't require a $ preface.

In addition to path, time, date and text, here are some other goodies you can include in your command prompt:

Command Prompt	How You Get It
$	$$
<	$L
=	$Q
¦	$B

Command Prompt	How You Get It
Backspace	$H
Current drive	$N
DOS version #	$V

Whenever you change a prompt from the command line, the new prompt starts working immediately. But to keep it working, you need to include the new PROMPT command in your AUTOEXEC.BAT file.

NERDY DETAILS

Don't get too carried away—the **PROMPT** information has to sit in a tiny memory area called the Environment Space. If it gets too big, DOS won't work until you increase its size. And that's a whole other lecture.

Name That Disk with LABEL and VOL

When you format a disk of any kind, it automatically gets a serial number made up of eight random numbers and letters, which, by my count, means that you could conceivably format 5.4 trillion diskettes before you would get a duplicate.

You might, however, want a more personal way of tracking your diskettes. After formatting, you're also asked if you want to name a diskette:

```
Volume label (11 characters, ENTER for none)?
```

It's a bit like naming a file, but you don't have to worry about an extension, and you *can* use spaces. Don't use these characters, though—DOS has other plans for them:

* ? / \ | . , ; : + = [ ] ( ) & ^ < > "

You can also name or rename a disk later using the LABEL command with the correct drive name. Let's say you want to name the disk in drive A 1993 FILES. Type:

```
LABEL A: 1993 FILES
```

Want to delete the label? Easy. Type:

```
LABEL A:
```

Press Enter, and DOS responds:

```
Volume in drive A is 1993 FILES
Volume Serial Number is 1A56-422A
Volume label (11 characters, ENTER for none)?
```

Press Enter. DOS asks you to confirm:

```
Delete current volume label (Y/N)?
```

Press **Y**. The deed is done.

If you just want to *see* the current volume serial number and label, the VOL command will do the same job:

```
VOL A:
```

Voila! The DIR command also displays the label.

If you don't include a drive name, VOL (and LABEL) changes the label of the disk in your current drive.

Giving a New Name to a File with REN

Now that you know how to rename a disk, I'll show you something you'll probably do more often: how to rename a *file*.

Let's say you've got a file called NEWFILE.DOC in the subdirectory D:\ALLFILES. You want to rename it OLDFILE.BAK. Here's how:

```
REN D:\ALLFILES\NEWFILE.DOC OLDFILE.BAK
```

If you don't include a path for the original file name, REN looks in the current directory. You don't need a path for the new name, however, because it always stays the same as the original.

TRICKS

You can change both the file name and the extension at the same time. If you only want to change part of the name, REN doesn't skimp on support for wild cards:

```
REN D:\ALLFILES\*.DOC *.BAK
```

This changes the extension of *all* DOC files in the D:\ALLFILES subdirectory.

REN is the rare DOS command that actually looks out for your interests, rather than assuming that you know what you're doing. If you try to rename a file to use the same name as another file in the same directory, it'll stop you:

```
Duplicate file name or file not found
```

REN *looks* as if it might move files, too. No such luck. For that, you need the spanking-new DOS 6 command MOVE. This seems like a good time to MOVE on...

MOVEing and Shaking Files and Directories in DOS 6

The DOS 6 MOVE command moves files, but it only renames directories. To move a file, first specify the path and name of the file; then show where you want DOS to stick it:

```
MOVE C:\CURRENT\NOV1992.DOC C:\OLDFILES
```

This moves the file NOV1992.DOC from the subdirectory C:\CURRENT into the subdirectory C:\OLDFILES.

That's the basic MOVE. Now let's add some steps...

To MOVE all the files in C:\CURRENT into C:\OLDFILES, type:

```
MOVE C:\CURRENT\*.* C:\OLDFILES
```

To rename the single file NOV1992.DOC while moving it:

```
MOVE C:\CURRENT\NOV1992.DOC C:\OLDFILES\ARCH1192.DOC
```

But you *can't* rename several files while moving them. (Use REN first, then MOVE them.)

Got all that? Then get this: MOVE *renames* directories. But it doesn't actually move them. Well, we'll take what we can get— before MOVE, even renaming a directory was a major hassle. Now, all you have to do is type:

```
MOVE C:\NEWDIR OLDDIR
```

NERDY DETAILS

Actually, when you rename a subdirectory, its entry *does* get moved within DOS' internal structure. But *you* don't see any movement, and if you try to move one subdirectory into a different directory or onto a different disk, it won't work.

And, just like that, you've got another 11 DOS commands under your belt. Heck, why stop now? Read on to learn even more!

PART 7

Resources for Non-Nerds

PTOOEY

Where Do You Go Now?

By now, you are beginning to make sense of all that DOS and PC information that's out there. And maybe you're thinking that this computing business isn't going to be so painful after all, now that you know the basics. Good for you!

User, Educate Thyself!

Don't stop now! You're ready to build on your new-found computer smarts, and here's a quick overview of some good sources for continuing your DOS education (and no, friend, we promise you won't transmogrify into a... a... a computer *nerd*!).

Magazines

Years ago, circa 1983 B.D.T.P. (Before Desktop Publishing), I edited a small magazine that had *nothing* to do with computers. The magazine was *so* small, I had to do everything—including graphic design.

Knowing nothing whatsoever about magazine design, I went out and bought an armful of magazines to look at, including a whole bunch of those weird new computer magazines for nerds. Lo and behold, I got interested in the stuff... and what do you know? *Now I'm an author.*

It could happen to you, too. Here's a guide to some current computer magazines that will, at the least, teach you some good stuff, and—who knows?—may lead you to become one of my competitors.

Note that all prices are the introductory prices you get by sending in one of those annoying blow-in cards.

PC Novice, $24.00/year, monthly, Peed Communications. If you're still feeling *really* insecure, here's a good place to start. It has clear and simple explanations of very basic topics. Recent articles include: "What are Memory Chips?" "How to Install and Delete Programs," and "What You Can Do With a PC." There's also a glossary of terms in every issue.

DOS Resource Guide, $23.70/year, bimonthly, IDG. Good, strong, hands-on information about using MS-DOS; full of batch files and tips, though a bit expensive at almost $4/issue—$4.95 on the newsstand. Think of it as almost a cross between a specialized newsletter and a magazine.

Home Office Computing, $10.99/year, monthly, Scholastic. Brief reviews of selected PC and Macintosh products combined with ways to run your own small business using computers, faxes, and other technologies.

PC Computing, $19.97/year, monthly, Ziff-Davis. A wide-ranging overview of PC-based systems for non-experts who are still willing to read a moderately technical explanation here and there. *PC Computing* spices its offerings with the occasional literary excerpt, such as unauthorized biographies of (Microsoft founder and wunderkind) Bill Gates, and surprisingly amusing columns by Penn & Teller's Penn Jillette.

PC Magazine, $29.97/year, twice monthly, Ziff-Davis. This is the preeminent source of comprehensive review information, which is generated in a sophisticated test laboratory. Add to that an extensive section of hints on operating environments, word processing, spreadsheets, databases, graphics, networking, and programming, and you have an industry-leading source of information for the corporate power user.

Computer Shopper, $19.97/year, monthly, Ziff-Davis. *Computer Shopper* is the heart and soul of the incredibly competitive mail-order computer business. It often comes within a hair of 1,000 tabloid-size pages. (That twenty bucks comes to roughly 75 cents a pound. If you subscribe, you may want to up your mailman's Christmas tip.) There's no better resource for finding hardware bargains.

In the past few years, the *Computer Shopper* (and its younger, smaller brother, *PC Sources*) has also become quite a good source of information about new technologies. With hundreds of pages of editorial space to fill, *Computer Shopper* is also a good source for up-to-date bulletin board and user group information.

If you're running Windows, you'll want to read *Windows Magazine*, $14.97/year, CMP Publications, and *Windows Sources*, $19.97/year, Ziff-Davis.

Finally, if you're interested in how the other half (well, more precisely, the other *eighth*) lives, here are two Macintosh monthlies. *MacUser*, $19.97/year, monthly, Ziff-Davis, focuses on reviews and how-to info. *Macworld*, $24.00/year, monthly, PCW Communications, leans toward more general-interest Macintosh coverage.

Of course, you may not want to spend a small fortune, buying these publications for months, as you try to decide which one(s) are for you. No problem. Most public and university libraries carry a decent selection of computer magazines. The Holy Grail of PC poop is yours for a pittance.

Books (Ours, Of Course)

A technical step up from this book is *Inside DOS 6,* from New Riders Publishing. It contains roughly 1400 pages of information on making the most of DOS 6, with very detailed coverage of all the new DOS 6 features, including MemMaker, Microsoft Anti-Virus, Microsoft Backup, and DoubleSpace.

You may also be interested to know that *DOS 6 for Non-Nerds* is part of a growing family of New Riders Publishing titles for "non-nerds", which currently includes:

 *Windows for Non-Nerds*

 *PCs for Non-Nerds*

 *OS/2 for Non-Nerds*

So you can upgrade or migrate to your heart's content and still remain a non-nerd!

Television

With a little bit of digging, even you couch potatoes can find TV shows that can further your computer education.

These programs include *The Computer Chronicles* from PBS, which are broadcast at various times throughout the country. *PCTV* and *MacTV,* available on the Mind Extension University cable channel, are produced by PC Connection, the leading mail order software house. Check your local listings or cable distributor (where applicable) for broadcast times and channels.

Daily Newspapers

Many daily newspapers now carry a weekly syndicated column on computers, often as part of a science/health section.

On-Line Services

Several commercial on-line services offer specific PC and DOS support information. (Non-commercial bulletin boards are covered in Chapter 24.)

Sometimes you can access official information from the manufacturers of hardware and software, including Microsoft. You can also learn from the hard-won experience of other users who know the answer to your question because they've been down that road themselves.

For DOS 6 itself, the best source is *CompuServe*, which contains Microsoft Connection (a set of forums run by Microsoft). You can search a database of more than 14,000 articles about Microsoft products; download new device drivers and other software from the Microsoft Software Library; or enter the DOS and Windows forums, browse the messages, and ask specific questions.

CompuServe currently costs $8.95 a month, which buys unlimited access to a wide range of basic services and roughly 60 free electronic mail messages (you don't get access to Microsoft Connection or to dozens of other software support forums). For those, you pay another $8 per hour if you're using a 1200-bps or 2400-bps modem. For information about joining CompuServe, call 1-800-848-8199.

Other commercial on-line sources for support on PC topics follow (phone numbers are voice numbers for information):

- *America On-Line*, 1-800-227-5938, Computing & Software Section, Industry Connection, Microsoft Support area. An up-and-coming on-line service.
- *BIX* (Byte Interactive Exchange), 1-800-544-4005. PC and DOS operating systems (`ibm.dos` section). BIX is a bit on the technical side, and you might find less patience for "how do I format a disk"-type questions.
- *Delphi* (General Videotex Corporation), 1-800-544-4005, Computing Groups menu, PC Compatibles/IBM Special Interest Group. Offers very good deals if you spend a lot of time on-line.
- *GEnie* (General Electric Information Services), 1-800-638-9636. Microsoft RoundTable, PC Support section. Basic service is only $4.95 per month—a good deal.
- *Prodigy* (Prodigy Services Corporation, a joint venture of IBM and Sears), 1-800-PRODIGY. Computers & Technology Section, Info, Experts & Bulletin Boards areas. Prodigy may be a good choice for beginners—it's highly visual, and it caters to non-experts. The downside is that it can be very slow if you're running a slow PC, and there's a lot of advertising.

In Your PC

Just a reminder that DOS 6 itself comes with basic help, examples of ways that every command can be used, and information about critical system files such as `AUTOEXEC.BAT` and `CONFIG.SYS`. Just type **HELP** followed by the command name, as in:

```
HELP INTERLNK
```

or

```
HELP CONFIG.SYS
```

NERDY DETAILS

Microsoft's DOS 6 manual, although not nearly as complete as it used to be (or as it ought to be), does offer some useful information about the new features, such as InterLnk, Anti-Virus, DoubleSpace, and Microsoft Backup.

THE
REALLY
BIG
DICTIONA
VOLUME 87

Glossary

This chapter describes the words and phrases that you're most likely to encounter as you start hanging out with DOS, and offers up some common-sense—*not* theoretical or nerdy!—definitions.

80x86. A family of microprocessors first manufactured by Intel and used in nearly all PCs and PC-compatibles.

Application. A program that does something you'd consider useful, in contrast to system software, which simply helps the computer run.

ASCII. A communication code that changes numbers, letters, and symbols so that different hardware and software can talk to each other and swap unformatted files between programs or computers.

Attribute. A notation that accompanies a file, telling DOS whether it's a system file, a hidden file, or a read-only file. It also notes whether the file has been changed since you last backed it up.

AUTOEXEC.BAT. A batch file that DOS runs every time you start up. You can customize AUTOEXEC.BAT so that DOS performs the commands you want when you start it up—for example, loading a specific program.

Backup. To make extra copies of your files, so if and when your originals are damaged, you'll still have copies. Backing up files is like cutting the Federal deficit: it's so important that maybe we'll all start doing it one of these days. DOS 6 contains programs that make it somewhat easier. Perhaps that'll help.

Batch file. A file containing quasi-English-language commands that DOS executes one-by-one.

Baud rate. A measurement of a modem's speed. It counts how many times a signal changes per second.

BBS (Bulletin Board System)**.** A computer that stores information and messages that are accessible to people who call in by modem.

BIOS. A program built into IBM PCs and compatibles that kickstarts your computer when you first switch it on.

Boot. To start your computer. Switching on a computer begins a byzantine set of steps that result in the computer figuratively picking itself up by its bootstraps and getting ready to work. A **warm boot**—the kind you get by pressing Ctrl-Alt-Del—reloads DOS but doesn't necessarily clear out all your memory. A **cold boot** runs through the whole shebang, including hardware diagnostics.

Buffer. A chunk of memory in which information sits while it's waiting to go somewhere else. *Disk buffers*, which are controlled by the BUFFERS command, hold information on the way to and from the disk.

Bug. A defect in a program that makes it behave strangely or not at all.

Byte. A set of eight bits, often corresponding to a single character.

CGA (Color Graphics Adapter)**.** The first primitive IBM standard for color graphics. To be avoided at all costs (which, fortunately, is not hard to do these days).

CHKDSK. A DOS program that checks to see if your disk's logical structure is OK—for example, that your files all have a beginning and an end, and that your File Allocation Table makes sense.

Click. To press a mouse button once. (**Double-click** means to press the button twice in quick succession.)

Clone. A computer that is designed to run the same programs and work with the same hardware as the IBM PC.

COM. DOS' word for a serial port. Serial port #1 is COM1, serial port #2 is COM2, and so on.

COMMAND.COM. An important program that DOS loads while it's booting. It's called the *command processor*, and (among other things) it's the program that displays your C:> prompt.

Command Prompt. The C:> (or A:> or B:>) prompt that sits there on screen, eagerly waiting to follow your every whim.

CVF (Compressed Volume File**).** A hidden file that contains all of the contents of a DoubleSpace compressed drive.

CONFIG.SYS. A DOS program that sets up your computer's configuration, including any device drivers you have to run.

Conventional Memory. Memory within the 640K limit that DOS programs can use directly, without any tricks.

CPU (Central Processing Unit)**.** Also called a microprocessor. Your computer's brains, such as they are.

Cursor. The marker that indicates where you are on screen.

Data. Information, translated into the digital 1 or 0 bits that a computer can understand.

Database. A collection of information, usually arranged into records and capable of being sorted in many ways.

DBLSPACE.BIN. An extension of DOS 6, designed to recognize DoubleSpace compressed drives.

DBLSPACE.SYS. A DOS program that runs at startup, and decides whether to plunk DBLSPACE.BIN in conventional or upper memory.

Default. A setting your system will use unless you specifically tell it otherwise.

Defragmentation. The process of rearranging the way your files are kept on disk, so that entire files and directories are kept together, and therefore can be loaded faster. DOS 6s DEFRAG command does this.

DELTREE. A DOS 6 command that nukes a directory and all its contents, including subdirectories within it.

Directory. A set of files grouped together.

Disk compression. The use of a specialized program that reduces the amount of space required to store files, often by as much as 50 percent.

Display adapter. Video circuitry, usually on a separate card, that makes your computer work with your monitor.

DOS Shell. A simple, mouse-based graphical user interface built into DOS 4, 5, and 6.

Dot-matrix printer. A printer that works by hammering tiny dots onto the page.

DoubleSpace. The disk-compression program that comes with DOS 6.

Download. To receive files from another computer, usually by modem.

EGA (Enhanced Graphic Adapter). The second-generation IBM color video standard. Not as awful as CGA, but still not up to the job.

Environment. A bunch of settings DOS needs to keep in memory so that they're always available.

Expanded memory. RAM above 640K that can be used by programs only by a complicated rigamarole called *swapping page frames*.

Extended memory. A flexible kind of RAM above 640K that can be used directly by 80386, 80486 and Pentium systems.

Extension. The three letters that appear after the period in most file names. In REPORT.DOC, the extension is DOC.

FAT (File Allocation Table). A table that tells DOS exactly where every file on your disk is stored. No FAT, no files!

Fax/Modem. A contraption that not only sends and receives data, but also sends and/or receives fax transmissions.

FDISK. A DOS program that lets you create or change disk partitions (destroying all the data on those partitions in the process).

File. A bunch of bytes that you want to keep *together*—such as a program or a document.

Floppy disk. A removable magnetic storage device containing a relatively small amount of data (usually 360K, 720K, 1.2M, 1.44M or 2.88M).

Font. A set of characters that all share a consistent style.

Format. To prepare a disk for use.

Fragmentation. The process by which files are split into many smaller pieces as they are saved and resaved.

GUI (Graphical User Interface)**.** A set of visual standards and methods by which a computer presents itself to you—generally involving menus, windows, icons, and using a mouse.

Hard disk. An unremovable magnetic data storage device that nearly always can store much more information than a floppy disk.

Hardware. Your computer's *physical components*, in contrast to software, the programs that make it run.

Icon. A small picture that represents a program, file, or other object.

Inkjet printer. A printer that sprays tiny jets of ink on paper—often creating output that's almost as good as a laser printer, at a much lower cost.

Intel-based. A computer based on one of the 80×86 family of chips made by Intel or one of its clone competitors such as AMD or Cyrix. Most computers that can run DOS are Intel-based.

InterLnk. A DOS 6 program that allows you to connect two computers together for file exchange.

Kilobyte. 1,024 bytes of data (2*2*2*2*2*2*2*2*2*2).

Laptop. A portable computer that is roughly small enough to fit on your lap.

Laser printer. A printer that uses a laser mechanism to produce very high-quality output, usually at 300 or 600 dots-per-inch.

Loading high. Loading a program into memory above the conventional 640K limit.

Macintosh. An Apple personal computer with a sophisticated, easy-to-use graphical interface.

Macro. A set of instructions that can all be executed by pressing a single key, thereby automating a procedure.

Mainframe. A huge, expensive, and extremely powerful computer (kind of like those behemoths you see in old sci-fi films).

Math coprocessor. A chip that can work with the microprocessor to handle specialized math stuff.

Media. Anything you can stick data on—floppy disks, hard disks, optical disks, CD-ROM, or tape backup units.

MemMaker. A DOS 6 utility program that figures out where best to stick all your programs so you hold onto as much precious conventional memory as possible.

Memory management. The black art of finding and liberating every last scrap of conventional memory.

Menu. A list of options, from which you're expected to choose one (usually, a pull-down menu).

Microprocessor. The brains of your computer. Same as CPU.

Microsoft. The rags-to-riches company that sells MS-DOS, Windows, and many leading applications programs.

Modem. MOdulator/DEModulator—a device that converts digital data to analog sound that can travel across a phone line and be reconverted to digital data at the other end.

Mouse. A device that allows you to "point" at an area on screen, and then "click" to take action there.

`MSDOS.SYS`. A hidden file that contains DOS' *kernel*, the program at the very heart of DOS, which handles most of its core functions.

Multimedia. Any mixture of text, graphics, sound, animation and video assembled and delivered via computer.

Multitasking. What DOS ain't—a system that can run more than one process at the same time.

Operating System. A set of programs that manage your computer.

OS/2. An advanced operating system, sold by IBM, that runs DOS and Windows programs, but also offers multitasking and many other advanced features.

Parallel port. A PC connector that sends data eight bits at a time. Mostprinters use parallel ports.

Parameters. What nerdy computer types sometimes also refer to as *switches*.

Path. A description of the directories and subdirectories that DOS needs to follow to find a specific program.

PC. Personal computer. It often refers to the original IBM PC and compatibles.

PC/AT. An IBM PC based on the Intel 80286 microprocessor. Clone 286 systems were often called AT-compatibles.

Pixel. Picture element—a single electronic dot on your screen. (The IBM variant is *pel*.)

PostScript. A computer language, designed specifically to build pages, which is built into many laser printers and typesetting machines.

Program. The set of instructions that the computer follows to carry out a specific task.

PS/2. IBM's brand name for its current line of personal computers, some of which contain IBM's proprietary Micro Channel Architecture.

QBASIC. The version of the BASIC programming language built into DOS 6.

RAM (Random Access Memory). The memory chips that store programs and data while you are using them.

RAMDrive. A section of RAM that behaves like a hard disk, but works much faster (and also disappears when you shut your computer off).

Remark. To add the word REM at the beginning of a line in a batch file. This tells DOS that a line in a batch file is simply a comment, not a command to be executed.

ROM. Read-only memory.

Root. The main directory on each drive (the "top" of the DOS filing cabinet).

Scan. To check a disk for viruses.

Scanner. A device used to read an image from paper and store that image in a computer file.

Select. To choose an item before performing an action on it.

Serial port. A PC connection that transmits information one bit at a time. External modems and many mice use serial ports.

SETVER. A DOS program that lies to applications that need to think they're running another version of DOS.

SmartDRIVE. DOS' disk-caching program that allows you to store frequently used data in RAM, where it can be retrieved much faster than from disk.

Software. The programs that transform your computer from a doorstop into something useful.

Spreadsheet. A program that looks like an old-fashioned ledger sheet but automatically does the arithmetic for you.

Stacker. A widely-used DOS disk-compression program.

Subdirectory. Any directory contained within the overall `root` directory.

Supplemental disk. A disk that includes several rarely-used DOS commands and files to customize DOS for use by the disabled.

Switch. An optional parameter that changes the way a command works. In this book switches are referred to as **parameters**.

Syntax. The precise order, language, and punctuation you must use to execute a command.

System disk. A disk that contains the files DOS needs to run.

Tape backup. A unit that allows you to archive old files on a special tape cassette.

Task swapper. A feature built into the DOS Shell that allows you to halt a program in mid-stream, switch to another one, and then return to where you were in the first one whenever you're ready.

Tree. A visual depiction of your `root` (parent) directory and all the baby directories that have grown from it.

Trojan Horse. A virus that sneaks into your computer and hides inside something that looks really neat.

TSR (Terminate-and-Stay-Resident)**.** A program that hangs out in memory after it finishes running—ready for you to run it again, even from within another program, with a single keystroke command.

UMB (Upper Memory Block)**.** A chunk of memory, between 640K and 1024M, which can be used for video, the computer's BIOS, and as a way to access *expanded memory*.

Undelete. To restore a file you previously deleted.

Unformat. To restore the contents of a disk you have formatted.

Uninstall. To remove the current version of DOS.

Upload. To send data "up" to another computer, generally via modem.

VGA (Video Graphics Array)**.** The current basic graphics standard for monitors.

Virus. A computer program designed to cause mayhem as it spreads from one computer to another.

Volume label. The specific name of a disk or disk partition.

Wild card. The * or ? characters, which are used with certain commands to make them apply to all files in a specific category.

Windows. 1. On-screen boxes containing specific programs or tasks. 2. Microsoft Windows, a specific program that provides a graphical user interface for DOS.

Windows for Workgroups. A local area network, built around Windows 3.1, that lets Windows and DOS computers communicate.

Windows NT. An advanced Microsoft operating system that looks and feels like Windows 3.1, but swaps DOS' 1982-vintage guts for a new multitasking, multithreading, networking architecture that's intended to be real hot stuff.

Workgroup Connection. A DOS add-on, originally intended to be part of MS-DOS 6.0, that lets MS-DOS computers act as clients on Windows for Workgroups networks.

Fifth Annual
COMPUTER
DINN
& DANCE
CHIPS

Contacting PC User Groups and Bulletin Boards

Maybe by now, you've learned so much about DOS that you're wondering if you're becoming a computer dork. Well, I'm sure you're not nerdy, but you may be ready and brave enough to venture into a territory often frequented by them: user's groups and bulletin boards, which are excellent sources of information about your computer.

Is There Anybody Out There?

One misnomer is the *personal* in personal computing. And that's because there's a whole world of people out there with whom you can interact via your computer. This chapter shows you the way.

User's groups are clubs that share information about a particular type of computer or software. Some are enormous and have become extremely sophisticated. It's not uncommon, for example, for top management at a major software company to speak to a large user group gathering about new products—and sometimes even give out free samples! Other smaller user groups can be just as helpful, though. User's groups tend to attract people who are willing to share their knowledge and help newcomers. If you have trouble finding one for your favorite software, contact the software company that produced it.

Bulletin board systems (BBSs) are accessed via computer modems. They're usually either non-profit or low-profit enterprises, run by an individual for the love of it. Visitors to a bulletin board may share a specific computer interest. Or, for that matter, a specific interest that has nothing to do with computers.

So you're wondering how to find out about a BBS if the only way to reach it is through a modem? We've included a starter list. If that's not enough, check out *Boardwatch Magazine* ($36/year, $3.95/single copy). If you can't find it on the newsstand, write to: *Boardwatch Magazine*, 7586 West Jewell Avenue, Suite 200, Lakewood, CO 80232.)

Boardwatch Magazine lists hundreds of bulletin boards each month, and tells you what's going on in the bulletin-board community. And what a community it is—bulletin boards are at the heart of a growing phenomenon, called *cyberspace*. By one estimate, there are 100,000 bulletin boards that cater to different interests and subcultures.

In addition, there is CompuServe, a huge BBS (actually much more than a BBS) where you can find "forums" on nearly any computer topic, product, or software package. Many of these are sponsered by software and hardware manufacturers, and provide the best user support you will find anywhere. See Chapter 22 for information on CompuServe.

User Groups

Here's a list of user's groups known to focus on PC- and DOS-oriented topics, as of January 1993. Both user's groups and bulletin boards have a fairly high attrition rate. If you can't reach one of these, or if we haven't listed an organization in your area, contact the Association of PC User's Groups in Scotts Valley, California.

Alabama

South Alabama Computer Society
#11 Grove Street On The Square
Headland, AL 36345

Alaska

IBM PC & Compatible User's Group
P.O. Box 240945
Anchorage, AK 99524

Arizona

Arizona Society for Computer Information
Suite 110-129, 4212 West Cactus
Phoenix, AZ 85029

South Mountain Users Group
P.O. Box 50002
Phoenix, AZ 85076

Arkansas

South Arkansas PC User Group
2206 North Jackson
Magnolia, AR 71753

Twin Lakes Computer Users Group
HC 61 Box 263
Norfolk, AR 72658

Rogers PC Users Group
P.O. Box 1251
Bentonville, AR 72712

California

Desert Users Group
P.O. Box 1179
Indio, CA 92201

Gold Country PC Users Group
1260 Taylor Lane
Auburn, CA 95603

Golden Gate Computer Society
P.O. Box 151696
San Rafael, CA 94915-1696

Madera County PC Users Group
P.O. Box 216
Madera, CA 93639

Long Beach IBM Users Group
4156 Woodruff Avenue, Suite 517
Lakewood, CA 90713

Diablo Valley PC Users Group
P.O. Box 8040, #117
Walnut Creek, CA 94596

Santa Barbara PC Users Group
281 Oak Road
Santa Barbara, CA 93108

Valley Computer Club
P.O. Box 6545
Burbank, CA 91510-6545

South Orange County Computer Club
P.O. Box 5246
Huntington Beach, CA 92646

Colorado

PC Users Group of Colorado
P.O. Box 944
Boulder, CO 80306

Metro Area Computer Enthusiasts
P.O. Box 440247
Aurora, CO 80044

Colorado Springs PC Users Group
P.O. Box 1028
Colorado Springs, CO 80901

Electric Locksmith Users Group
P.O. Box 17272
Colorado Springs, CO 80935

Front Range PC Users Group
305 West Magnolia #152
Fort Collins, CO 80521

Connecticut

Connecticut Computer Society
P.O. Box 370032
West Hartford, CT 06137-0032

Fairfield County Computer User's Group
14 Wakefield Road
Wilton, CT 06897

Delaware

Delaware Valley User's Group
24 Cawdor Lane
New Castle, DE 19720

Florida

Broward County Personal Computer Association
4410 S.W. 22nd Street
Fort Lauderdale, FL 33317

PC Users Group of Boca Raton
P.O. Box 273421
Boca Raton, FL 33427-3421

Manatee Personal Computer Users Group
P.O. Box 14190
Bradenton, FL 34280

Central Florida Computer Society
P.O. Box 948019
Maitland, FL 32794

IBM Users Group
917 39th Street N.
St. Petersburg, FL 33713

PC User's Group of Jacksonville
P.O. Box 47197
Jacksonville, FL 32247

Georgia

Atlanta PC Users Group
P.O. Box 28788
Atlanta, GA 30358

Hawaii

Aloha Computer Club
P.O. Box 4470
Honolulu, HI 96812

Idaho

Coeur d'Alene PC User Group
P.O. Box 561
Coeur d'Alene, ID 83814

Illinois

Chicago Computer Society
P.O. Box 27
Deerfield, IL 60015

Computers Are Easy Users Group
P.O. Box 2727
Glen Ellyn, IL

McHenry County IBM PC Users Group
1078 Plum Tree Drive
Crystal Lake, IL 60014

Indiana

Terre Haute PC User Group
P.O. Box 3174
Terre Haute, IN 47803

PC Abusers Group
P.O. Box 441171
Indianapolis, IN 46244

Iowa

Quad-Cities Computer Society
P.O. Box 2456
Davenport, IA 52809

Central Iowa Computer User Group
P.O. Box 672
Ankeny, IA 50021

Kansas

Topeka PC Users Club
P.O. Box 1279
Topeka, KS 66601

Kentucky

Kentucky Indiana PC Users Group
P.O. Box 3564
Louisville, KY 40201

Central Kentucky Computer Society
2050 Idle Hour Center, #160
Lexington, KY 40502

Louisiana

Acadiana Microcomputer Users Group
P.O. Box 51142
Lafayette, LA 70505

Maine

Downeast Computer Society
P.O. Box 348
Deer Isle, ME 04627

Island Reach Computer Users
P.O. Box 1029
Blue Hill, ME 04614

Maryland

Johns Hopkins University Mac & IBM User Group
Box 0432, Johns Hopkins University
Baltimore, MD 21218

Massachusetts

Boston Computer Society
Boston, MA 02134

Pioneer Valley PC Users Group
P.O. Box H
North Amherst, MA 01002

Pioneer Valley Computer Club
Box 87
Westfield, MA 01086

Michigan

*.DOS User Group of Southeastern Michigan
P.O. Box 1942
Dearborn, MI 48121

User's Personal Computer Organization
P.O. Box 80086
Lansing, MI 48908

Midland Computer Club
P.O. Box 132
Midland, MI 48640

Missouri

ICON
2353 E. Bennett
Springfield, MO 65802

New Jersey

PC Club of South Jersey
P.O. Box 427
Cherry Hill, NJ 08003

South Jersey IBM PC Users Group
P.O. Box 1117
Ocean City, NJ 08226

Morris Micro Computer Club
P.O. Box 161
Chatham, NJ 07928

Amateur Computer Group of New Jersey
2047 Elizabeth Avenue
Scotch Plains, NJ 07090

New York

New York Amateur Computer Club
P.O. Box 3442
New York, NY 10008

Creative Computing Club
153 E. 57th Street, #8G
New York, NY 10022

Long Island Computer Society
P.O. Box 2440
Patchogue, NY 11772

Suffolk County Computer Association
244 Mill Road
Yaphank, NY 11980

Buffalo IBM PC User Group
P.O. Box 609
Buffalo, NY 14226

Hudson Valley Personal Computer Club
P.O. Box 6057
Kingston, NY 12401

North Carolina

Blue Ridge Computer Users Group
Rt. 4, Box 445
Sparta, NC 28675

Personal Computer Club of Charlotte
600 Regency Drive
Charlotte, NC 28211

Fayetteville Area PC User's Group
P.O. Box 35375
Fayetteville, NC 28303

North Dakota

PC Users Association
2498 30th Ave. S., #123
Grand Forks, ND 58201

Ohio

Toledo Area Computer Society
5752 Normandy Drive
Sylvania, OH 43560

Cincinnati PC Users Group
P.O. Box 3097
Cincinnati, OH 45201

Oklahoma

Oklahoma City PC Users Group
P.O. Box 12027
Oklahoma City, OK 73157

Pennsylvania

Exton PC Council, Inc.
310 North High Street
West Chester, PA 19380

N.E.A.T. Atari & IBM PC Users Group
P.O. Box 18150
Philadelphia, PA 19116

Pittsburgh Area Computer Club
P.O. Box 6440
Pittsburgh, PA 15212

Harrisburg PC Users Group
1195 Fairmont Drive
Harrisburg, PA 17112

Rhode Island

South County Computer Users Group
P.O. Box 493
Wakefield, RI 02880

South Carolina

Palmetto PC Club
P.O. Box 2046
Columbia, SC 29202

IBM PC User Group of Charleston
P.O. Box 520
Charleston, SC 29402-0520

Tennessee

Southeast Tennessee Computer Association
323 TN Nursery Road
Cleveland, TN 37311

Memphis PC Users Group
P.O. Box 241756
Memphis, TN 38124

Texas

South Texas Computer Users Group
4009 Heatherglen Drive
Bay City, TX 77414

CAUG-PC
P.O. Box 270711
Corpus Christi, TX 78427

Central Texas Computer Users Group
3803 Griffin Drive
Killeen, TX 76543

Virginia

Fredericksburg PC User's Group
P.O. Box 5096
Falmouth, VA 22403

Richmond PC Users' Group
P.O. Box 8331
Richmond, VA 23226

Washington

Vancouver PC Users Group
3011 NE 135th Avenue
Vancouver, WA 98682

West Virginia

Morgantown IBM PC Users Group
P.O. Box 1085
Morgantown, WV 26507-1085

Personal Computer Huntington User Group
P.O. Box 2173
Huntington, WV 25722-2173

Wisconsin

FVTC PC User Group
P.O. Box 2277 - MR 318
Appleton, WI 54913

Wyoming

Sheridan Microcomputer Users' Group
1752 Meadowlark
Sheridan, WY 82801

Bulletin Boards

As mentioned above, bulletin boards can be transient, and there's no telling what you'll find on them.

Some contain computer programs and graphics files for downloading. Others are primarily a conversational medium or a meeting ground—often helping to develop a real sense of community. A few are directly involved in helping new PC users. And some others traffic in the seedier sides of the human condition. If you see or hear something you're not comfortable with, sign off.

We'll give you a few pointers, and then you're on your own:

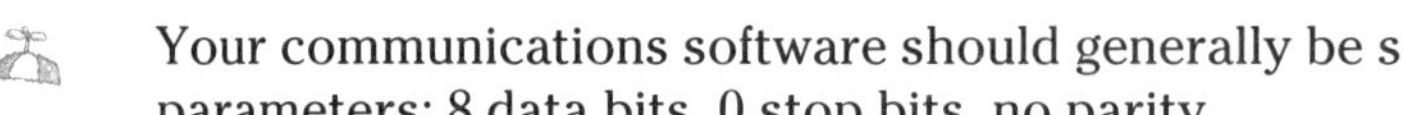

- Your communications software should generally be set to these parameters: 8 data bits, 0 stop bits, no parity.

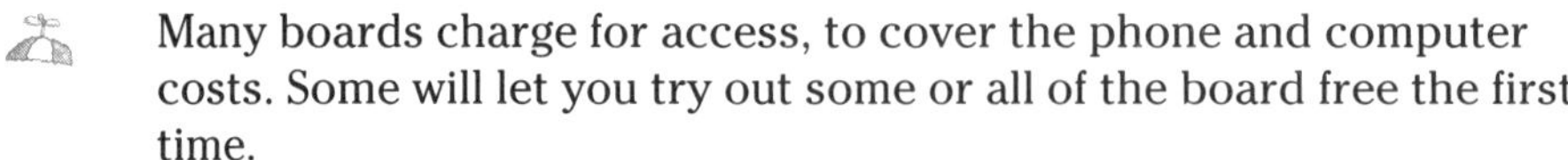

- Many boards charge for access, to cover the phone and computer costs. Some will let you try out some or all of the board free the first time.
- Boards come and go—some reverting to telephone lines. So call at a reasonable hour, at least the first time.
- If you download software, run it through a good anti-virus program. If you download shareware that you decide to keep using, pay the author for it.

Don't ever give your password to anyone.

You'll be surprised how much of your meaning can get lost when you communicate in pure ASCII text. These and other "emoticons" (emote = to express, icon = symbol, get it?) can help unseen and unheard others to understand your frame of mind:

G>	Grin
<BG>	Big grin
:)	Smile (look sideways)
;)	Wink (see the face?)
:(	Frown (cute, huh?)

You may also come across a few unusual abbreviations, such as:

IMO	In my opinion
IMHO	In my humble opinion
RTFM	Read the F——— manual

If you overhear discussions of illegal activity—pirating software and worse—leave the BBS immediately.

Current BBS Numbers

This list was current as of January 1993. It's just a sampling, of course—not even one percent of the boards that are out there.

Alabama

The Byte House, Andalusia, (205) 222-3097
The Byte Swap, Decatur, (205) 355-2983

Alaska

The FredBox, Anchorage, (907) 344-8437

Arizona

The High Mountain, Flagstaff, (602) 527-8404
The Nucleus II, Ft. Huachuca, (602) 459-3653

California

The WELL, Sausalito, (415) 332-7190
B C S BBS, Los Angeles, (213) 962-2902
Data Core BBS, Los Angeles, (310) 842-6880
Fido Software BBS 1, San Francisco, (415) 863-2739
HoloNet, Berkeley, (510) 704-1058
Root Connection, Modesto, (209) 576-1606
The Lighthouse, Palmdale, (805) 272-1812
Zero Wait States, San Diego, (619) 283-3507

Colorado

Fast Track, Denver, (303) 922-0766

Connecticut

Bruce's Bar & Grill, West Hartford, (203) 236-3761
Sam-I-Am's BBS, Enfield, (203) 741-6736

Delaware

PC-PUG BBS, Wilmington, (302) 477-0324

Florida

Online Connections!, Orlando, (407) 841-3533
Road Runner BBS, Hialeah, (305) 557-5357
Seniors Board, Gainesville, (904) 336-9588
Shareware Online, Miami, (305) 271-4467

Georgia

Graffiti, Atlanta, (404) 972-4999
The Local Link, LaGrange, (404) 883-8100

Hawaii

Techno Tronic, Mililani, (808) 625-0291

Idaho

Night Flight, Idaho Falls, (208) 529-4248

Illinois

Aquila BBS, Aurora, (708) 820-8344
Computerized Bulletin Board System, Chicago, (708) 849-1132
Heartland Freenet, Peoria, (309) 674-1100

Indiana

Synergistic BBS, Indianapolis, (317) 549-1835
Tech, New Carlisle, (219) 654-3210

Iowa

Computer Support Hot-Line, Des Moines, (515) 244-7745
Macky Blue, Burlington, (319) 754-7511

Kansas

New World Information Service, Wichita, (316) 262-1829

Kentucky

Bear Waller Holler, Pikeville, (606) 437-4321
Hugboard, Paducah, (502) 554-0614

Louisiana

American Silver Dollar, Alexandria, (318) 443-0271
The MainStay, New Orleans, (504) 734-0461

Maine

Defcon II, Lewiston, (207) 783-8064

Maryland

Advanced Data Services, Frederick (301) 695-5116
Capital PC User's Group BBS, Rockville, (301) 738-9060
Sub Comm Systems, Baltimore, (410) 284-0565

Massachusetts

BCS Zi/Tel Remote Access System, Boston, (617) 965-7046
Channel 1, Cambridge, (617) 354-8873
Cul-de-Sac Bar & Grill, Holliston, (508) 429-1784

Michigan

Gateway On-Line, Rockwood, (313) 291-5571
HAL 9000, Ann Arbor, (313) 663-4173
Michigan Online, St. Joseph, (616) 429-3414

Minnesota

PC Support, Duluth, (218) 724-9626
Short Circuit, Walls, (612) 781-1886
Spare Computer, Minneapolis, (612) 824-1209

Missouri

Computers Plus, St. Louis, (314) 942-5932
The Goose's Nest, Kansas City, (816) 587-3373

Nebraska

Abort, Retry, Fail?, Bellevue, (402) 292-8290

Nevada

The Skunk Works, Las Vegas, (702) 894-9619

New Hampshire

North Country, Lancaster, (603) 788-2251
The Cereal Port, Rindge, (603) 899-3335

New Jersey

Bytes 'n' Bits BBS, Bayonne, (201) 437-4355
Millennium, Newark, (201) 374-2730
1984 BBS, Princeton, (609) 921-1984

New Mexico

The Electronic Trib, Albuquerque, (505) 823-7700

New York

Computers & Dreams, New York, (212) 888-6565
DataShack, Eastchester, (914) 961-7032
Executive Network, Mt. Vernon, (914) 667-4567

Hi Teck's Place, Deer Park, (516) 757-0210
MindVox, New York, (212) 988-5030
The Forum, Ithaca, (607) 272-1371
The Times, Albany, (518) 452-4757

North Carolina

Air Raid, Gastonia, (704) 865-3063
Micro Message Service, Raleigh, (919) 779-6674

North Dakota

The Above Board II, Minot Air Force Base, (701) 727-4842

Ohio

Multisystem TBBS, Cincinnati, (513) 231-7013
The Information Exchange, Athens, (614) 593-0432
Toledo's TBBS, Toledo, (313) 854-6001

Oklahoma

Black Gold, Tulsa, (918) 272-7779

Oregon

Computer Time Online, Wilsonville, (503) 682-1619

Pennsylvania

Computer Shop, Allentown, (215) 395-9823
MCR Tech System, Exton, (215) 889-0448
Pennsylvania Online/The Other BBS, Harrisburg, (717) 657-8699

Rhode Island

Terminal Madness, Middletown, (401) 848-9069

South Carolina

Orangeburg Computer Club, Orangeburg, (803) 531-5734

South Dakota

YEEB, Sioux Falls, (605) 331-5831

Tennessee

Dataworld, Knoxville, (615) 675-3282
Orion's Rift, Nashville, (615) 824-3871

Texas

Atomic Cafe, Houston, (713) 530-8875
BBS America, Richardson, (214) 680-3406
Byte Back!, Dallas, (214) 361-6756
GIRC BBS, Amarillo, (806) 359-3542
Laid Back BBS, San Antonio, (210) 822-5868

Utah

Rocky Mountain Software, Salt Lake City, (801) 963-8721

Vermont

Bit O' Bytes, St. Albans, (802) 524-7294

Virginia

CommunityLink, Alexandria, (703) 765-0501
Info*Express, Chesapeake, (804) 488-1327
Red Dwarf, Centreville, (703) 631-0041

Washington

Northwest's Best BBS, Auburn, (206) 939-6337
Quicksilver, Moses Lake, (509) 762-6845

West Virginia

21st Century Connection, Dunbar, (304) 768-5036
Mindless Ones, Weirton, (304) 748-0491

Wisconsin

Boardwalk, Madison, (608) 257-0486
EXEC-PC, Elm Grove, (414) 789-4210
Ye Olde Board, Albany, (414) 862-3708

Symbols

A

B

C

D

E

F

G

H

M

N

O

P

Q

R

S

T

U

V

W-Z

DOS Crossword by Terry Hall

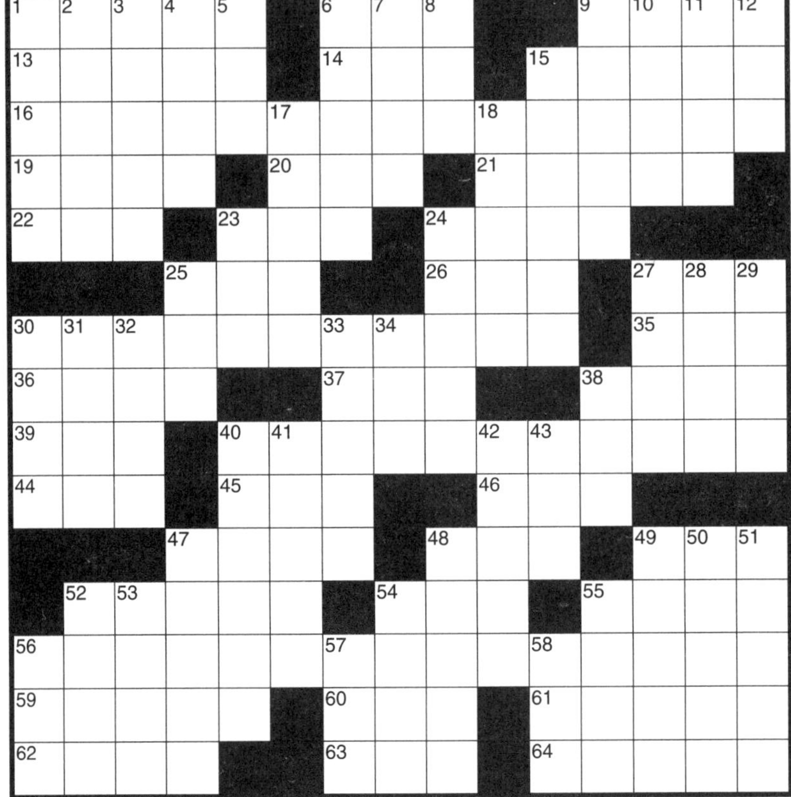

ACROSS

1 Slants, as italics
6 Photographic film DIN
9 Bit-mapped graphics format
13 Small image within a larger
14 Bot. line
15 Type of E-mail
16 New PC program platform (pt. 1): 5 wds
19 Discharged debt
20 Three in Italy
21 Choose
22 ___-fi (fiction)
23 Smallest monitor display item
24 Iraqi missile
25 Del. work from RAM
26 Printer's speed rating
27 Setup, for short
30 New disk-compression program
35 Tumor suffix
36 MCA computers
37 Electronic learning cs.
38 Combines with gamate
39 Confederate soldier
40 Problem-analysis program
44 CONFIG.___ (startup file)
45 Make bigger, in brief
46 "Short" publication
47 St. John's province
48 Fed. nuclear regulator
49 System information reporter
52 Sleep sound
54 365-day per.
55 Bishop Desmond ___
56 New PC program platform (cont. from 16-A)
59 Correct program errors
60 Makes lemon into a drink
61 Competitive field
62 Finances, for short
63 Hard disk unit: abbr.
64 Bill Gates' original program

DOWN

1 Falters
2 First large computer
3 Plain text
4 Whom this book's not for
5 Narrative rept.
6 ___, Retry, Fail?
7 Data-preserving format
8 Ctrl-___-Del
9 Presented, as a problem
10 LaserWriter model
11 Fax-modem standards setter
12 TI's state
15 Disk label
17 Save to disk
18 Computer brand: 2 wds.
23 Dynamic Linking Library
24 Madrid's country
25 Network
27 Serial port
28 Fed. Mediation and Conciliation
29 Four-quart measures
30 Disk indices: abbr.
31 Follow rules
32 Spaces above 640K
33 Hot liquid burn
34 Pennsylvania German
38 Adobe Type Manager
40 Compact hard disk
41 Entrance
42 Makes file ready to edit
43 Fluid-filled bag
47 Won't execute: slang (2 wds)
48 Heavenly helper
49 Reduced color intensity
50 Shorthand writer
51 *Three Musketeers'* author
52 Detailed description
53 Mt. where Moses saw Promised Land
54 Amos' partner
55 Ram-ready pgms.
56 ___ *on a Grecian Urn*
57 Inter-application communication
58 Sweet potato

DOS Wordsearch by Terry Hall

Find these DOS words hidden in the puzzle above. Words may be hidden diagonally, horizontally, vertically, backwards, or forwards. Hint: Some words share letters and may be found more than once. Can you find the three extra DOSs?

Y D E L E T E S E N T R Y S W I T C H E S
E N M L I A F Y R T E R T R O B A Q D S C
K I S E H V K O D M O V E L R C R E C O S
S F A T T R I B U T E K L E K E L I N T T
O U A P A S L R C Z C E B J G T T F A P D
D P P M A S Y E U A H A Z A R S I R M D D
S P E P P R R S R S T T N E O G T O I N N
M R O A E I E T G C S A E N U U R S E O S
G L C W D R E N H N M C G R P P K P I O R
N E E T E T M L T Y I A A U C C P T D S E
I M O B E R A E R D I T L N O A A C D E V
T O O L A N M O M D I L A M N T D I T L I
R S E C G L M A M O D R P R N E S S P I R
A D W U D E E E N O R R E E E K R A M F D
T T A O M N T M W A E Y M C C P P B O N E
S G R J D S A N U S G G B A T O O Q R E C
E D E V Y N M M S L A E C L I O P K P D I
T O V S A E I I M R O H M T O T R Y S D V
D S T G N S O W F O E V H E N C I Y O I E
O O E U B N M E B A C K U P N T K D D H D
S R S U M B D E L I F E L B A T U C E X E

Abort-Retry-Fail
append
attribute
backup
batch language
C-prompt
COMMAND.COM
configuration manager
copy
Dblspace
defragmentation
Delete Sentry
Delete Tracker
DELTREE
device drivers
diagnostics
directory
disk cache
disk compression
disk operating system
DOS
DOS prompt
DOSKEY
EDIT
executable file
files
find
hidden files
memory manager
menu
MOVE
MSAV
MSD
parent directory
path
power management
pull-down menu
Qbasic
remark
root directory
SETVER
Shell
starting MSDOS
startup
switches
system diagnostics
tree
TSR
UMB
upper memory block
virus scanner
volume label
Windows
workgroup connection

L	E	A	N	S		A	S	A			P	I	C	T
I	N	S	E	T		B	A	L		V	O	I	C	E
M	I	C	R	O	S	O	F	T	D	O	S	S	I	X
P	A	I	D		T	R	E		E	L	E	C	T	
S	C	I		D	O	T		S	C	U	D			
			C	L	R			P	P	M		C	F	G
D	O	U	B	L	E	S	P	A	C	E		O	M	A
I	B	M	S			C	A	I			A	M	A	L
R	E	B		D	I	A	G	N	O	S	T	I	C	S
S	Y	S		E	N	L			P	A	M			
			N	F	L	D		A	E	C		M	S	D
	S	N	O	R	E		A	N	N		T	U	T	U
O	P	E	R	A	T	I	N	G	S	Y	S	T	E	M
D	E	B	U	G		A	D	E		A	R	E	N	A
E	C	O	N			C	Y	L		M	S	D	O	S

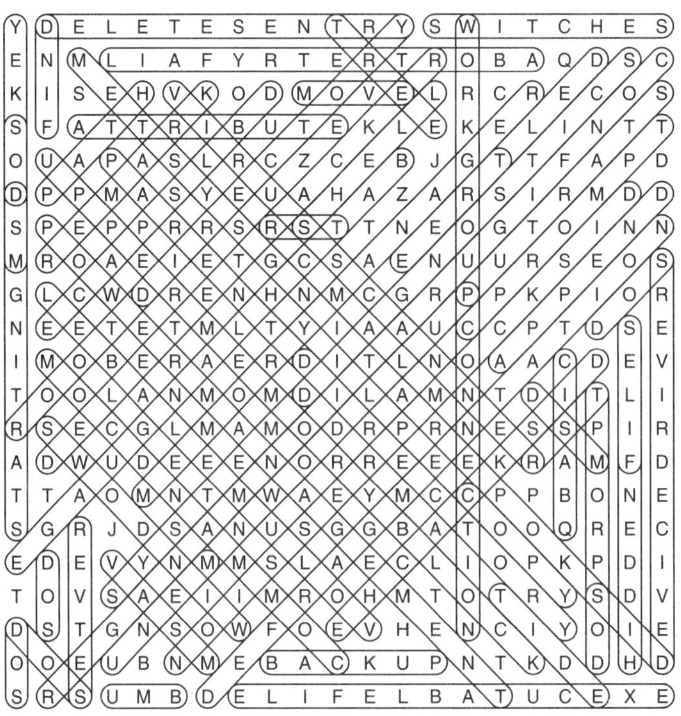

This is to certify that

____

is a graduate of the Non-Nerds School of DOS, and has successfully completed all training, testing, and behavior modification counseling necessary for this course.

But that doesn't mean much.

Awarded this ______ day of _______, Nineteen-hundred-ninety- __________

____

Chief Executive Non-Nerd

Here's a chart with the sizes and capacities of popular floppy disks:

Disk Size	Density	Capacity
5 1/4	Double Density	360K
5 1/4	High Density	1.2M
3 1/2	Double Density	720K
3 1/2	High Density	1.44M
3 1/2	Very High Density	2.88M

Things to do to format a disk:

1. Place the disk, label side up and toward you, into your A drive. (Close the door's latch if you are using a 5 1/4-inch disk.)
2. Type the following:

```
C>FORMAT A:
```

3. Press Enter. You are then asked to insert the disk. Because you've already done that, go ahead and press Enter again.
4. After formatting is complete, you are asked to enter a volume label for the disk. Unless you want to type a label name, just press Enter.
5. You can also format disks in drive B. Use the following command and follow the steps for drive A.

```
C>FORMAT B:
```

STOP!

> The FORMAT command should be used only with drives A and B to format floppy disks. ***Never*** type just **FORMAT** or **FORMAT C:** (or any drive letter higher than C). If you do, you could wipe out the contents of that drive.

The most important and most frequently used DOS commands are right here at your fingertips (in no particular order):

The Top Ten (Commands, That Is)

Type this...	*If you want to...*
CD	Change to another directory
DIR	View the list of files on a disk
MD	Make a directory
RD	Remove a directory
FORMAT	Format a disk
	Example: **FORMAT A:**
COPY	Make a copy of a file
	Example: **COPY C:REPT1 A:REPT2**
DEL	Delete one or more files
	Example: **DEL REPORT92.DOC**
TYPE	Display a file on the screen
	Example: **TYPE NOTES.DOC**
REN	Rename a file
	Example: **REN OLD.DOC NEW.DOC**
CLS	Clear the screen, erasing the display

Things To Do with That Darned CTRL Key

Press these keys...	*To do this...*
Ctrl-E, or up arrow	Move the cursor up one line
Ctrl-X, or down arrow	Move the cursor down one line
Ctrl-S, or left arrow	Move the cursor left (back) one character
Ctrl-D, or right arrow	Move the cursor right (forward) one character
Ctrl-R, or PgUp	Move up to the previous page (screen)
Ctrl-C, or PgDn	Move down to the next page
Ctrl-A, or Ctrl-Left	Move left one word
Ctrl-F, or Ctrl-Right	Move right one word
Ctrl-W, or Ctrl-Up	Scroll the screen up one line
Ctrl-Z, or Ctrl-Down	Scroll the screen down one line
Ctrl-G, or delete	Delete current character
Ctrl-T, or Ctrl-backspace	Delete current word (or Ctrl-Del)
Ctrl-H, or backspace	Delete previous character